UNFAIR DISMISSAL

A GUIDE TO RELEVANT CASE LAW

THIRTY-THIRD EDITION

Text of the first 24 editions by
Michael Rubenstein and Yvonne Frost

Subsequent editions revised by
Tony Gould

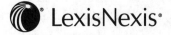

United Kingdom	LexisNexis, a Division of Reed Elsevier (UK) Ltd, Lexis House, 30 Farringdon Street, LONDON, EC4A 4HH, and 9-10, St. Andrew Square, EDINBURGH, EH2 2AF
Australia	Reed International Books Australia Pty Ltd trading as LexisNexis, CHATSWOOD, New South Wales
Austria	LexisNexis Verlag ARD Orac GmbH & Co KG, VIENNA
Benelux	LexisNexis Benelux, AMSTERDAM
Canada	LexisNexis Canada, MARKHAM, Ontario
China	LexisNexis China, BEIJING and SHANGHAI
France	LexisNexis SA, PARIS
Germany	LexisNexis GmbH, DUSSELDORF
Hong Kong	LexisNexis Hong Kong, HONG KONG
India	LexisNexis India, NEW DELHI
Italy	Giuffrè Editore, MILAN
Japan	LexisNexis Japan, TOKYO
Malaysia	Malayan Law Journal Sdn Bhd, KUALA LUMPUR
New Zealand	LexisNexis New Zealand Ltd, WELLINGTON
Singapore	LexisNexis Singapore, SINGAPORE
South Africa	LexisNexis, DURBAN
USA	LexisNexis, DAYTON, Ohio

© Reed Elsevier (UK) Ltd 2015
Published by LexisNexis

A CIP Catalogue record for this book is available from the British Library.

ISBN 978-1-4057-9809-9

9 781405 798099

13 digit ISBN: 9781405798099

Printed and bound in Great Britain by Hobbs the Printers Ltd, Totton, Hampshire

Visit LexisNexis at www.lexisnexis.co.uk

CONTENTS

Contents continued

CASE INDEX

INTRODUCTION

This is the 33rd edition of the *IRLR Unfair Dismissal Guide* and it takes account of the effect on the case law of 14 cases dealing with unfair dismissal reported in *Industrial Relations Law Reports* during 2014.

One of the most important legislative changes which took place in 2014 relating to unfair dismissal was the introduction of mandatory early conciliation by Acas. It is impossible to say whether this development has had a major impact on preventing unfair dismissal claims from reaching a tribunal, given the dramatic drop in employment tribunal claims following the introduction of fees in July 2013. Early figures do, however, show that 18% of cases dealt with by early conciliation result in settlement.

A further interesting legislative change in 2014 was to the TUPE Regulations, so that a dismissal that occurs at or around the time of a transfer is deemed automatically unfair for the purposes of an unfair dismissal claim only where the transfer was the "sole or principal" reason for the dismissal and no longer also if it was for a reason "connected with" the transfer. The meaning of "changes in the workplace" in the context of an ETO reason for dismissal was also amended to include changes in the place of employment.

Relevant major case law developments during 2014 included the confirmation by the Court of Session in Scotland in *McNeill v Aberdeen City Council (No.2)*, and later in the EAT in England in *Atkinson v Community Gateway Association*, that an employee who has committed a fundamental repudiatory breach of the implied term of trust and confidence remains entitled to bring a claim of constructive dismissal based on a breach of contract by his employer provided that, for whatever reason, the breach by the employee has not already been accepted by the employer. There was also a helpful review by the Court of Appeal in *Creditsights Ltd v Dhunna* of the case law relating to whether an employee working abroad can bring an unfair dismissal claim (or other claim under the ERA 1996) before a UK employment tribunal.

The aim of the *Unfair Dismissal Guide* remains to assist those acting, advising or adjudicating on this subject on the current approach of the courts to the range of problems of interpretation posed by statute. In doing so, it analyses the most important decisions of the courts and tribunals and extracts the main relevant findings. Fifteen new principles have been added from the cases reported in 2014 and principles in 24 cases have been removed, including all those relating to the default retirement age (which have been removed from this edition of the Guide because the number of cases to which it has remained relevant has dwindled with the passage of time).

This edition of the Guide has adopted the same methodology as for previous editions. Where the emphasis in the judicial interpretation of the statutory language has shifted, this has been taken into account. Consideration has also been given as to whether the relevant principle for the reported case would still be regarded as authoritative were it to be scrutinised by the appeal courts today.

Where the same point has been dealt with in more than one reported case, the highest authority is cited or, if that is not possible, the most recent or the most frequently quoted decision. For this and other purposes, therefore, the Guide distinguishes between the principle and the case. The principle, if still relevant, should be found in the Guide. A particular case may not be referred to either because it is no longer relevant or because the principle contained within it is captured better by another reference.

If there are conflicting lines of authority, both sets of decisions are referred to unless a clear trend has been established in favour of one or the other.

Some matters are specifically not dealt with, for example the statutory definition of redundancy, employment tribunal procedure and exclusions and qualifications for bringing a claim where they are not based on the statutory provisions (eg whether or not a contract is illegal, or who is or is not an employee). That is because they are outside the remit of the Guide as they involve statutes or common law older than the concept of unfair dismissal and/or case law outside the area of unfair dismissal itself.

The statutory extracts included in the Guide are generally those in force at the end of 2014. Footnotes also indicate where the statutory provisions have been and/or are likely to be amended in some way.

Tony Gould
Solicitor
LexisNexis
January 2015

1. STATUTORY EXCLUSIONS AND QUALIFICATIONS

Claim in time

111. *(2) Subject to the following provisions of this section, an employment tribunal shall not consider a complaint under this section unless it is presented to the tribunal –*

    (a) before the end of the period of three months beginning with the effective date of termination, or

    (b) within such further period as the tribunal considers reasonable in a case where it is satisfied that it was not reasonably practicable for the complaint to be presented before the end of that period of three months.

    (5) Where the dismissal is alleged to be unfair by virtue of section 104F (blacklists),

    (a) subsection (2)(b) does not apply, and

    (b) an employment tribunal may consider a complaint that is otherwise out of time if, in all the circumstances of the case, it considers that it is just and equitable to do so.

            EMPLOYMENT RIGHTS ACT 1996 (as amended)

Radakovits v   **[2010] IRLR 307 CA**
Abbey National plc
The time limits applicable to unfair dismissal claims go to jurisdiction, and jurisdiction cannot be conferred on a tribunal by agreement or waiver. An employment judge considering a jurisdictional issue at an early stage in proceedings should declare expressly whether jurisdiction is accepted, or whether the issue is being left open.

Hammond v   **[1973] IRLR 91 NIRC**
Haigh Castle Ltd
A period of three months beginning with the effective date of termination includes that date as part of the period.

Pruden v   **[1993] IRLR 317 EAT**
Cunard Ellerman Ltd
The correct way to calculate the period of three months beginning with the effective date of termination is first to find the effective date of termination, take the date before it, and then go forwards three months. If there is no corresponding date in that month, the last day of the month should be taken. Thus, if the effective date of termination was 1 September, the date before would be 31 August, and the three-month period would expire on 30 November.

Kirklees Metropolitan Council v   **[2009] IRLR 555 CA**
Radecki
If an employee is dismissed summarily the effective date of termination for the purposes of s.111 ERA 1996 is the date of summary dismissal as long as the employee knows of it.

Swainston v   **[1983] IRLR 164 CA**
Hetton Victory Club
The normal rule that the three-month time limit for presenting a complaint of unfair dismissal at the Regional Office of employment tribunals expires at midnight on the last day of that period, applies even where that is a non-working day if the application can be placed through a letter box or dealt with in some other way held out by the Regional Office as a means by which it will receive communications. The principle set out in *Pritam Kaur v S Russell & Sons Ltd* that where a statutory time limit expires on a non-working day, it is taken as expiring on the next working day, does not apply to the presentation of unfair dismissal claims because the "presentation" does not require any action on the part of the body to whom the presentation is made. However, if a complainant or his solicitor arrives at the Office and finds that there is no letter box, he may be able to show that it was not reasonably practicable for the complaint to be presented within the relevant period.

Hammond v   **[1973] IRLR 91 NIRC**
Haigh Castle Ltd
A claim is "presented" to a tribunal when it is received by the tribunal, not when it is dealt with by the tribunal or when it is posted by the claimant.

Tyne and Wear Autistic Society v   **[2005] IRLR 336 EAT**
Smith
Where a claimant presents his claim online, a claim is "presented" to an employment tribunal for the purposes of s.111(2) when it is successfully submitted online to the Employment Tribunals Service website. If an application is successfully submitted to the website in time, it does not matter if it is forwarded by the website host to the tribunal office computer on a later date, or date stamped on a later date.

Hart v   **[2006] IRLR 915**
English Heritage (Historic Buildings &
  Monuments Commission for England)
A complaint has been presented in time if all the elements of it have been pleaded in a claim presented in time even if the appropriate label has not been attached to it.

Gillick v   **[1993] IRLR 437 EAT**
BP Chemicals Ltd
There is no time limit which applies as such when it is proposed to add a new or substitute respondent to a claim which has been lodged timeously. The employment tribunal should treat an application to amend the complaint by the addition of a new respondent as a question of discretion, having regard to all the circumstances, and not as one to be settled by the application of the rules of time-bar. (Followed in *Drinkwater Sabey Ltd v Burnett and another* [1995] IRLR 239 EAT.)

Hart v   **[2006] IRLR 915**
English Heritage (Historic Buildings &
  Monuments Commission for England)
Under rule 10 of the Employment Tribunals Rules of Procedure, a tribunal can reconsider any case management decision, including a decision whether a complaint has already been presented in time or should be treated as a fresh claim. This does not allow parties several bites at the cherry. Parties should run all their legal arguments at one hearing (as per

Henderson v Henderson (1843) 3 Hare 100), and unless there has been a material change in circumstances it will only be in exceptional cases that a reconsideration will be merited in accordance with the overriding objective.

Reasonably practicable

Marks & Spencer plc v   **[2005] IRLR 562 CA**
Williams-Ryan
Section 111(2) should be given a liberal interpretation in favour of the employee.

Palmer and Saunders v   **[1984] IRLR 119 CA**
Southend-on-Sea Borough Council
The meaning of the words "reasonably practicable" in [s.111(2)] lies somewhere between reasonable on the one hand and reasonably physically capable of being done on the other. The best approach is to read "practicable" as the equivalent of "feasible" and to ask "Was it reasonably feasible to present the complaint to the employment tribunal within the relevant three months?"

Biggs v   **[1996] IRLR 203 CA**
Somerset County Council
The words "reasonably practicable" in the context of [s.111(2)] are directed to a temporary impediment or hindrance faced by an individual claimant, such as illness, rather than a mistake of law. Therefore, the fact that it was not until March 1994 that the House of Lords, in *R v Secretary of State for Employment ex parte EOC*, declared that the hours per week qualifying condition for bringing an unfair dismissal claim was contrary to European law, could not be taken into account as a ground for arguing that it was not "reasonably practicable" before that date for a part-time worker to present a claim within the time limit.

Palmer and Saunders v   **[1984] IRLR 119 CA**
Southend-on-Sea Borough Council
Whether it was reasonably practicable for a complaint to be presented in time is pre-eminently an issue of fact for the employment tribunal, taking all the circumstances of the given case into account and it is seldom that an appeal from its decision will lie. Depending upon the circumstances of the particular case, an employment tribunal may wish to consider the substantial cause of the employee's failure to comply with the statutory time limit; whether he had been physically prevented from complying with the limitation period, for instance by illness or a post strike or something similar. It may be relevant for the tribunal to investigate whether, at the time of dismissal, and if not when thereafter, the employee knew that he had the right to complain of unfair dismissal; in some cases the tribunal may have to consider whether there was any misrepresentation about any relevant matter by the employer to the employee. It will frequently be necessary for the tribunal to know whether the employee was being advised at any

material time and, if so, by whom; of the extent of the adviser's knowledge of the facts of the employee's case; and of the nature of any advice which they may have given him. It will probably be relevant in most cases for the employment tribunal to ask itself whether there was any substantial failure on the part of the employee or his adviser which led to the failure to comply with the time limit. The employment tribunal may also wish to consider the manner in which and the reason for which the employee was dismissed, including the extent to which, if at all, the employer's conciliatory appeals machinery had been used. However, the mere fact that an employee was pursuing an appeal through the internal machinery does not mean that it was not reasonably practicable for the unfair dismissal application to be made in time.

Schultz v   **[1999] IRLR 488 CA**
Esso Petroleum Company Ltd
Whenever a question arises as to whether a particular step or action was reasonably practicable or feasible, the injection of the qualification of reasonableness requires the answer to be given against the background of the surrounding circumstances and the aim to be achieved. The surrounding circumstances will always include whether or not the claimant was hoping to avoid litigation by pursuing alternative remedies, such as an internal appeal. In that context, the end to be achieved is not so much the immediate issue of proceedings as issue of proceedings with some time to spare before the end of the limitation period. Accordingly, in assessing whether or not something could or should have been done within the limitation period, while looking at the period as a whole, attention will in the ordinary way focus upon the closing rather than the early stages. Thus, in cases where illness is relied upon, a period of disabling illness should not be given similar weight regardless of in what part of the period of limitation it falls. The approach should vary according to whether the illness falls in the earlier weeks or in the far more critical weeks leading up to expiry of the limitation period.

Consignia plc v   **[2002] IRLR 624 CA**
Sealy
In determining whether it was reasonably practicable to present an unfair dismissal application within the prescribed time period, a complainant is entitled to rely on the ordinary course of post. Thus, if an application is sent by first class post, it can be assumed that it will be delivered on the second day after it was posted (excluding Sundays and public holidays). If, in fact, it did not arrive when it was expected to arrive, it can be regarded as not reasonably practicable to be presented within the prescribed period. Giving the claimant the benefit of the ordinary course of post provides a workable (if generous) test of what is reasonably practicable and one which is familiar in analogous contexts.

Consignia plc v   **[2002] IRLR 624 CA**
Sealy
Until a simpler regime for the service of documents such as that which is now available to the courts is introduced in

respect of employment tribunals, the following guidance may be helpful in determining whether an unfair dismissal application was presented within the prescribed time period:

1. Section 111(2) of the Employment Rights Act 1996 refers to "presenting" a complaint to a tribunal. It is now well established that a complaint is "presented" when it arrives at the Central Office of Employment Tribunals or at an office of the tribunals.

2. If a complainant or his or her agent proves that it was impossible to present a complaint in this way before the end of the time prescribed by s.111(2)(a) – for example because the office was found to be locked at a weekend and it did not have a letter-box – it will be possible to argue that it was not reasonably practicable for the complaint to be presented within the prescribed period.

3. If a complainant chooses to present a complaint by sending it by post, presentation will be assumed to have been effected, unless the contrary is proved, at the time when the letter would be delivered in the ordinary course of post.

4. If the letter is sent by first class post, it is now legitimate to adapt the approach contained in Civil Procedure Rule 6.7 and conclude that in the ordinary course of post it will be delivered on the second day after it was posted (excluding Sundays, Bank Holidays, Christmas Day and Good Friday).

5. If the letter does not arrive at the time when it would be expected to arrive in the ordinary course of post, but is unexpectedly delayed, a tribunal may conclude that it was not reasonably practicable for the complaint to be presented within the prescribed period.

6. If a form is date-stamped on a Monday by a tribunal office so as to be outside a three-month period which ends on the Saturday or Sunday, it will be open to a tribunal to find as a fact that it was posted by first class post not later than the Thursday and arrived on the Saturday, alternatively to extend time as a matter of discretion if satisfied that the letter was posted by first class post not later than the Thursday.

7. This regime does not allow for any unusual subjective expectation, whether based on inside knowledge of the postal system or on lay experience of what happens in practice, to the effect that a letter posted by first class post may arrive earlier than the second day after it is posted. The "normal and expected" result of posting a letter must be objectively, not subjectively, assessed and it is that the letter will arrive at its destination in the ordinary course of post. A complainant knows that he or she is taking a risk if the complaint is posted by first class post on the day before the guillotine falls, and it would be absurd to hold that it was not reasonably practicable for it to be presented in time if it arrives in the ordinary course of post on the second day after it was posted. The post will have taken its usual course and nothing unexpected will have occurred.

8. The strict litigation rule in *Godwin v Swindon Borough Council*, that even if it can be proved that a document arrived by post on a day earlier than the deemed date of service, it must nevertheless be deemed to have been served on the deemed date of service, does not apply in employment tribunal cases. If a complainant takes a chance and the letter containing

the complaint happens to arrive at the tribunal office on the day after it was posted and therefore within the permitted three-month period, it will have been presented in time.

Initial Electronic Security   [2005] IRLR 671 EAT
Systems Ltd v
Avdic

Applying the principle established by the Court of Appeal in *Consignia plc v Sealy*, the reasonable expectation of the sender of an electronic mail communication is that, in the absence of any indication to the contrary, it will be delivered and will arrive within a very short time after transmission, normally 30 or 60 minutes. Although, as with the post, there are occasions when e-mails are delayed or disappear, the vast majority of them do not. Accordingly, in the present case, the tribunal was entitled to conclude that when the claimant emailed her claim form some eight hours before the expiry of the time limit it was reasonable for her to assume that the claim form would be received on that date, and since it was not until a few days afterwards that she discovered that her claim form had not been received, it was not reasonably practicable for her to present her complaint in time.

Initial Electronic Security   [2005] IRLR 671 EAT
Systems Ltd v
Avdic

Observed: Unless the *Consignia* defence becomes available, it will always matter why the claimant has left the presentation of the claim form until the last moment.

Machine Tool Industry Research   [1988] IRLR 212 CA
Association v
Simpson

An employment tribunal is entitled to find that it was not reasonably practicable for a complaint to have been presented timeously where during the period of the three-month limitation, there were crucial or important facts unknown, and reasonably unknown, to the claimant which then became known as facts to him such as to give him a belief, and a genuine belief, that he had a claim to be brought before the employment tribunal.

In determining whether or not it was reasonably practicable for an employee to present his complaint in time where initially he took the view that he had no grounds for complaining of unfair dismissal, fundamentally the exercise to be performed is a study of the subjective state of mind of the employee when, at a late stage, he decides that after all there is a case to bring. In order to be relieved of the strict time limit it is not necessary for the employee to establish in evidence the veracity of the reason which led him to make his claim. The expression "reasonably practicable" in [s.111(2)] imports three stages, the proof of which rests on the claimant. First, that it was reasonable for him not to be aware of the factual basis upon which he could bring an application to the tribunal during the three-month limitation period. It cannot be reasonably practicable to expect a claimant to bring a case based upon facts of which he is ignorant. Second, there is an objective qualification of reasonableness in the circumstances to the subjective test of the claimant's state of mind. The claimant must establish that the knowledge which he gains has been reasonably gained by him in the circumstances and that that knowledge is crucial, fundamental or important to his change of belief from one in which he does not believe that he has grounds for an application, to a belief which he reasonably and genuinely holds that he has a ground for making such application. Third, the acquisition of that knowledge must be crucial to the decision to bring a claim in any event.

London Underground Ltd v   **[1999] IRLR 621 CA**
Noel
The essential matter or matters about which the claimant is mistaken or ignorant must relate to the right to bring a claim, not to something that simply goes either to the quality of the claim in financial terms, or the advisability of bringing the claim in commercial and industrial relations terms.

Hart v   **[2006] IRLR 915**
English Heritage (Historic Buildings &
  Monuments Commission for England)
It would be a factor in considering whether it was reasonably practicable to have presented a claim in time if a claimant considered that an individual complaint had already been presented.

Marley (UK) Ltd and another v   **[1996] IRLR 163 CA**
Anderson
Issues of reasonable practicability under [s.111(2)] depend upon awareness of specific grounds for complaint, not upon awareness of the right to complain at all. There is no statutory restriction on the number of complaints which may be brought by a complainant in respect of one dismissal. Where there is more than one ground for complaint, each ground must be looked at separately.

Therefore, if an application alleging unfair dismissal on a particular ground is time-barred, an employment tribunal is entitled to find that there was jurisdiction to consider the complaint on a different ground which had subsequently come to light and which the employee had raised within a reasonable period after acquiring the relevant knowledge. The moment at which an employee first developed a belief in a right to claim unfair dismissal, on any ground, does not fix the point at which it became reasonably practicable for the employee to present a complaint, for all time and for all purposes, including any independent grounds of complaint then still unknown but subsequently discovered.

James W Cook & Co (Wivenhoe) Ltd   **[1990] IRLR 386 CA**
  (in liquidation) v
Tipper and others
That an employee dismissed on grounds of redundancy justifiably believed that work would pick up and he would be re-employed was a relevant factor in determining whether or not it was reasonably practicable for his unfair dismissal complaint to be presented in time.

London Underground Ltd v   **[1999] IRLR 621 CA**
Noel
An offer of re-employment in a new job representing a significant demotion and with a significant cut in salary does not make it reasonably impracticable to present a complaint of unfair dismissal within the statutory time limit. The existence of the offer of a new job is not a fact which is fundamental to the employee's right to present a claim in the sense of affecting the factual basis upon which an application could be brought. If it was unfair for the employee to have been dismissed, the employee had the right to present a complaint even if the offer had matured into another job with the employer.

Wall's Meat Co Ltd v   **[1978] IRLR 499 CA**
Khan
Ignorance or mistaken belief in respect of essential matters can be regarded as grounds for an employment tribunal to hold that a claim in time was not reasonably practicable if it can be shown that the ignorance or mistaken belief was itself reasonable. Either ignorance or mistaken belief will not be reasonable if it arises from the fault of the complainant in not making such inquiries as he reasonably should have made in all the circumstances, or from the fault of his solicitors or other professional advisers in not giving him all the information which they reasonably should have given him in the circumstances.

Dedman v   **[1973] IRLR 379 CA**
British Building and Engineering
  Appliances Ltd
In deciding whether it was practicable for a complaint of unfair dismissal to be presented within the stipulated time period, the employment tribunal should inquire into the circumstances and ask themselves whether the claimant or his advisers were at fault in allowing the time period to pass by without presenting the complaint. If either were at fault, then it could not be said to have been impracticable for the complaint to have been presented in time.

Marks & Spencer plc v   **[2005] IRLR 562 CA**
Williams-Ryan
There is no binding authority which extends the principle in *Dedman* to a situation where advice is given by a Citizens Advice Bureau. The mere fact of seeking advice from the CAB cannot, as a matter of law, rule out the possibility of demonstrating that it was not reasonably practicable to make a timely application to an employment tribunal. It may well depend on who it was who gave the advice and in what circumstances.

Riley v   **[1980] IRLR 103 CA**
1. Tesco Stores Ltd and
2. Greater London Citizens Advice
  Bureau Service Ltd
Where an employee who presents his complaint of unfair dismissal out of time alleges ignorance of his right or of how

and when he should pursue it, or is under some mistaken belief about these matters, an employment tribunal must look at the circumstances of his ignorance or belief and any explanation that he can give for them, including any advice he took, and then ask itself whether the ignorance or mistake is reasonable on his or his adviser's part, or whether it was his or his adviser's fault. If either was at fault or unreasonable, it was reasonably practicable to present the complaint in time. When considering the effect of going to an adviser, the employee cannot necessarily prove that it was not reasonably practicable by saying that he took advice. A third party, skilled or otherwise, only comes to be considered a possible excuse for the employee's delay if he gives advice or is authorised to act in time and he fails to act or advise acting in time.

London International College v [1993] IRLR 333 CA
Sen

A prospective complainant who consults a solicitor does not thereby lose for all time his right to rely on the "not reasonably practicable" defence. The cases which suggest that after consulting a solicitor, or a trade union official or similar adviser, the complainant can no longer say that it was not reasonably practicable for him to comply with the time limit, even if he was advised wrongly, were not really purporting to lay down a rule of law to govern what is essentially a question of fact. Accordingly, the complainant in the present case was not precluded from relying on the defence in circumstances in which he distrusted the advice as to the time limit given by his solicitor and immediately sought advice from another source.

Northamptonshire County Council v [2010] IRLR 740 EAT
Entwhistle

In a case where a claimant has consulted skilled advisers and been given incorrect advice, there is a difference between where the adviser's failure to give correct advice is reasonable, such as where the adviser was misled by the employer as to a material matter like the date of dismissal, and where the error is negligent. The question of reasonable practicability is to be judged by what the claimant could have done if he had been given such advice as the adviser should reasonably in all the circumstances have given him.

Siraj-Eldin v [1989] IRLR 208 CS
Campbell Middleton Burness &
Dickson

To succeed in a claim for damages against solicitors for failing to present an unfair dismissal complaint in time, an employee has to show that the complaint possessed more than mere nuisance value. Where there is no evidence that the employers would have settled with the employee if the complaint had been presented in time, the complainant has to satisfy the court that it would have been open to a reasonable employment tribunal to hold that no reasonable employer would have dismissed the employee in the circumstances of the case, and to make an award.

Further reasonable period

Marley (UK) Ltd and another v [1994] IRLR 152 EAT
Anderson

If a tribunal is satisfied that it was not reasonably practicable for a complaint to be presented before the end of the statutory three-month period, there are no time limits on what it can regard as a further reasonable period for presenting the complaint.

Biggs v [1996] IRLR 203 CA
Somerset County Council

In deciding what is a reasonable further period, the tribunal has to take all the circumstances into account in order to achieve a fair balance. It is not concerned only with difficulties faced by the claimant. Therefore, an extended further period may be unreasonable if the employer would face difficulties of substance in answering the claim.

Service qualification

108. *(1) Section 94 does not apply to the dismissal of an employee unless he has been continuously employed for a period of not less than two years* ending with the effective date of termination.*

. . .

(3) Subsection (1) does not apply if –

   (a) . . . ,

   (aa) subsection (1) of s.98B (read with subsection (2) of that section) applies,

   (b) subsection (1) of s.99 (read with any regulations made under that section) applies,

   (c) subsection (1) of s.100 (read with subsections (2) and (3) of that section) applies,

   (d) subsection (1) of s.101 (read with subsection (2) of that section) or subsection (3) of that section applies,

   (dd) s.101A applies,

   (e) s.102 applies,

   (f) s.103 applies,

   (ff) s.103A applies,

   (g) subsection (1) of s.104 (read with subsections (2) and (3) of that section) applies,

   (gg) subsection (1) of s.104A (read with subsection (2) of that section) applies,

   (gh) subsection (1) of s.104B (read with subsection (2) of that section) applies,

   (gi) s.104C applies,

   (gj) subsection (1) of section 104D (read with subsection (2) of that section) applies,

   (gk) s.104E applies,

   (gl) subsection (1) of s.104F (read with subsection (2) of that section) applies,

   (h) s.105 applies,

   (hh) paragraph (3) or (6) of reg. 28 of the Transnational Information and Consultation of Employees Regulations 1999 (read with paras. (4) and (7) of that regulation) applies,

   (i) paragraph (1) of reg. 7 of the Part-Time Workers (Prevention of Less Favourable Treatment) Regulations 2000 applies,

   (j) paragraph (1) of reg. 6 of the Fixed-term Employees (Prevention of Less Favourable Treatment) Regulations 2002 applies,

   (k) paragraph (3) or (6) of reg. 42 of the European Public Limited-Liability Company Regulations 2004 applies,

   (l) paragraph (3) or (6) of reg. 30 of the Information and Consultation of Employees Regulations 2004 (read with paragraphs (4) and (7) of that regulation) applies,

   (m) paragraph 5(3) or (5) of the Schedule to the Occupational and Personal Pension Schemes (Consultation by Employers and Miscellaneous Amendment) Regulations 2006 (read with para. 5(6) of that Schedule) applies,

   (n) . . .

   (o) paragraph (3) or (6) of reg. 31 of the European Cooperative Society (Involvement of Employees) Regulations 2006 (read with paras. (4) and (7) of that regulation) applies,

   (p) regulation 46 or 47 of the Companies (Cross-Border Mergers) Regulations 2007 applies,

   (q) paragraph (1)(a) or (b) of reg. 29 of the European Public Limited-Liability Company (Employee Involvement) (Great Britain) Regulations 2009 (SI 2009/2401) applies, or

   (r) paragraph (1) of regulation 17 of the Agency Workers Regulations 2010 applies.

(4) Subsection (1) does not apply if the reason (or, if more than one, the principal reason) for the dismissal is, or relates to, the employee's political opinions or affiliation.

EMPLOYMENT RIGHTS ACT 1996 (as amended)

Leicester University   **[1995] IRLR 292 EAT**
  Students' Union v
Mahomed
If an employment tribunal decides on the evidence that the qualifying period is established, that decision is not rendered a nullity for want of jurisdiction if there is subsequent evidence showing that the qualifying period had not been served.

Redfearn v   **[2013] IRLR 51 ECHR**
UK
The absence in British law of a remedy against dismissal on grounds of political opinion or affiliation for those who do not have the necessary qualifying period of service contravenes Article 11 of the ECHR (freedom of association with others), read in light of Article 10 (freedom of expression).

Computation of period of continuous employment

210. *(1) References in any provision of this Act to a period of continuous employment are (unless provision is expressly made to the contrary) to a period computed in accordance with this Chapter.*

(2) In any provision of this Act which refers to a period of continuous employment expressed in months or years –

   (a) a month means a calendar month, and

   (b) a year means a year of 12 calendar months.

(3) In computing an employee's period of continuous employment for the purposes of any provision of this Act, any question –

   (a) whether the employee's employment is of a kind counting towards a period of continuous employment, or

   (b) whether periods (consecutive or otherwise) are to be treated as forming a single period of continuous employment,

shall be determined week by week; but where it is necessary to compute the length of an employee's period of employment it shall be computed in months and years of 12 months in accordance with s.211.

(4) Subject to sections 215 to 217, a week which does not count in computing the length of a period of continuous employment breaks continuity of employment.

(5) A person's employment during any period shall, unless the contrary is shown, be presumed to have been continuous.

---

* Or one year in any case where the period of continuous employment began before 6 April 2012.

211. *(1) An employee's period of continuous employment for the purposes of any provision of this Act –*

    (a) (subject to subsection (3)) begins with the day on which the employee starts work, and

    (b) ends with the day by reference to which the length of the employee's period of continuous employment is to be ascertained for the purposes of the provision.

. . .

(3) If an employee's period of continuous employment includes one or more periods which (by virtue of s.215, 216 or 217) while not counting in computing the length of the period do not break continuity of employment, the beginning of the period shall be treated as postponed by the number of days falling within that intervening period, or the aggregate number of days falling within those periods, calculated in accordance with the section in question.

212. *(1) Any week during the whole or part of which an employee's relations with his employer are governed by a contract of employment counts in computing the employee's period of employment.*

          EMPLOYMENT RIGHTS ACT 1996 (as amended)

Pacitti Jones v   **[2005] IRLR 888 CS**
O'Brien

In determining whether an employee has the necessary continuous employment to claim unfair dismissal, s.211(1)(a) makes it clear that the day on which the employee started work is to be included in the reckoning.

The General of the Salvation Army v **[1984] IRLR 222 EAT**
Dewsbury

The phrase "starts work" in [s.211(1)(a)] is intended to refer to the beginning of the employee's employment under the relevant contract. It is not intended to be interpreted literally as referring to when the employee first undertook the duties of the employment.

Presumption of continuity

Wood v   **[1978] IRLR 228 CA**
York City Council

A period with the same employer is to be treated as continuous unless it comes within one of the specified exceptions. A man may change his job, his place of work or the terms of his employment, he may even enter a new contract of employment, but provided he is employed by the same employer this change in the contractual terms will not affect his period of continuous employment.

Carrington v   **[1998] IRLR 567 EAT**
Harwich Dock Co Ltd

The provisions of s.212(1) are mandatory and do not cease to apply where an employee resigns voluntarily at the end of one week and is re-engaged at the beginning of the next.

Sweeney v   **[1999] IRLR 306 EAT**
J & S Henderson (Concessions) Ltd

Employment is continuous in accordance with s.212(1), where, during any part of successive weeks, the employee was working

for the employer under a contract of employment, even if there is a gap in the employment created by the employee obtaining alternative employment. So long as, during the relevant weeks, there is at least one day governed by a contract of employment with the relevant employer, it does not matter how the gap was created nor what the employee did during its currency. Any inequity as far as the employer is concerned is easily resolved by declining to take the employee back until there has been a gap of at least two weeks where the employee has not worked under a contract of employment with the employer.

Tipper v   **[1989] IRLR 419 EAT**
Roofdec Ltd

Where there are successive employments in successive weeks by the same employer, if the statutory requirements for computing periods of continuous employment are satisfied, the precise reason why the first employment ceased is of no significance. Therefore, to the catalogue of events which do not break continuity set out in *Wood v York City Council* can be added frustration of the first contract as opposed to its termination by other means.

Collison v   **[1998] IRLR 238 EAT**
British Broadcasting Corporation

Continuity of employment is a purely statutory concept. There is nothing in the statutory provisions relating to compromise agreements which permits the parties to contract out of the statutory provisions governing the computation of continuous employment.

Secretary of State for Employment v **[1979] IRLR 327 HL**
Globe Elastic Thread Co Ltd

Continuity of employment and the presumption of continuity means continuity with the dismissing employer. The only exceptions to this are when a business or undertaking is transferred or when an employee is taken into employment by an associated company. Apart from these exceptions, continuous employment must be with one employer – otherwise continuity is broken.

Secretary of State for Employment v **[1987] IRLR 169 EAT**
1. Cohen and 2. Beaupress Ltd

Employment with successive employers cannot be presumed to be continuous unless the case can be brought within [s.218]. The statutory presumption of continuity in [s.210.(5)] cannot be applied so as to enable the condition expressed in the relevant sub-paragraphs of [s.218] to be satisfied. Since the presumption does not apply unless the condition is satisfied, it cannot be right to apply the presumption in order to satisfy the condition.

Preservation of continuity

212. *(3) Subject to subsection (4), any week (not within subsection (1)) during the whole or part of which an employee is –*

    (a) incapable of work in consequence of sickness or injury, or

    (b) absent from work on account of a temporary cessation of work, or

(c) absent from work in circumstances such that, by arrangement or custom, he is regarded as continuing in the employment of his employer for any purpose,

counts in computing the employee's period of employment.

(4) Not more than 26 weeks count under subsection (3)(a) between any periods falling under subsection (1).

EMPLOYMENT RIGHTS ACT 1996 (as amended)

Pearson v   **[1992] IRLR 110 EAT**
Kent County Council

For [s.212(3)] to apply, there must have been an original contract of employment; termination of that contract; a period when no contract of employment exists; and finally a subsequent contract of employment with the same employer. In respect of the period when there is no contract, the question to be determined is, "Why was there no contract of employment in each of the statutory weeks?"

SICKNESS OR INJURY

Pearson v   **[1993] IRLR 165 CA**
Kent County Council

[Section 212(3)(a)] requires a causal link between the employee's absence from work and his incapacity in consequence of sickness or injury. The tribunal has to look backwards and decide what was the reason for the employee's absence considered week by week during the relevant period. "Incapable of work" in this context does not mean incapable of work generally. Nor, however, in all circumstances does it refer to the particular work provided for in the contract of employment which has been terminated. Where during a particular week, the work on offer by the employer differs from that for which the employee was previously employed, the tribunal has to consider whether the work offered was of a kind which the employee was willing to accept or, even though unwilling, was suitable for his particular circumstances. The tribunal then has to decide whether the employee's absence from that work was in consequence of sickness or injury.

Accordingly, a gap of 10 days between an employee retiring from his original job on medical grounds and being re-employed in a less arduous position was not a period when he was incapable of work in consequence of sickness or injury within the meaning of [s.212(3)(a)] since his incapacity related only to his ability to perform the original job and did not prevent him from carrying out the new position.

Donnelly v   **[1992] IRLR 496 EAT**
Kelvin International Services

The mere fact that the employee works for another employer during that period does not necessarily mean that he has ceased to be incapable of work by reason of sickness for the purposes of [s.212(3)(a)]. If the employment is only of a nature intended to bridge the gap in his employment with the first employer – for example, if it is a period of light work undertaken in the hope or expectation that in time he will be able to return to his previous full-time employment – it may not interrupt continuity. On the other hand, if it appears that

the intervening employment was undertaken as full-time permanent employment, the appropriate conclusion may well be that the employee is no longer absent from his first employment because of incapacity.

TEMPORARY CESSATION

Ford v   **[1983] IRLR 127 HL**
Warwickshire County Council

The period of time described by the phrase "absent from work on account of a temporary cessation of work" in [s.212(3)(b)] must refer to the interval between (i) the date on which the employee who would otherwise be continuing to work under an existing contract of employment is dismissed because for the time being his employer has no work for him to do; and (ii) the date on which work for him to do having become available again, he is re-engaged under a fresh contract of employment to do it.

In the context of [s.212(3)(b)], the word "temporary" is used in the sense of "transient", that is lasting for only a relatively short time. Whether an interval can be so characterised is a question of fact for the employment tribunal to determine. The words "on account of" a temporary cessation of work refer to the reason when the employer dismissed the employee and make it necessary to inquire what the reason for dismissal was. The fact that the unavailability of work was foreseen by the employer sufficiently far in advance to enable him to anticipate it by giving the employee the period of notice of termination to which he was entitled, cannot alter the reason for the dismissal or prevent the absence from work following upon the expiry of the notice being "on account of a temporary cessation of work". [Section 212(3)(b)] is not concerned with the means employed for bringing the employment to an end temporarily but with the reason for bringing it to an end.

The requirement that the absence be on account of a temporary cessation of work can be satisfied equally by a cessation which was anticipated when a fixed term was introduced into the contract. If it is irrelevant to the employee's right to claim unfair dismissal whether his work has ended owing to the expiry of the fixed term of the contract or owing to the expiry of the term of the notice of dismissal, it is consistent that the "counting" process under [s.212(3)(b)] should likewise have no regard to the question whether the "absence from work" was the immediate result of the dismissal notice, or the immediate result of the expiry of a fixed term specified in the contract. In the case of a fixed term contract, the employer in effect gives notice when the contract is signed of the date when the employment is to cease, instead of reserving to himself the right to give such notice at a later date. If [s.212(3)(b)] is intended to apply to a case where notice of dismissal is served during the currency of the contract on account of an anticipated cessation of work, there is no logical reason why it should be supposed not to apply where the contract itself indicates when the employment is to cease, if that is on account of a temporary cessation of work.

Observed (per Lord Diplock): In cases of employment under a succession of contracts with intervals between them, continuity of employment for the purposes of the Act is not broken until, looking backwards from the date of expiry of the contract on which the employee's claim was based, there can be found between one contract and its immediate predecessor an interval which cannot be characterised as short relative to the combined duration of the two contracts.

Flack and others v   **[1986] IRLR 255 CA**
Kodak Ltd
In deciding whether a gap in an employee's employment during which he is absent from work on account of a cessation of work is a temporary cessation for the purposes of [s.212(3)(b)], the correct approach is to take account of all the relevant circumstances and, in particular, to consider the length of the period of employment as a whole. The leading authority is the House of Lords' decision in *Fitzgerald v Hall, Russell & Co* which makes it clear that the relativity in terms of time between an absence due to a cessation of work and its antecedent and subsequent periods of employment is no more than one relevant consideration. Whether a cessation during the statutory qualifying period can be characterised as temporary may be affected by the whole history of the employment. The speech of Lord Diplock in *Ford v Warwickshire County Council* in which he advocated the purely mathematical approach of comparing each gap in employment with the antecedent and subsequent periods of employment was *obiter* and was not intended as laying down a test in all cases.

Sillars v   **[1989] IRLR 152 CA**
Charringtons Fuels Ltd
It has been made clear in a series of decisions of the courts that "temporary" in relation to a cessation of work under [s.212(3)(b)] has to be construed in the sense of a relatively short period of time compared with the period in work. The employment tribunal were entitled to apply the mathematical approach set out in obiter in *Ford v Warwickshire County Council* rather than the broad approach advocated in *Flack v Kodak Ltd* to the case of a seasonal employee who, over a total period of 15 years, had spent roughly half of each year in the company's employment and half of each year out of it, since whatever the period considered the answer would be the same. Taking the final two years in isolation, it was not possible to regard the periods out of employment as short in relation to the periods in work and that pattern was not altered by looking back over the whole 15-year period.

The Bentley Engineering Co Ltd v   **[1976] IRLR 146 HC**
Crown and Miller
In determining whether an employee's absence from work is on account of a temporary cessation of work within the meaning of [s.212(3)(b)], three questions are posed: was there a cessation of the employee's work, was the cessation a temporary one, and was the employee absent on account of that cessation? In determining whether the cessation was temporary, relevant criteria include the nature of the employment, the length of prior and subsequent service, the duration of the

break, what was said when the break occurred, what happened during the break and what was said on re-engagement. The fact that the employee had taken up another job during his absence did not mean that he could not be said to be absent on account of the cessation.

Hussain v   **[2011] IRLR 463 EAT**
Acorn Independent College
When considering whether there was continuity of employment because an employee was only absent from work on account of a temporary cessation of work, the nature of the contract either side of the interval does not matter and the correct approach is to find the reason for the termination of the first contract, looking back from the end of the second contract. There is no difficulty arising in the application of section 212 to cases where the interval consists of the summer holidays.

Sillars v   **[1989] IRLR 152 CA**
Charringtons Fuels Ltd
The fact that a cessation is not permanent does not mean that it must be temporary for the purposes of [s.212(3)(b)].

Lewis v   **[1987] IRLR 509 HL**
Surrey County Council
An interval between separate contracts, as distinct from between successor and predecessor contracts in the same series, cannot amount to a temporary cessation of work within the meaning of [s.212(3)(b)]. Each series of contracts has to be considered in isolation from any other series.

Byrne v   **[1987] IRLR 191 CA**
City of Birmingham
   District Council
The expression "cessation of work" in [s.212(3)(b)] must denote that some quantum of work had for the time being ceased to exist and therefore was no longer available to the employer to give to the employee. It does not apply to a situation where the work that was available was given to someone else. Therefore, a period during which a member of a "pool" of casual workers is not allocated work under the pool arrangement cannot be described as a temporary cessation of work.

ARRANGEMENT OR CUSTOM

Curr v   **[2003] IRLR 74 CA**
Marks & Spencer plc
For s.212(3)(c) to apply to preserve continuity of employment during a week when there is no contract of employment, the ex-employee must, by arrangement (which can, but need not, be a contract) or custom, be regarded by each of the parties as continuing in the employment of the employer for any purpose during that period. Without there being a meeting of minds by the arrangement that both parties regard the ex-employee as continuing in that employment for some purpose, s.212(3)(c) will not be satisfied.

London Probation Board v   **[2005] IRLR 443 EAT**
Kirkpatrick

There is no reason why an "arrangement" to preserve continuity within the meaning of s.212(3)(c) cannot be made retrospectively. An arrangement can be in place without ever being put into operation in any specific case or it can be made and applied in a specific case. Although logically a "custom" should exist prior to a gap in employment, there was no reason to add words to the statute so as to limit arrangements to those made in advance of the gap. Accordingly, a gap of about two months between the date a claimant was dismissed and the date an appeal panel decided to reinstate him was covered by an arrangement to preserve continuity in terms of s.212(3)(c), notwithstanding that it was made after the gap. Alternatively, the discipline and appeal procedure which gave the claimant a contractual right to have an appeal heard by an independent body with the power to put right a wrong or unfair decision, could aptly be described as an "arrangement" which was in place prior to the gap in the claimant's employment and under which he was regarded as being in the employment of the employers for at least the purposes of an appeal.

Morris v   **[1997] IRLR 562 EAT**
Walsh Western UK Ltd

An arrangement to preserve continuity made after a period of absence cannot fall within s.212(3)(c). Continuity is a creature of statute. As a matter of construction, the statutory provision envisages that the arrangement is in place when the employee is absent from work, not afterwards. Accordingly, the fact that an employee had been told on re-employment that the absence would be treated as unpaid leave did not amount to an arrangement to regard him as continuing in employment within the meaning of s.212(3)(c). The reasoning of the EAT in *Murphy v A Birrell & Sons* was correct. The view of the EAT in *Ingram v Foxon*, that a retrospective arrangement could be held to preserve continuity within the meaning of s.212(3)(c) where the employer recognised that the employee had been unfairly dismissed and reinstated him, had been reached without the benefit of full argument and was not permissible.

Murphy v   **[1978] IRLR 458 EAT**
A Birrell & Sons Ltd

An arrangement under which an employee is regarded during a period when there is no contract of employment as continuing in the employment of the employer for all or any purposes within the meaning of [s.212(3)(c)] cannot be made retrospectively at the conclusion of the absence from work. The arrangement must exist at the time the absence began. For [s.212(3)(c)] to apply, during any relevant week of absence it must be in the minds both of the employer and the employee that he is regarded as still being in employment. [Section 212(3)(c)] does not cover a situation where an employee leaves his employer's service, apparently permanently, and returns at a later date, notwithstanding that at that later date there is an agreement between them that his service can be regarded as continuous for certain purposes.

Ingram v   **[1985] IRLR 5 EAT**
Foxon

An agreement to reinstate a dismissed employee and regard him as having been continuously employed throughout the period between dismissal and reinstatement can fall within [s.212(3)(c)]. Such a situation can be distinguished from that in *Murphy*'s case if there was no intention when making the retrospective arrangement to commit a calculated fraud.

Welton v   **[2013] IRLR 166 EAT**
Deluxe Retail (t/a Madhouse)

When determining whether, during the whole or part of any week, the employee was absent from work in circumstances such that, "by arrangement or custom, he is regarded as continuing in the employment of his employer for any purpose" (under section 212(3)(c)), an "arrangement" can only bridge the gap in continuity if it was in existence before, or arose contemporaneously with, the relevant weeks of absence from work.

Ingram v   **[1985] IRLR 5 EAT**
Foxon

That an employee was not paid during the period between dismissal and reinstatement did not mean that he could not be regarded as having been reinstated and his continuity of employment preserved. If the employee chose to waive the condition (wholly in his favour) that he should be paid for the period of absence, that could not affect the validity of his reinstatement if it was otherwise effective for the purpose of preserving his continuity.

Booth v   **[1999] IRLR 16 EAT**
United States of America

In the absence of an arrangement to treat a break in employment as continuous, employment could not be treated as continuing even where the underlying purpose of the break was to defeat the application of employment protection legislation. If, by so arranging their affairs, employers lawfully are able to employ people in such a manner that the employees cannot complain of unfair dismissal or seek a redundancy payment, that is a matter for them. It is for the legislators, not the courts, to close any loopholes that might be perceived to exist.

Employment abroad

215. *(1) This Chapter applies to a period of employment –*
    (a) (subject to the following provisions of this section) even where during the period the employee was engaged in work wholly or mainly outside Great Britain, and
    (b) even where the employee was excluded by or under this Act from any right conferred by this Act.
        EMPLOYMENT RIGHTS ACT 1996

Weston v   **[1989] IRLR 429 EAT**
Vega Space Systems Engineering Ltd

The effect of [s.215(1)] is that an employee is entitled to count a period of employment wholly or mainly outside Great Britain for the purpose of determining whether he meets the service qualification set out in [s.108(1)].

Effect of industrial dispute

216. *(1) A week does not count under s.212 if during the week, or any part of the week, the employee takes part in a strike.*

(2) The continuity of an employee's period of employment is not broken by a week which does not count under this Chapter (whether or not by virtue only of subsection (1)) if during the week, or any part of the week, the employee takes part in a strike; and the number of days which, for the purposes of s.211(3), fall within the intervening period is the number of days between the last working day before the strike and the day on which work was resumed.

(3) The continuity of an employee's period of employment is not broken by a week if during the week, or any part of the week, the employee is absent from work because of a lock-out by the employer; and the number of days which, for the purposes of s.211(3), fall within the intervening period is the number of days between the last working day before the lock-out and the day on which work was resumed.

EMPLOYMENT RIGHTS ACT 1996

Hanson v   **[1980] IRLR 393 EAT**
Fashion Industries (Hartlepool) Ltd
The effect of [s.216] is that whilst the weeks that an employee is on strike do not count towards his continuous service, continuity is preserved even where the employee was dismissed during the strike and subsequently re-engaged under a new contract.

Change of employer

218. *(1) Subject to the provisions of this section, this Chapter relates only to employment by the one employer.*

(2) If a trade or business, or an undertaking (whether or not established by or under an Act), is transferred from one person to another –

> *(a) the period of employment of an employee in the trade or business or undertaking at the time of the transfer counts as a period of employment with the transferee, and*
>
> *(b) the transfer does not break the continuity of the period of employment.*

(3) If by or under an Act (whether public or local and whether passed before or after this Act) a contract of employment between any body corporate and an employee is modified and some other body corporate is substituted as the employer –

> *(a) the employee's period of employment at the time when the modification takes effect counts as a period of employment with the second body corporate, and*
>
> *(b) the change of employer does not break the continuity of the period of employment.*

(4) If on the death of an employer the employee is taken into the employment of the personal representatives or trustees of the deceased –

> *(a) the employee's period of employment at the time of the death counts as a period of employment with the employer's personal representatives or trustees, and*
>
> *(b) the death does not break the continuity of the period of employment.*

(5) If there is a change in the partners, personal representatives or trustees who employ any person –

> *(a) the employee's period of employment at the time of the change counts as a period of employment with the partners, personal representatives or trustees after the change, and*

> *(b) the change does not break the continuity of the period of employment.*

(6) If an employee of an employer is taken into the employment of another employer who, at the time when the employee enters the second employer's employment, is an associated employer of the first employer –

> *(a) the employee's period of employment at that time counts as a period of employment with the second employer, and*
>
> *(b) the change of employer does not break the continuity of the period of employment.*

(7) If an employee of the governing body of a school maintained by a local authority is taken into the employment of the authority or an employee of a local authority is taken into the employment of the governing body of a school maintained by the authority –

> *(a) his period of employment at the time of the change of employer counts as a period of employment with the second employer, and*
>
> *(b) the change does not break the continuity of the period of employment.*

(8) If a person employed in relevant employment by a health service employer is taken into relevant employment by another such employer, his period of employment at the time of the change of employer counts as a period of employment with the second employer and the change does not break the continuity of the period of employment.

(9) For the purposes of subsection (8) employment is relevant employment if it is employment of a description –

> *(a) in which persons are engaged while undergoing professional training which involves their being employed successively by a number of different health service employers, and*
>
> *(b) which is specified in an order made by the Secretary of State.*

(10) The following are health service employers for the purposes of subsections (8) and (9) –

> *(za) the National Health Service Commissioning Board,*
>
> *(zb) a clinical commissioning group established under section 14D of the National Health Service Act 2006,*
>
> *(a) . . .*
>
> *(b) Special Health Authorities established under s.28 of that Act or s.22 of the National Health Service (Wales) Act 2006,*
>
> *(bb) . . .*
>
> *(c) National Health Service trusts established under the National Health Service Act 2006 or the National Health Service (Wales) Act 2006,*
>
> *(ca) NHS foundation trusts,*
>
> *(cb) Local Health Boards established under s.11 of the National Health Service (Wales) Act 2006,*
>
> *(d) . . .*
>
> *(dd) . . .*
>
> *(e) . . .*

(11) In subsection (7) "local authority" has the meaning given by section 579(1) of the Education Act 1996.

231. *For the purposes of this Act, any two employers shall be treated as associated if –*

> *(a) one is a company of which the other (directly or indirectly) has control, or*
>
> *(b) both are companies of which a third person (directly or indirectly) has control;*

and "associated employer" shall be construed accordingly.

EMPLOYMENT RIGHTS ACT 1996 (as amended)

TRANSFER OF BUSINESS

Macer v   **[1990] IRLR 137 EAT**
Abafast Ltd

The preferred interpretation of [s.218(2)] is that which best gives effect to the preservation of continuity of service and obviates and discourages any attempt to avoid rights and obligations under the legislation by a tactical manoeuvre which seeks to avoid the clear intention of Parliament.

Macer v   **[1990] IRLR 137 EAT**
Abafast Ltd

[Section 218(2)] should be read as meaning that provided that there has been a valid transfer of a business from A to B, the continuous period of service of an employee with A may be added to the continuous period of service with B so as to establish a qualifying period of continuous employment for the purpose of jurisdiction under [s.108]. [Section 218(2)] can be understood to have four essentials: the transfer and therefore the continuation of the business; employment by the owner before the transfer or change of ownership and by the owner afterwards; the period of service with the former and likewise the period of service with the latter must be continuous within the statutory provisions; and the combined periods of service must satisfy the statutory qualification period.

Justfern Ltd v   **[1994] IRLR 164 EAT**
D'Ingerthorpe and others

There may be a transfer of a business in terms of [s.218(2)] even where, prior to the transfer, the business closes down and the employee's employment is terminated. However, it is a necessary implication of [s.218(2)] that the business and the employment of the relevant employee should survive sufficiently as to be susceptible to transfer. If the old employer closes down the business so completely that the new employer was effectively starting a new business, the necessary implication would not be satisfied.

Secretary of State for Employment v   **[1987] IRLR 169 EAT**
1. Cohen and
2. Beaupress Ltd

Although the onus of satisfying the employment tribunal that there has been a transfer of the business from one employer to another lies with the claimant, it may be sufficient to justify the inference of a transfer if the employee gives evidence that his employment continued in the same place, under the same directors, with the same customers and the same stock being used. Documentary evidence of the true nature of the transaction between the employer and the successor employer would not in the ordinary way be available to an employee and it is not necessarily essential for the employee to place such evidence before the tribunal. An employee can do no more than give evidence of that which he knows. To require him to do more in order to discharge some strict standard of proof in effect would be to deprive him of the chance of claiming a right to which he might be entitled.

Dabell v   **[1988] IRLR 439 CA**
Vale Industrial Services
    (Nottingham) Ltd

In order for there to be a transfer of a business, it is not essential that there has been a written sales agreement or that the disposition of the ownership of the business is final and conclusive. Since whether there has been a transfer must be determined as at the date when the act of which the employee complains occurred, it follows that there can be a change in ownership of the business even though there is still the possibility of a future re-transfer if negotiations fall through.

Melon and others v   **[1980] IRLR 477 HL**
Hector Powe Ltd

The essential distinction between the transfer of a business, or part of a business, and a transfer of physical assets is that in the former case the business is transferred as a going concern so that (per Lord Denning in *Lloyd v Brassey*) "the business remains the same business but in different hands". In the case of a transfer of physical assets, the assets are transferred to the new owner to be used in whatever business he chooses.

Jeetle v   **[1985] IRLR 227 EAT**
Elster

Whether or not there has been a transfer of the goodwill of the business or undertaking is only one of the factors to be taken into consideration in determining whether there has been a transfer within the meaning of [s.218(2)].

SI (Systems & Instruments) Ltd v   **[1983] IRLR 391 EAT**
Grist and Riley

There is no change in ownership of a business within the meaning of [s.218(2)] where no legal rights, shares or assets have been acquired, notwithstanding that the day to day running of the business has been taken over by the alleged transferee. For a change in ownership to occur, the transferee must acquire something, whether by sale or other disposition.

Allen & Son v   **[1979] IRLR 399 EAT**
Coventry

Transfer of part of the equity of a partnership so that a person who formerly owned part of it now owns it all is a transfer of a business within the meaning of [s.218(2)] such as to preserve the continuity of employment of employees of the partnership.

Clark & Tokeley Ltd v   **[1998] IRLR 577 CA**
Oakes

The 'time of the transfer' in s.218(2) refers to the period of time over which the transfer extends, not to the point in time at which the legal formalities of transfer are completed. Accordingly, an employee dismissed during the process of transfer who was later re-employed by the transferee could count his employment as continuous.

Macer v   **[1990] IRLR 137 EAT**
Abafast Ltd
The words "at the time of the transfer" in [s.218(2)] do not require the employee to have been in the employment of the transferor "immediately before the transfer".

Clark & Tokeley Ltd v   **[1997] IRLR 564 EAT**
Oakes
Section 218 (2) requires that the employee has still to be in the employ of the previous employer at the point of change. It does not bridge a gap in employment. If, before the transfer, an employee has ceased to be in the employment of the business, then his earlier period of employment does not count as a period in the employment of the transferee.

Justfern Ltd v   **[1994] IRLR 164 EAT**
D'Ingerthorpe and others
Where the employee's employment is terminated by the original employer prior to the transfer, the motive for doing so is not of direct significance for the purposes of [s.218(2)].

Justfern Ltd v   **[1994] IRLR 164 EAT**
D'Ingerthorpe and others
That the employee received unemployment benefit between the time the business in which he was lately employed closed and the time when it reopened under new ownership is not inconsistent with a finding that he was employed in the business "at the time of the transfer", in that he was available for employment in it.

A & G Tuck Ltd v   **[1994] IRLR 162 EAT**
Bartlett and A & G Tuck (Slough) Ltd
[Section 218(2)] does not require the employee to enter the employment of the transferee at "the moment" of the transfer. Although legal documentation may be complete, the machinery of transfer of an undertaking may take a more extended period.

Lord Advocate v   **[1974] IRLR 215 HL**
De Rosa and John Barrie
   (Contractor) Ltd
Where an employee changes employers as a result of a transfer of ownership in the business, he is entitled to count his period of employment with both employers, notwithstanding that he was re-engaged by the new employer under different terms and conditions.

Gale v   **[1994] IRLR 292 CA**
Northern General Hospital NHS Trust
[Section 218(3)] is directed to a situation where one employer replaces another and employees pass from the one to the other almost as if part of the premises or the stock in trade.

Stevens v   **[2004] IRLR 957 CA**
Bower
Section 218(5) applies when two partners are succeeded by one of them as sole principal.

Observed (per Maurice Kay LJ): Section 218(2) is also capable of applying where partners A and B dissolve their partnership and the business is thereafter carried on by B alone. Sections (2) and (5) are not mutually exclusive.

ASSOCIATED EMPLOYERS

Gardiner v   **[1980] IRLR 472 CA**
London Borough of Merton
The definition of "associated employer" in [s.231] applies only where one of the employers concerned is a company. Though the Act does not contain a definition of "company", it means "limited company". Local authorities are not limited companies and therefore do not come within the [s.231] definition. Thus [s.218(6)] cannot apply to preserve a local government worker's continuity of employment over periods of service with different authorities.

Hancill v   **[1990] IRLR 51 EAT**
Marcon Engineering Ltd
The decision in *London Borough of Merton* that "company" means "limited company" does not require the company concerned to be a UK company formed and registered under the Companies Act, which would exclude all overseas companies. An overseas company can fall within the definition if it can be likened in its essentials to a company limited under the Companies Act.

Pinkney v   **[1989] IRLR 425 EAT**
Sandpiper Drilling Ltd and others
Where one of the two employers is a partnership consisting of limited companies, the second limb of [s.231] may apply to preserve the employee's continuity of employment. Were that not so, a number of companies by forming themselves into a partnership would be able to avoid certain legal and statutory obligations.

South West Launderettes Ltd v   **[1986] IRLR 305 CA**
Laidler
The provision in [s.231] that two employers are to be treated as associated if both are companies of which a third person, directly or indirectly, has control requires the control of the two companies to be in the hands of the same third person.

Strudwick v   **[1988] IRLR 457 EAT**
IBL
The decision of the Court of Appeal in *South West Launderettes* was binding authority for the proposition that, if the third person is more than one individual, it must be the same combination of those individuals which has voting control over each relevant company.

Secretary of State for Employment v   **[1981] IRLR 305 EAT**
1. Newbold and
2. Joint Liquidators of David
   Armstrong (Catering Services) Ltd
Whether two employers are controlled by the same third per-

son and thus are associated employers within the meaning of [s.231] depends upon whether that third person has control in terms of majority ownership. The word "control" in [s.231] is used in the context of the limited company. In company law, control is well recognised to mean control by the majority of votes attaching to shares, exercised in general meetings. It is not how and by whom the enterprise is actually run.

Payne v [1989] IRLR 352 CA
Secretary of State for Employment
Observed (per Balcombe LJ): Whereas voting control is undoubtedly the usual and normal test, exceptionally there may be other circumstances to be taken into account. It *might*, in certain circumstances, be relevant to know about *de facto* control.

South West Launderettes Ltd v [1986] IRLR 305 CA
Laidler
Observed (per Mustill LJ): In determining the identity of the possessor of control, the register of shares cannot be conclusive since the person registered as owner of the majority may be a nominee or trustee, or might be a party to a contract which conferred the right to determine the way in which the voting rights were exercised. It was debatable, however, whether anything short of a legally binding agreement to that effect would ever justify the conclusion that control resided in someone other than the registered owner of the shares.

Payne v [1989] IRLR 352 CA
Secretary of State for Employment
The observations of Mustill LJ in *South West Launderettes Ltd v Laidler* concerning the identity of the possessor of control indicated that a person who has the legal right to control the exercise of votes by another or others, himself has "control" within [s.231].

Hair Colour Consultants Ltd v [1984] IRLR 387 EAT
Mena
The definition of "control" within the meaning of [s.231] established in Secretary of State for Employment v Newbold means that unless there is a holding of more than 50% of the shares in a company, there is no control. That definition of control does not extend to "negative control" so as to mean that a person who has a 50% shareholding has control because he can thwart the wishes of the person or persons holding the remaining 50%. If negative control was permissible in this context, then where two people each had 50% of the shares in a company they would both "control" it. The language of the statute is inconsistent with there being two controllers at the same time.

Excluded cases

Employment outside GB

Ravat v [2012] IRLR 315 SC
Halliburton Manufacturing and Services
In deciding whether an employee who works abroad is entitled to bring a claim for unfair dismissal before a UK employment tribunal, (1) the question in each case is whether the unfair dismissal provisions apply to the particular case, notwithstanding its foreign elements, (2) the starting point is that the employment relationship must have a stronger connection with Great Britain than with the foreign country where the employee works, (3) the general rule is that the place of employment is decisive, but the open-ended language of the statute leaves room for some exceptions where the connection with Great Britain is sufficiently strong, (4) as regards whether a case falls within these exceptions, (a) there is no hard and fast rule, and the examples provided in *Lawson v Serco* are merely examples of the application of the general principle, (b) the case of those who both work and live outside Great Britain requires an especially strong connection with Great Britain and British employment law before an exception can be made for them, whereas the burden on a commuter who lives in Great Britain of showing a sufficient connection is less onerous, (c) the proper law of the employee's contract is relevant but not determinative, and (d) any reassurances given to the employee by the employer about the availability to him of UK employment law are likewise relevant but not determinative.

Lawson v [2006] IRLR 289 HL
Serco Ltd
Botham v
Ministry of Defence
Crofts v
Veta Ltd
The correct test of the right to claim unfair dismissal for employees with some foreign element to their employment, in most cases, will be whether the employee is employed in Great Britain at the time of their dismissal (not taking into account casual visits).

In the case of peripatetic employees, such as airline pilots, a "base" test should be applied to determine where the employee should be regarded as ordinarily working.

Expatriate employees can claim unfair dismissal if they are:
1. working in an extra-territorial British enclave in a foreign country, as was the case in *Lawson*, where the employee was working in an RAF base on Ascension Island; or
2. working abroad for a British employer for the purposes of a business carried out in Great Britain, for example a foreign correspondent on the staff of a British newspaper.

Any other cases relating to expatriate employees "would have to have equally strong connections with Great Britain and British employment law." The *Lawson* formulation can be seen as endorsing a "substantial connection" approach.

Whether, on given facts, a case falls within the territorial scope of s.94(1) of the Employment Rights Act 1996 should be treated as a question of law.

Creditsights Ltd v Dhunna
[2014] IRLR 953 CA

Proof that an employee's relationship with his employer has a sufficiently strong connection with Great Britain and British employment law such that it can be presumed that Parliament must have intended that s.94(1) should apply to that employee is not established by making a comparison of the relevant merits of British and any competing system of labour law.

YKK Europe Ltd v Heneghan
[2010] IRLR 563 EAT

In determining whether it has jurisdiction to hear an unfair dismissal claim a tribunal must focus on what was happening as at the date of dismissal rather than at the outset of the relationship. Where the employee is absent from work for whatever reason at the date of dismissal, in addition to considering the category into which an employee falls, the following factors will in general be relevant: (1) why the employee was absent from work, and the length of his absence before dismissal; (2) where the employee was ordinarily working, or based, and for how long, before his absence from work began; (3) where the employee would have been working at dismissal, if he had not been absent from work; (4) whether there was an active employment relationship between the date of his absence from work and the date of dismissal; (5) from where the contract was being operated at dismissal; and (6) whether the tribunal would have had territorial jurisdiction as at the date on which the claimant became absent from work.

Ministry of Defence v Wallis
[2010] IRLR 1035 EAT

The special connection between the employment and Great Britain, as referred to in *Lawson v Serco*, need not be some inherent feature of the work. It need not relate to some characteristic of the claimants' work which connected it peculiarly with Great Britain. Accordingly, servicemen's wives who were employed at international schools situated in NATO headquarters in the Netherlands and Belgium, who qualified for that employment only because their spouses had been posted to NATO as part of the British military contingent, had a sufficiently special connection between their employment and Great Britain to come within the scope of the unfair dismissal legislation. Parliament must be taken to have intended that employment relationships of this kind, parasitic as they are on the employee's spouse's status as a member of the armed forces posted abroad, should fall within the scope of British employment law.

Duncombe v SoS for Children, Schools and Families
[2011] IRLR 840 SC

Four factors were relevant in determining that British teachers at European Schools were another example of an exceptional case where the employment had such an overwhelmingly closer connection with Britain and with British employment law than with any other system of law that it was right to conclude that Parliament must have intended that the employees should enjoy protection from unfair dismissal. First, their employer was based in Britain, and was not just based there but was the Government of the United Kingdom. That was the closest connection with Great Britain that any employer could have, for it could not be based anywhere else. Second, they were employed under contracts governed by English law; the terms and conditions were either entirely those of English law or a combination of those of English law and the international institutions for which they worked. Although this factor was not mentioned in *Serco*, it was relevant to the expectation of each party as to the protection which the employees would enjoy. Third, they were employed in international enclaves, having no particular connection with the countries in which they happened to be situated and governed by international agreements between the participating states. They did not pay local taxes and were there because of commitments undertaken by the British Government. Fourth, it would have been anomalous if a teacher employed by the British Government to work in the European School in England were to have enjoyed different protection from those employed in the same sort of school in other countries.

Duncombe v SoS for Children, Schools and Families
[2010] IRLR 331 CA

The principle of effectiveness in EC law requires that the implied territorial limitation in domestic law, as identified in *Lawson v Serco*, on the right not to be unfairly dismissed should be modified to permit such a claim to be made where that is necessary for the effective vindication of a right derived from EC law, ie so that the employees had a remedy for the termination of their contracts which the Fixed-term Employees Regulations (giving effect to the Fixed-term Workers Directive) had converted from fixed-term contracts into permanent contracts.

Bleuse v MBT Transport Ltd and another
[2008] IRLR 264 EAT

Employees working abroad who would not otherwise be covered by unfair dismissal law cannot gain the right to bring a claim by virtue of a choice of law clause in their employment contract. The only issue is whether, as a matter of fact, the employee is based in the UK, and neither the terms of the contract, nor its proper law, determine that question.

Employment on ships

---

199. (7) The provisions mentioned in subsection (8) apply to employment on board a ship registered in the register maintained under section 8 of the Merchant Shipping Act 1995 if and only if –

(a) the ship's entry in the register specifies a port in Great Britain as the port to which the vessel is to be treated as belonging,

(b) under his contract of employment the person employed does not work wholly outside Great Britain, and

(c) the person employed is ordinarily resident in Great Britain.

(8) The provisions are –

...

(f) Part X.

EMPLOYMENT RIGHTS ACT 1996 (as amended)

Diggins v   **[2010] IRLR 119 CA**
Condor Marine Crewing Services Ltd

Section 199(7) of the ERA 1996 regulates the statutory rights of those employed on ships registered in Great Britain. For those employed on ships registered outside Great Britain a tribunal has jurisdiction provided the claimant can establish the necessary link with the UK stipulated by the House of Lords in *Lawson v Serco*. In the case of a peripatetic employee such as a seaman, this requires determining where the employee is based rather than where the employer is based.

Employee shareholders

205A   Employee shareholders

(1) An individual who is or becomes an employee of a company is an "employee shareholder" if –

(a) the company and the individual agree that the individual is to be an employee shareholder,

(b) in consideration of that agreement, the company issues or allots to the individual fully paid up shares in the company, or procures the issue or allotment to the individual of fully paid up shares in its parent undertaking, which have a value, on the day of issue or allotment, of no less than £2,000,

(c) the company gives the individual a written statement of the particulars of the status of employee shareholder and of the rights which attach to the shares referred to in paragraph (b) ("the employee shares") (see subsection (5)), and

(d) the individual gives no consideration other than by entering into the agreement.

(2) An employee who is an employee shareholder does not have –

...

(c) the right under section 94 not to be unfairly dismissed

...

(5) The statement referred to in subsection (1)(c) must –

(a) state that, as an employee shareholder, the individual would not have the rights specified in subsection (2),

(b) specify the notice periods that would apply in the individual's case as a result of subsections (3) and (4),

(c) state whether any voting rights attach to the employee shares,

(d) state whether the employee shares carry any rights to dividends,

(e) state whether the employee shares would, if the company were wound up, confer any rights to participate in the distribution of any surplus assets,

(f) if the company has more than one class of shares and

any of the rights referred to in paragraphs (c) to (e) attach to the employee shares, explain how those rights differ from the equivalent rights that attach to the shares in the largest class (or next largest class if the class which includes the employee shares is the largest),

(g) state whether the employee shares are redeemable and, if they are, at whose option,

(h) state whether there are any restrictions on the transferability of the employee shares and, if there are, what those restrictions are,

(i) state whether any of the requirements of sections 561 and 562 of the Companies Act 2006 are excluded in the case of the employee shares (existing shareholders' right of pre-emption), and

(j) state whether the employee shares are subject to drag-along rights or tag-along rights and, if they are, explain the effect of the shares being so subject.

(6) Agreement between a company and an individual that the individual is to become an employee shareholder is of no effect unless, before the agreement is made –

(a) the individual, having been given the statement referred to in subsection (1)(c), receives advice from a relevant independent adviser as to the terms and effect of the proposed agreement, and

(b) seven days have passed since the day on which the individual receives the advice.

(7) Any reasonable costs incurred by the individual in obtaining the advice (whether or not the individual becomes an employee shareholder) which would, but for this subsection, have to be met by the individual are instead to be met by the company.

...

(9) The reference in subsection (2)(c) to unfair dismissal does not include a reference to a dismissal –

(a) which is required to be regarded as unfair for the purposes of Part 10 by a provision (whenever made) contained in or made under this or any other Act, or

(b) which amounts to a contravention of the Equality Act 2010.

(10) The reference in subsection (2)(c) to the right not to be unfairly dismissed does not include a reference to that right in a case where section 108(2) (health and safety cases) applies.

EMPLOYMENT RIGHTS ACT 1996 (as amended)

Claim prior to dismissal

111. (3) Where a dismissal is with notice, an employment tribunal shall consider a complaint under this section if it is presented after the notice is given but before the effective date of termination.

(4) In relation to a complaint which is presented as mentioned in subsection (3), the provisions of this Act, so far as they relate to unfair dismissal, have effect as if –

(a) references to a complaint by a person that he was unfairly dismissed by his employer included references to a complaint by a person that his employer has given him notice in such circumstances that he will be unfairly dismissed when the notice expires,

(b) references to reinstatement included references to the withdrawal of the notice by the employer,

(c) references to the effective date of termination included references to the date which would be the effective date of termination on the expiry of the notice, and

(d) references to an employee ceasing to be employed included references to an employee having been given notice of dismissal.

EMPLOYMENT RIGHTS ACT 1996 (as amended)

Throsby v　　　　　　　　　　　**[1977] IRLR 337 EAT**
Imperial College of Science and
　Technology

The provisions of [s.111(3)] which allow a complaint to be made before the effective date of termination but after notice of termination has been given do not apply in a situation where an employee has been informed that a contract for a fixed period will not be renewed when it expires.

Patel v　　　　　　　　　　　　**[1995] IRLR 370 CA**
Nagesan

The jurisdiction given to an employment tribunal under [s.111(3)] to consider a complaint of unfair dismissal which is presented after an employee has been given notice of termination but before that termination takes effect is unaffected by a subsequent summary dismissal during the notice period.

Presley v　　　　　　　　　　　**[1979] IRLR 381 EAT**
Llanelli Borough Council

[Section 111(3)] applies whether the notice is given by the employer or the employee and so applies where the employee terminates his contract by notice and claims constructive dismissal.

Agreement precluding complaint

18. *(1) In this section and sections 18A to 18C "relevant proceedings" means employment tribunal proceedings –*

...

(b) under section...111... of the Employment Rights Act 1996...

(1A) Sections 18A and 18B apply in the case of matters which could be the subject of relevant proceedings, and section 18C applies in the case of relevant proceedings themselves.

(2) ...

(2A) ...

(3) ...

(4) ...

(5) ...

(6) In proceeding under any of sections 18A to 18C a conciliation officer shall, where appropriate, have regard to the desirability of encouraging the use of other procedures available for the settlement of grievances.

(7) Anything communicated to a conciliation officer in connection with the performance of his functions under any of sections 18A to 18C shall not be admissible in evidence in any proceedings before an employment tribunal, except with the consent of the person who communicated it to that officer.

18A. *(1) Before a person ("the prospective claimant") presents an application to institute relevant proceedings relating to any matter, the prospective claimant must provide to ACAS prescribed information, in the prescribed manner, about that matter.*

This is subject to subsection (7).

(2) On receiving the prescribed information in the prescribed manner, ACAS shall send a copy of it to a conciliation officer.

(3) The conciliation officer shall, during the prescribed period, endeavour to promote a settlement between the persons who would be parties to the proceedings.

(4) If –

　(a) *during the prescribed period the conciliation officer concludes that a settlement is not possible, or*

　(b) *the prescribed period expires without a settlement having been reached,*

the conciliation officer shall issue a certificate to that effect, in the prescribed manner, to the prospective claimant.

(5) The conciliation officer may continue to endeavour to promote a settlement after the expiry of the prescribed period.

(6) In subsections (3) to (5) "settlement" means a settlement that avoids proceedings being instituted.

(7) A person may institute relevant proceedings without complying with the requirement in subsection (1) in prescribed cases.

The cases that may be prescribed include (in particular) –
cases where the requirement is complied with by another person instituting relevant proceedings relating to the same matter;
cases where proceedings that are not relevant proceedings are instituted by means of the same form as proceedings that are;
cases where section 18B applies because ACAS has been contacted by a person against whom relevant proceedings are being instituted.

(8) A person who is subject to the requirement in subsection (1) may not present an application to institute relevant proceedings without a certificate under subsection (4).

(9) Where a conciliation officer acts under this section in a case where the prospective claimant has ceased to be employed by the employer and the proposed proceedings are proceedings under section 111 of the Employment Rights Act 1996, the conciliation officer may in particular –

　(a) *seek to promote the reinstatement or re-engagement of the prospective claimant by the employer, or by a successor of the employer or by an associated employer, on terms appearing to the conciliation officer to be equitable, or*

　(b) *where the prospective claimant does not wish to be reinstated or re-engaged, or where reinstatement or re-engagement is not practicable, seek to promote agreement between them as to a sum by way of compensation to be paid by the employer to the prospective claimant.*

(10) In subsections (1) to (7) "prescribed" means prescribed in employment tribunal procedure regulations.

(11) The Secretary of State may by employment tribunal procedure regulations make such further provision as appears to the Secretary of State to be necessary or expedient with respect to the conciliation process provided for by subsections (1) to (8).

(12) Employment tribunal procedure regulations may (in particular) make provision –

　(a) *authorising the Secretary of State to prescribe, or prescribe requirements in relation to, any form which is required by such regulations to be used for the purpose of providing information to ACAS under subsection (1) or issuing a certificate under subsection (4);*

　(b) *requiring ACAS to give a person any necessary assistance to comply with the requirement in subsection (1);*

(c) for the extension of the period prescribed for the purposes of subsection (3);

(d) treating the requirement in subsection (1) as complied with, for the purposes of any provision extending the time limit for instituting relevant proceedings, by a person who is relieved of that requirement by virtue of subsection (7)(a).

18B. (1) This section applies where –

(a) a person contacts ACAS requesting the services of a conciliation officer in relation to a matter that (if not settled) is likely to give rise to relevant proceedings against that person, and

(b) ACAS has not received information from the prospective claimant under section 18A(1).

(2) This section also applies where –

(a) a person contacts ACAS requesting the services of a conciliation officer in relation to a matter that (if not settled) is likely to give rise to relevant proceedings by that person, and

(b) the requirement in section 18A(1) would apply to that person but for section 18A(7).

(3) Where this section applies a conciliation officer shall endeavour to promote a settlement between the persons who would be parties to the proceedings.

(4) If at any time –

(a) the conciliation officer concludes that a settlement is not possible, or

(b) a conciliation officer comes under the duty in section 18A(3) to promote a settlement between the persons who would be parties to the proceedings,

the duty in subsection (3) ceases to apply at that time.

(5) In subsections (3) and (4) "settlement" means a settlement that avoids proceedings being instituted.

(6) Subsection (9) of section 18A applies for the purposes of this section as it applies for the purposes of that section.

18C. (1) Where an application instituting relevant proceedings has been presented to an employment tribunal, and a copy of it has been sent to a conciliation officer, the conciliation officer shall endeavour to promote a settlement –

(a) if requested to do so by the person by whom and the person against whom the proceedings are brought, or

(b) if, in the absence of any such request, the conciliation officer considers that the officer could act under this section with a reasonable prospect of success.

(2) Where a person who has presented a complaint to an employment tribunal under section 111 of the Employment Rights Act 1996 has ceased to be employed by the employer against whom the complaint was made, the conciliation officer may in particular –

(a) seek to promote the reinstatement or re-engagement of the complainant by the employer, or by a successor of the employer or by an associated employer, on terms appearing to the conciliation officer to be equitable, or

(b) where the complainant does not wish to be reinstated or re-engaged, or where reinstatement or re-engagement is not practicable, and the parties desire the conciliation officer to act, seek to promote agreement between them as to a sum by way of compensation to be paid by the employer to the complainant.

(3) In subsection (1) "settlement" means a settlement that brings proceedings to an end without their being determined by an employment tribunal.

EMPLOYMENT TRIBUNALS ACT 1996 (as amended)

203. (1) Any provision in an agreement (whether a contract of employment or not) is void in so far as it purports –

(a) to exclude or limit the operation of any provision of this Act; or

(b) to preclude a person from bringing any proceedings under this Act before an employment tribunal.

(2) Subsection (1) –

. . .

(b) does not apply to any provision in a dismissal procedures agreement excluding the right under s.94 if that provision is not to have effect unless an order under s.110 is for the time being in force in respect of it,

(c) does not apply to any provision in an agreement if an order under s.157 is for the time being in force in respect of it,

. . .

(e) does not apply to any agreement to refrain from instituting or continuing proceedings where a conciliation officer has taken action under any of sections 18A to 18C of the Employment Tribunals Act 1996, and

(f) does not apply to any agreement to refrain from instituting or continuing any proceedings within the following provisions of s.18(1) of the Employment Tribunals Act 1996 (cases where conciliation available) – (i) paragraph (b) (proceedings under this Act) ... if the conditions regulating compromise agreements under this Act are satisfied in relation to the agreement.

(3) For the purposes of subsection (2)(f) the conditions regulating settlement agreements under this Act are that –

(a) the agreement must be in writing,

(b) the agreement must relate to the particular proceedings,

(c) the employee or worker must have received advice from a relevant independent adviser as to the terms and effect of the proposed agreement and, in particular, its effect on his ability to pursue his rights before an employment tribunal,

(d) there must be in force, when the adviser gives the advice, a contract of insurance, or an indemnity provided for members of a profession or professional body covering the risk of a claim by the employee or worker in respect of loss arising in consequence of the advice,

(e) the agreement must identify the adviser, and

(f) the agreement must state that the conditions regulating settlement agreements under this Act are satisfied.

(3A) A person is a relevant independent adviser for the purposes of subsection (3)(c) –

(a) if he is a qualified lawyer,

(b) if he is an officer, official, employee or member of an independent trade union who has been certified in writing by the trade union as competent to give advice and as authorised to do so on behalf of the trade union,

(c) if he works at an advice centre (whether as an employee or volunteer) and has been certified in writing by the centre as competent to give advice and as authorised to do so on behalf of the centre, or

(d) if he is a person of a description specified in an order made by the Secretary of State.

(3B) But a person is not a relevant independent adviser for the purposes of subsection (3)(c) in relation to the employee or worker –

(a) if he is, is employed by or is acting in the matter for the employer or an associated employer,

(b) in the case of a person within subsection (3A)(b) or (c), if the trade union or advice centre is the employer or an associated employer,

(c) *in the case of a person within subsection (3A)(c), if the employee or worker makes a payment for the advice received from him, or*

(d) *in the case of a person of a description specified in an order under subsection (3A)(d), if any condition specified in the order in relation to the giving of advice by persons of that description is not satisfied.*

(4) In subsection (3A)(a) qualified lawyer means –

(a) *as respects England and Wales, a person who, for the purposes of the Legal Services Act 2007, is an authorised person in relation to an activity which constitutes the exercise of a right of audience or the conduct of litigation (within the meaning of that Act), and*

(b) *as respects Scotland, an advocate (whether in practice as such or employed to give legal advice) or a solicitor who holds a practising certificate.*

EMPLOYMENT RIGHTS ACT 1996 (as amended)

Agreement rendered void

Sutherland v   **[2001] IRLR 12 EAT**
Network Appliance Ltd
Where a compromise agreement which is expressed as being in full and final settlement of "any claim" an employee may have fails to comply with s.203, the agreement is made void only in respect of statutory claims. It remains enforceable to the extent to which it contains a compromise of contractual claims.

Igbo v   **[1986] IRLR 215 CA**
Johnson Matthey Chemicals Ltd
A provision for automatic termination upon a failure to report for work on a specified future date is void because it has the effect of limiting the employee's statutory right not to be unfairly dismissed.

Logan Salton v   **[1989] IRLR 99 EAT**
Durham County Council
An agreement providing for termination of the employee's employment which was entered into freely and included financial benefits for the employee was not rendered void by [s.203(1)]. Such a case was distinguishable on its facts from *Igbo v Johnson Matthey Chemicals Ltd.* The agreement was not a contract of employment or a variation of an existing contract. It was a separate contract which was entered into willingly, without duress and after proper advice and for good consideration. Termination of the employment did not depend upon the happening of some future event which may have been envisaged, nor upon the possible happening of events which were not envisaged and which, had they been, might well have caused the employee not to agree with the proposed terms.

Hennessy v   **[1986] IRLR 300 CA**
Craigmyle & Co Ltd and ACAS
Economic duress is a ground for avoiding a contract only if the duress is such as to amount to a coercion of will vitiating consent. It must be shown that the payment made or the contract entered into was an involuntary act. It must be very rare to encounter economic duress of an order which renders action involuntary. Whether economic duress of that order did exist in a particular case is entirely a question of fact for the tribunal. The possibility of economic duress is made more remote where the agreement was reached after the employee received independent advice and assistance from a skilled conciliation officer.

Freeman v   **[1991] IRLR 408 EAT**
Sovereign Chicken Ltd
A settlement reached under the auspices of a conciliation officer by a barrister, solicitor, CAB adviser or member of a law centre, named as representative by a party to proceedings before an employment tribunal, is binding upon the client, whether or not the adviser had actual authority to enter into it. In the absence of any notice to the contrary, such an adviser has ostensible, or implied, authority.

Gloystarne & Co Ltd v   **[2001] IRLR 15 EAT**
Martin
Ostensible authority to enter into a binding settlement of a claim can arise only by the claimant himself holding out that a person was authorised to act on his behalf, and not by anything that was said by that person. B does not become A's agent in dealings with C, nor does B acquire authority from A to act on A's behalf in relation to C by way only of what B says to C. If that was the case, principals could have agents completely unknown to them and over whom they had no control. Rather, B becomes A's agent in dealings with C by reason, in general, of what A says to C on the point or if A conducts himself in some way that reflects on the possibility of B's agency.

Scott and others v   **[1988] IRLR 131 EAT**
Coalite Fuels and Chemicals Ltd
Observed: An agreement to resign by accepting voluntary early retirement as an alternative to redundancy was not rendered unlawful by [s.203(1)] since it did not exclude or limit the operation of any provision of the Act or prevent or preclude the employee from presenting a complaint to an employment tribunal. The employment tribunal still had jurisdiction to hear the application.

Courage Take Home Trade Ltd v   **[1986] IRLR 427 EAT**
Keys
[Section 203(1)(b)] renders void an agreement under which an employee accepts a sum of money in full and final settlement of his unfair dismissal claim which was reached after the employment tribunal found his dismissal unfair but before the question of remedy was settled. [Section 203(1)(b)] does not cease to have effect either after proceedings have been commenced or after liability, as opposed to remedy, has been determined. Nor do the duties of an ACAS conciliation officer cease until all questions of liability and remedy have been determined by the tribunal.

Fitzgerald v   **[2004] IRLR 300 CA**
University of Kent at Canterbury
An agreement between the parties to backdate the employee's effective date of termination is caught by the restriction on contracting-out in s.203. A consensual arrangement to antedate the date of termination falls squarely within the description of a "provision in an agreement [which] . . . purports to limit the operation" of a provision of the Act. The word "purports" is not designed only to catch provisions which expressly claim to have such an effect. It is there to take account of the fact that s.203(1) makes such provisions void.

M & P Steelcraft Ltd v   **[2008] IRLR 355 EAT**
Ellis and another
A clause specifying that there was no intention to create legal relations was not effective to exclude the tribunal's jurisdiction because whilst it did not limit or exclude any rights, it did have the effect of limiting or excluding the rights and was therefore void under s.203. In so finding, Mr Justice Elias pointed out that in order for a clause to be said to infringe s.203, "the only purpose of the clause must be to alter, or seek to alter, what would, absent the clause, be the legal effect of the contractual arrangements".

Action by conciliation officer

Gilbert v   **[1984] IRLR 52 EAT**
Kembridge Fibres Ltd
In order for there to be a binding agreement on the parties so as to exclude an unfair dismissal application, there need be only an oral settlement reached through the intermediary of an ACAS conciliation officer.

Slack v   **[1983] IRLR 271 EAT**
Greenham (Plant Hire) Ltd
In attempting to reach a binding agreement between the parties such as to preclude an employee from thereafter claiming unfair dismissal, a conciliation officer is not obliged to follow any specific formula. The nature of a conciliation officer's function must depend upon the particular circumstances of each case. In some cases, a conciliation officer may deem it necessary in his attempt to promote agreement of the payment of compensation to give a brief description to the employee of the relevant framework of his statutory rights. However he is not under a statutory duty to do so.

Allmer Construction Ltd v   **[2011] IRLR 204 EAT**
Bonner
The communication by an ACAS officer to the respondent of the claimant's acceptance of an offer is enough to satisfy the statutory requirement that he has "taken action" to promote settlement of the claim. "Taking action" covers "any action taken by an ACAS officer in relation to the claim". The threshold is very low indeed.

Clarke and others v   **[2006] IRLR 324 EAT**
Redcar & Cleveland Borough Council
Wilson and others v
Stockton-on-Tees Borough Council
There is no duty on a conciliation officer to advise on the merits of a claim before an employee enters into a binding settlement agreement.

Hennessy v   **[1986] IRLR 300 CA**
Craigmyle & Co Ltd and ACAS
Where an issue arises under [s.203(2)(e)] it is not for the tribunal or court to consider whether a conciliation officer correctly interpreted his duties under [ss.18 to 18C of the Employment Tribunals Act]. It is sufficient that he intended and purported to act under any of those sections.

Moore v   **[1982] IRLR 31 HL**
Duport Furniture Products Ltd
   and others
The provisions of [s.203(2)(e)] of the Act, which preclude an employee from claiming unfair dismissal where he has agreed not to make such a claim as part of a settlement in which an ACAS conciliation officer has taken action in accordance with the requirements of [s.18 of the Employment Tribunals Act], apply not only where the employee has made some express or formal claim of unfair dismissal but also where an implied claim can be inferred from the overt acts or attitudes of the employee concerned in the particular circumstances of the case.

Moore v   **[1982] IRLR 31 HL**
Duport Furniture Products Ltd and others
The requirement that the conciliation officer take action to endeavour to promote reinstatement or re-engagement or an agreement as to a sum of compensation does not necessarily involve the taking of a positive initiative by the conciliation officer concerned. The requirement is limited by implication by the words "so far as applicable by the circumstances of the particular case". Thus, faced with an agreement between the parties as to the amount of compensation and faced with the fact that reinstatement or re-engagement was not practicable, the conciliation officer fulfilled as much of his duty as was open to him by ascertaining that the parties had truly agreed and reducing the agreement on form COT3 into clear writing for signature by the parties.

Moore v   **[1980] IRLR 158 CA**
Duport Furniture Products Ltd and others
[Section 18C(2)(b) of the Employment Tribunals Act] does not impose a duty on the conciliation officer to promote an agreement which he considers fair. [Section 18C(2)(a)] requires the conciliation officer to seek to promote reinstatement or re-engagement of the complainant by the employer on terms appearing to him to be equitable. But where no such possibility exists, the conciliation officer is left to act without regard to what is equitable. His duty under [s.18C(2)(b)] is to promote agreement between the parties

as to a sum by way of compensation to be paid by the employer to the complainant.

Hennessy v   [1985] IRLR 446 EAT
Craigmyle & Co Ltd and ACAS

The conciliation officer's responsibility under [s.18(6) of the Employment Tribunals Act] is to encourage the use of internal procedures only "where appropriate". Where it is obvious that there was nothing to negotiate except the amount of compensation, it could not be said that the conciliation officer had failed to act in accordance with [s.18(6)] by not encouraging the use of the grievance procedure.

The Milestone School of English Ltd v   [1982] IRLR 3 EAT
Leakey

Where an employment tribunal makes an order recording the terms of a settlement between the parties and that order provides that "all further proceedings on the claim be adjourned generally until further order", the employment tribunal is not debarred from looking at the employee's complaint again if the employers fail to comply with the terms of the agreed settlement.

Settlement/compromise agreements

BCCI v   [2001] IRLR 292 HL
Ali

In a compromise agreement supported by valuable consideration, a party may agree to release claims or rights of which he is unaware and of which he could not be aware, even claims which could not on the facts known to the parties have been imagined, if appropriate language is used to make plain that that is his intention. However, a long and salutary line of authority shows that, in the absence of clear language, the courts will be very slow to infer that a party intended to surrender rights and claims of which he was unaware and could not have been aware.

Hinton v   [2005] IRLR 552 CA
University of East London

In order to meet the requirement in s.203(3)(b) that an agreement must "relate to the particular proceedings", the particular proceedings to which the compromise agreement relates must be clearly identified. The question to be asked is "How does the agreement relate to the particular proceedings in question?". Although one document can be used to compromise all the particular proceedings, it is not sufficient to use a rolled-up expression such as "all statutory rights". The particular claims or potential claims to be covered by the agreement must be identified either by a generic description such as "unfair dismissal" or by reference to the section of the statute giving rise to the claim. The conditions regulating compromise agreements should be construed, so far as is possible, to promote the purpose for which they were intended, namely to protect employees when agreeing to relinquish their right to bring proceedings under the Act in the employment tribunal.

Royal National Orthopaedic   [2002] IRLR 849 EAT
Hospital Trust v
Howard

As a matter of public policy, there is no reason why a party should not contract out of some future course of action. However, if the parties seek to achieve such an extravagant result that they release claims of which they have and can have no knowledge, whether those claims have already come into existence or not, they must do so in language which is absolutely clear and leaves no room for doubt as to what it is they are contracting for. An agreement which was stated to be "in full and final settlement of these proceedings and of all claims which the applicant has or may have against the respondent (save for claims for personal injury and in respect of occupational pension rights) whether arising under her contract of employment or out of the termination thereof", did not indicate any intention to contract out of future claims.

Rock-It Cargo Ltd v   [1999] IRLR 458 EAT
Green

An employment tribunal has jurisdiction to enforce a compromise agreement relating to the terms on which employment is to terminate.

Industrious Ltd v   [2010] IRLR 204 EAT
Vincent

An employment tribunal has jurisdiction to determine whether an otherwise valid compromise agreement is unenforceable because it was entered into on the basis of a misrepresentation.

Thompson and others v   [1997] IRLR 343 EAT
Walon Car Delivery

A compromise agreement between a transferor and its ex-employees concluded after the transfer cannot benefit the transferee which was not party to the agreement.

National security

10. *(1) If on a complaint under –*

 . . .

  (b) s.111 of the Employment Rights Act 1996 (unfair dismissal),

it is shown that the action complained of was taken for the purpose of safeguarding national security, the employment tribunal shall dismiss the complaint.

   EMPLOYMENT TRIBUNALS ACT 1996 (as amended)

B v   **[2005] IRLR 927 EAT**
BAA plc

Section 10(1) can arise in any context and in any employment. It is not restricted to Crown employment.

B v   **[2005] IRLR 927 EAT**
BAA plc

An employer seeking to rely on s.10(1) of the Employment Tribunals Act must prove what the reason was for a dismissal and whether the dismissal for such reason was for the purpose of safeguarding national security, rather than what the underlying facts were. Notwithstanding the national security context, however, s.3 of the Human Rights Act requires that s.10(1) should be construed so that the impact of the test of fairness in s.98(4) of the Employment Rights Act should not be excluded. The tribunal must conclude that the employer acted reasonably in dismissing.

Accordingly, an employer seeking to rely on s.10(1) must show not only that the removal of the employee was required for the purpose of national security, but also that the steps which were taken by way of dismissal were also so required, taking into account the issues which would normally need to be considered in a case of substantial other reason, such as whether it was within the range of reasonable responses of the reasonable employer to dismiss rather than redeploy.

2. MEANING OF DISMISSAL

Definition of dismissal

95. *(1) For the purposes of this Part, an employee is dismissed by his employer if (and, subject to subsection (2), only if) –*

   (a) the contract under which he is employed is terminated by the employer (whether with or or without notice),

   (b) he is employed under a limited-term contract and that contract terminates by virtue of the limiting event without being renewed under the same contract, or

   (c) the employee terminates the contract under which he is employed (with or without notice) in circumstances in which he is entitled to terminate it without notice by reason of the employer's conduct.

(2) An employee shall be taken to be dismissed by his employer for the purposes of this Part if –

   (a) the employer gives notice to the employee to terminate his contract of employment, and

   (b) at a time within the period of that notice the employee gives notice to the employer to terminate the contract of employment on a date earlier than the date on which the employer's notice is due to expire;

and the reason for the dismissal is to be taken to be the reason for which the employer's notice is given.

EMPLOYMENT RIGHTS ACT 1996 (as amended)

General principles

Martin v   **[1983] IRLR 198 CA**
MBS Fastenings (Glynwed)
  Distribution Ltd

Whether an employee has resigned or has been dismissed is for the employment tribunal to determine on the evidence. Whatever the respective actions of the employer and employee at the time of termination, the question always remains "who really terminated the contract of employment?" An employment tribunal's conclusions of fact must be accepted unless it is apparent that, on the evidence, no reasonable tribunal could have reached them.

Sandhu v   **[2007] IRLR 519 CA**
Jan de Rijk Transport

Negotiations leading to a better severance package will not change a dismissal into a resignation if the operative cause of the termination remains the pressure placed by the employer on the employee. If the employee has had the opportunity to take independent advice and then offers to resign, that fact would be powerful evidence pointing towards resignation rather than dismissal. In none of the cases in which the employee has been held to resign has the resignation occurred during the same interview/discussion in which the question of dismissal has been raised.

Caledonian Mining Co Ltd v   **[1987] IRLR 165 EAT**
Bassett and Steel

Whether termination of a contract is dismissal or constructive dismissal is not resolved simply by looking at the label put upon it. Thus, that there has been a resignation is not enough to say that the employer could not have terminated the contract save by way of constructive dismissal. If, as in this case, an employee is falsely inveigled by the employer into resigning, the reality of the matter is that it is the employer who terminates the contract of employment.

Morris v   **[1987] IRLR 182 CA**
London Iron & Steel Co

Where an employment tribunal is unable to make a decision on the facts as to whether there was a dismissal in law, it is permissible for them to fall back upon the burden of proof to decide the case. Where the decision can only be between two alternatives – dismissal or resignation – if the tribunal is unable to reach a decision on the facts, the case can be determined on the basis of the onus of proof.

Birch and Humber v   **[1985] IRLR 165 CA**
The University of Liverpool

The application of the primary facts to the meaning of the statutory definition of dismissal is a matter of law. The EAT can overrule the decision of an employment tribunal if it is shown that that decision was one which the employment tribunal were not entitled to reach on the facts as found by them.

Scott and others v   **[1988] IRLR 131 EAT**
Coalite Fuels and Chemicals Ltd

The decision of the Court of Appeal in *Birch v The University of Liverpool* does not mean that whether the employee was dismissed by the employer within the meaning of the statutory definition is a question of law. Although it is possible that questions of law will emerge when considering whether there has been a dismissal, in the majority of cases the issue is essentially one of fact.

Alcan Extrusions v   **[1996] IRLR 327 EAT**
Yates and others

Where an employer unilaterally imposes radically different terms of employment, there is a termination of the contract and a dismissal by the employer if, on an objective construction of the employer's conduct, there is a removal or withdrawal of the old contract. Whether the departure from the original contract is so substantial as to amount to the withdrawal of the whole contract, rather than a potential repudiatory breach giving the employee the option whether to remain or to resign and claim constructive dismissal, is a matter of fact and degree for the employment tribunal to decide.

Roberts v   **[2004] IRLR 788 CA**
West Coast Trains Ltd

An employee is not dismissed by his employers where, within the terms of a contractual disciplinary procedure, the initial sanction of dismissal is reduced on internal appeal to demotion to a lower grade. Demotion in such circumstances does not involve the termination of the existing contract or the entering into of a new contract. The effect of the decision on appeal is to revive retrospectively the contract of employment terminated by the earlier decision to dismiss so as to treat the employee as if he had never been dismissed. The fact that the employee made a complaint of unfair dismissal at a date between the initial dismissal and the hearing of his appeal does not affect the legal position in deciding whether or not he was dismissed for the purposes of an unfair dismissal claim.

Sarker v   **[1997] IRLR 328 EAT**
South Tees Acute Hospitals NHS Trust
A person engaged under a contract of employment to start work at a future date can claim unfair dismissal if the contract was terminated by the employer for an inadmissible reason before that date.

Termination by employer

Notice of termination

Stapp v   **[1982] IRLR 326 CA**
The Shaftesbury Society
A notice to terminate must be construed strictly against the employer who gives it and if there is any ambiguity it must be resolved in favour of the employee.

Walmsley v   **[1989] IRLR 112 CS**
C & R Ferguson Ltd
No particular terms of art are required to indicate notice of termination of employment.

Hughes v   **[1977] IRLR 436 EAT**
Gwynedd Area Health Authority
Notice of termination by an employee (as with notice of dismissal by an employer) must be specific. It must specify the date when it is to take effect or at least make it possible for the date to be deduced with certainty from what is said. The principle set out in *Morton Sundour Fabrics Ltd v Shaw* (1968) ITR 84 applied. Therefore, a statement by a pregnant woman that she would be leaving work to have her baby and not returning, made some three months before she stopped working, did not constitute a notice of resignation in law. It was no more than a statement of general intention and was not sufficient to constitute proper notice of termination by her because it neither specified a date nor did it contain or refer to other material from which it was possible to deduce with any certainty the effective date of termination.

The Burton Group Ltd v   **[1977] IRLR 351 EAT**
Smith
The requirement that the date of termination should be positively ascertainable is not met by a statement that the date of termination is to be some specific date or such earlier date as the employer may select, or such earlier date as the

employer may, consistent with his obligation to give the requisite notice, select.

Rai v   **[2004] IRLR 124 EAT**
Somerfield Stores Ltd
There is not a dismissal with notice where an employer delivers an ultimatum or conditional notice which says, for example, "If you do not come back to work by a certain date your contract of employment will be terminated on that date", and the contract of employment is then terminated as a result of the employee's failure to return to work by that date. Such a notice is not an unequivocal notice to terminate the employment. Nor is it one which is not capable of being unilaterally withdrawn.

Mowlem Northern Ltd v   **[1990] IRLR 500 EAT**
Watson
Once an employee has been given notice of dismissal for redundancy to take effect on a specified date, there is nothing in the statute to preclude the employer and employee from postponing that date by mutual agreement until the happening of an agreed event. The effective date can be brought forward or put back by mutual agreement but the dismissal for redundancy remains.

Haseltine Lake & Co v   **[1981] IRLR 25 EAT**
Dowler
It is not a dismissal in law to tell an employee that if he does not find a job elsewhere his employment will eventually be terminated. Such a statement, where the employer does not commit himself to an actual date for the termination of employment, can be distinguished from a case of "resign or be dismissed" such as *East Sussex County Council v Wall* (1972) ITR 280 where the employee was told her job was to be ended forthwith. Nor did the statement constitute a notice of dismissal within the principle of *Morton Sundour Fabrics Ltd v Shaw* (1968) ITR 84 since there was no specified or ascertainable future date for the employment ending.

International Computers Ltd v   **[1981] IRLR 28 EAT**
Kennedy
An announcement by the employers that a factory is to be closed down by a specified date and that the employees concerned should find alternative employment as quickly as possible was not equivalent to a statement "resign or be dismissed" and, therefore, was not a dismissal in law. Although the date of closure of the factory was precisely ascertainable, the relevant date which had to be ascertained was the date of termination of the employee's employment. As this was yet to be decided when the employee resigned, the case could not be distinguished from *Morton Sundour Fabrics Ltd v Shaw* (1968) ITR 84.

Dobie v   **[1981] IRLR 300 EAT**
Firestone Tyre and Rubber Co Ltd
A general announcement of plant closure given to union officials at the beginning of the statutory redundancy

consultation process is not a notice of dismissal to individual employees.

Harris & Russell Ltd v Slingsby [1973] IRLR 221 NIRC

It is not open to a party who has given notice determining a contract to withdraw the notice unilaterally before it expires. Although it is open to the other party to agree to the withdrawal of notice, in the absence of agreement the notice must stand and the contract of employment terminate when the notice period expires.

Springbank Sand & Gravel Co Ltd v Craig [1973] IRLR 278 NIRC

If an employer gives an employee notice of dismissal and at the same time makes it plain that he does not expect the employee to continue at his work, the fact that the employee does not return to work does not mean that the employee has terminated the contract.

Hindle Gears Ltd v McGinty and others [1984] IRLR 477 EAT

An uncommunicated decision to dismiss an employee is not sufficient to effect a dismissal. Communication of the decision to dismiss in terms which either bring it expressly to the attention of the employee or at least give him a reasonable opportunity of learning of it is essential.

Villella v MFI Furniture Centres Ltd [1999] IRLR 468 HC

Sending an employee his P45 is not sufficient to indicate that the employers are terminating the employment forthwith.

Stapp v The Shaftesbury Society [1982] IRLR 326 CA

The giving of a notice of termination does not deprive the employer of the right to dismiss the employee summarily before the notice expires. An employer has the right to change his mind after giving a notice of dismissal and to give another, shorter, notice.

Marshall (Cambridge) Ltd v Hamblin [1994] IRLR 260 EAT

Where an employee resigns with notice, there is no dismissal in law if the employer refuses to allow the employee to continue working and exercises its discretion under the contract of employment to pay wages in lieu of notice. An employee has no right to work out his notice.

Land and Wilson v West Yorkshire Metropolitan County Council [1981] IRLR 87 CA

The supplemental part of an employee's contract of employment relating to voluntary additional duties could be determined separately by the employers on reasonable notice without terminating the employee's whole-time service. Although the employee was employed under a single contract of employment, the contract was divisible into two distinct parts. There was no doubt that the employee could determine his voluntary additional duties without prejudicing his right of employment in regard to his whole-time duties. Therefore, the employers had the reciprocal right to terminate the additional duties without interfering with the full-time engagement.

Language of termination

Sothern v Franks Charlesly & Co [1981] IRLR 278 CA

When the words used by a person are unambiguous words of resignation and so understood by the employer, in the normal case the employer is entitled to accept the resignation. The question of what a reasonable employer might have understood does not arise. The natural meaning of the words and the fact that the employer understood them to mean that the employee was resigning cannot be overridden by appeals to what a reasonable employer might have assumed. The non-disclosed intention of a person using language as to his intended meaning is not properly to be taken into account in determining what the true meaning is.

Sovereign House Security Services Ltd v Savage [1989] IRLR 115 CA

Where unambiguous words of resignation are used by an employee to an employer and are so understood by the employer, generally the proper conclusion of fact is that the employee has resigned. In some cases, however, there may be something in the context of the exchange between the employer and employee, or in the circumstances of the employee himself, to entitle the tribunal of fact to conclude that there was no real resignation despite what it might appear to be at first sight. For example, if the case concerned decisions taken in the heat of the moment or involving an immature employee, then what otherwise might appear to be a clear resignation should not be so construed.

Kwik-Fit (GB) Ltd v Lineham [1992] IRLR 156 EAT

Where words or actions of resignation are unambiguous, an employer is entitled to treat them as such and accept the employee's repudiation of contract at once, unless there are special circumstances arising due to personality conflicts or individual characteristics. Words spoken or actions expressed in temper or in the heat of the moment or under extreme pressure, or the intellectual make-up of an employee may be such special circumstances.

Kwik-Fit (GB) Ltd v Lineham [1992] IRLR 156 EAT

Where special circumstances exist, before accepting a resignation at its face value, an employer should allow a reasonable period of time to elapse, such as a day or two, during which facts may arise that cast doubt upon whether the resignation was really intended and can properly be assumed. If the employer does not investigate those facts, it runs the risk that evidence may be forthcoming that in the special circumstances an intention to resign was not the correct interpretation when the facts are judged objectively.

J & J Stern v [1983] IRLR 52 EAT
Simpson
In order to decide whether or not there has been a termination, the words used should be construed in the context of the facts of the case. It is only if there is ambiguity after looking at the words in their context that a further test of whether any reasonable employer or employee might have understood the words to be tantamount to dismissal or resignation must be applied.

Martin v [1983] IRLR 49 EAT
Yeomen Aggregates Ltd
Where unambiguous words of dismissal are used in the heat of the moment and are withdrawn almost immediately, there is no dismissal in law. The contract does not irreversibly come to an end once clear and unambiguous words are used. It is a question of degree as to whether it is too late for an employer to recant words of dismissal spoken in the heat of the moment.

Willoughby v [2011] IRLR 985 CA
CF Capital plc
Where an employer, intending to dismiss an employee, sends a clear and unambiguous notice of dismissal, the normal rule applies that the employer is not entitled unilaterally to retract or withdraw the notice, and the so-called "special circumstances" exception, under which some such notices have, in the past, not been allowed to take effect, (a) is only relevant in cases where the true intention of the giver of the notice is not in tune with the words used, and (b) is not a true exception to that rule, but rather a category of cases in which the recipient of the notice (i) will be well advised to allow the giver a "cooling off" period before acting upon it, and (ii) may choose to afford the giver of the notice the opportunity to satisfy the recipient that he never intended to give it in the first place.

Sothern v [1981] IRLR 278 CA
Franks Charlesly & Co
The words "I am resigning" are not ambiguous. They are in the present tense and indicate a present intention of resigning. They have the same meaning as "I am resigning now" or "I resign". The words do not naturally mean "I am going to resign in the future". There was no indication of futurity in the words.

Employee's counter-notice

Ready Case Ltd v [1981] IRLR 312 EAT
Jackson
The reference in [s.95(2)] of the Act to the employee giving "notice" expiring on a date earlier than the date when the employer's notice is due to expire means notice of any period. In order to rely upon [s.95(2)] to say that he was dismissed at the end of the period of the employer's notice, the employee does not have to give either the contractual notice or the statutory minimum notice. *Quaere:* It may be that the employee's notice can be immediate.

Termination of limited-term contracts

British Broadcasting Corporation v [1979] IRLR 114 CA
Dixon
The words "fixed term" in the statutory definition of dismissal include a term for a specific stated period even though the contract is determinable by notice within that period. Therefore, an employee is dismissed in law when a fixed-term contract under which he is employed comes to an end without being renewed, notwithstanding that the contract contains a term that it could be determined by one week's notice.

Wiltshire County Council v [1980] IRLR 198 CA
NATFHE and Guy
A part-time teacher employed to teach such courses as should be required during an academic session was employed under a fixed-term contract so that when that contract expired without being renewed there was a dismissal in law. Although the employee was employed to teach particular courses and her work could end during the session if there were not enough students for a particular course, the correct construction of the contract was that it was for a fixed term for the academic session. During that period she was required to teach such courses as were required of her. Even though her work could cease, her contractual obligations would not cease because she was employed to work for the session.

Thames Television Ltd v [1979] IRLR 136 EAT
Wallis
There is a dismissal in law where an employee employed under a fixed-term contract, having been told that the contract will not be renewed, agrees to cease work at the end of the period and receive an ex gratia payment. Such an agreement is not a supervening event so as to make the case one of a consensual termination, since the agreement does not vary what was already an accomplished fact, that the contract was to end at its date of termination. It is difficult to comprehend an agreement whereby the employee, who has been told that the contract will end on a fixed date, agrees that it will end on the fixed date and receives a sum of money so that it can be said that the termination was not by reason of expiry on the fixed date but because of an agreement that it should expire on the fixed date.

Tansell v [2013] IRLR 174 EAT
Henley College Coventry
The expiry of a limited-term contract without it being renewed is one of the forms of termination falling within the definition of dismissal; it is not a designated reason for dismissal itself.

Termination by agreement

Birch and Humber v **[1985] IRLR 165 CA**
The University of Liverpool
The definition of dismissal in [s.95(1)(a)] is directed only to a case where the contract of employment is terminated by the employer alone. Dismissal, as it is defined in that section, is not consistent with a case where the contract has been terminated by the mutual, freely-given consent of the employer and the employee. In a case where the contract has been terminated by such mutual agreement, it may properly be said that the contract has been terminated by both the employer and the employee jointly, but it cannot be said that it has been terminated by the employer alone.

Lees v **[1974] IRLR 93 CA**
Arthur Greaves (Lees) Ltd
Termination by agreement should not be found unless it is proved that the employee agreed with full knowledge of the implications which it held for him. The dictum of the NIRC in *McAlwane v Boughton Estates Ltd* (1973) ICR 470 that, "it would be a very rare case, indeed, in which it could properly be found that the employer and the employee had got together and, notwithstanding that there was a current notice of termination of the employment, agreed mutually to terminate the contract, particularly when one realises the financial consequences to the employee involved in such an agreement," was correct.

Sheffield v **[1979] IRLR 133 EAT**
Oxford Controls Company Ltd
It is a principle of law that where an employee resigns because the employer has threatened that if he does not resign he will be dismissed, the mechanics of the resignation do not cause that to be other than a dismissal. In such a case, the principle is one of causation. It is the existence of the threat which causes the employee to be willing to resign.

Where, however, terms of resignation emerge which are satisfactory to the employee, the threat of dismissal is no longer the operative factor in the employee's decision to resign. The employee resigns because he is willing to resign as the result of being offered terms which are to him satisfactory terms on which to resign. Thus the actual causation of the resignation is no longer the threat of dismissal. It is the state of mind of the resigning employee, that he is willing and content to resign on the terms which he has negotiated. In such circumstances, therefore, the employee is not dismissed in law if he agrees to terminate his employment upon terms which are satisfactory to him, notwithstanding that he has been threatened with dismissal if he does not resign.

Jones v **[1997] IRLR 685 CA**
Mid-Glamorgan County Council
For there to be a dismissal by way of enforced resignation, the threat of dismissal need not be the sole factor inducing the resignation. The concept of dismissal by forced resigna-

tion is too valuable and too flexible to be constrained by such a pre-condition.

Staffordshire County Council v **[1981] IRLR 108 EAT**
Donovan
Although it is a dismissal in law if an employee resigns upon being told that unless he resigns he will be dismissed, there is no dismissal in law where the agreement which forms the basis of the employee's resignation was not arrived at under duress and there was no threat of dismissal. Where the parties are seeking to negotiate in the course of disciplinary proceedings and an agreed form of resignation is worked out, it would be most unfortunate if the fact that that agreement was reached in the course of disciplinary proceedings entitled the employee thereafter to say that there was a dismissal.

Hellyer Bros Ltd v **[1992] IRLR 540 EAT**
Atkinson and Dickinson
Where an employee's voluntary act in compliance with the employer's request is the physical event which marks the termination of the contract of employment, there is no rule of law that that amounts to an agreement to terminate the contract unless there is duress or pressurisation. Therefore, an employment tribunal was entitled to find that in signing off when asked to do so, an employee was agreeing to fill in the appropriate form and not to termination of his contract of employment.

Logan Salton v **[1989] IRLR 99 EAT**
Durham County Council
In the resolution of industrial disputes, it is in the best interests of all concerned that a contract made without duress, for good consideration, preferably after proper and sufficient advice and which has the effect of terminating a contract by mutual agreement should be effective between the contracting parties, in which case there probably will not have been a dismissal.

Logan Salton v **[1989] IRLR 99 EAT**
Durham County Council
Whether a mutual agreement to terminate a contract of employment is rendered void by the fact that the employee entered into it under duress and that the reality of the situation is that there was a dismissal is a matter of fact for the employment tribunal to determine.

Burton, Allton & Johnson Ltd v **[1975] IRLR 87 HC**
Peck
That an employee has agreed to be dismissed on grounds of redundancy or has volunteered for redundancy does not mean that the termination of employment is by mutual consent. In such circumstances, the termination, when it occurs, is a dismissal by the employer.

Birch and Humber v **[1985] IRLR 165 CA**
The University of Liverpool
The dictum in the *Burton, Allton & Johnson Ltd* case was designed to make it clear that the fact that an employee has no

objection to being dismissed, or even volunteers to be dismissed, does not prevent it from being a dismissal within the meaning of the Act. The judgment did not encroach upon the distinction which exists in law between a contract which is terminated unilaterally (albeit without objection and perhaps even with encouragement from the other party) and a contract which is terminated by mutual agreement.

Birch and Humber v   **[1985] IRLR 165 CA**
The University of Liverpool
There was a termination by mutual agreement where the employee's application for retirement under an early retirement scheme was accepted by the employers, notwithstanding that the retirement was at the employers' request and subject to the employers' approval.

Scott and others v   **[1988] IRLR 131 EAT**
Coalite Fuels and Chemicals Ltd
There was no dismissal in law where employees, having received notice of dismissal on grounds of redundancy, accepted an option of voluntary early retirement as an alternative to redundancy.

Igbo v   **[1986] IRLR 215 CA**
Johnson Matthey Chemicals Ltd
A provision for automatic termination upon a failure to report for work on a specified future date is void because it has the effect of limiting the statutory right not to be unfairly dismissed. Therefore, the employee was dismissed in law when, in accordance with a contractual provision for extended holiday leave, the employers treated her employment as automatically terminated when she failed to return to work on the due date.

Logan Salton v   **[1989] IRLR 99 EAT**
Durham County Council
Notwithstanding that when an employee agreed that his employment would terminate by mutual agreement he was aware that a recommendation had been made that he be summarily dismissed, there was no dismissal in law in circumstances in which the employee entered into the agreement freely and without duress and under which he benefited from financial consideration.

Employee repudiation

London Transport Executive v   **[1981] IRLR 166 CA**
Clarke
Contracts of employment are not an exception to the general rule that a repudiated contract is not terminated unless and until the repudiation is accepted by the innocent party.

If a worker walks out of his job and does not thereafter claim to be entitled to resume work, then he repudiates the contract and the employer accepts that repudiation by taking

no action to affirm the contract. No question of unfair dismissal can arise unless the worker claims that he was constructively dismissed.

If a worker walks out of his job or commits any other breach of contract, repudiatory or otherwise, but at any time claims that he is entitled to resume or to continue his work, then his contract of employment is only determined if the employer expressly or impliedly asserts and accepts repudiation on the part of the worker. Acceptance can take the form of formal writing or can take the form of refusing to allow the worker to resume or continue his work. The acceptance by an employer of repudiation by a worker who wishes to continue his employment notwithstanding his repudiatory conduct constitutes the determination of the contract of employment by the employer. The employer relying on the repudiatory conduct of the worker must satisfy the employment tribunal, in accordance with the test of [s.98(4)].

Constructive dismissal

General principles

Western Excavating (ECC) Ltd v   **[1978] IRLR 27 CA**
Sharp
Whether an employee is "entitled" to terminate his contract of employment "without notice by reason of the employer's conduct" and claim constructive dismissal must be determined in accordance with the law of contract. The words "entitled" and "without notice" in the statute are the language of contract connoting that as a result of the employer's conduct the employee has a right to treat himself as discharged from any further performance of the contract. A test of "unreasonable conduct" similar to the concept of "unfairness" and not dependent upon a contract test was incorrect since it would not give effect to the words "without notice".

Per Lord Denning MR: An employee is entitled to treat himself as constructively dismissed if the employer is guilty of conduct which is a significant breach going to the root of the contract of employment; or which shows that the employer no longer intends to be bound by one or more of the essential terms of the contract. The employee in those circumstances is entitled to leave without notice or to give notice, but the conduct in either case must be sufficiently serious to entitle him to leave at once.

Per Lawton LJ: Sensible persons have no difficulty in recognising conduct by an employer which under law brings a contract of employment to an end. Persistent and unwanted amorous advances by an employer to a female member of his staff would, for example, clearly be such conduct.

McNeill v   **[2014] IRLR 113 CSIH**
Aberdeen City Council (No.2)
As a matter of Scots law, an employee who is in prior repudiatory breach of the implied term of trust and confidence

remains entitled to terminate their contract of employment by reason of the employer's breach of that term and claim constructive unfair dismissal.

Atkinson v   **[2014] IRLR 834 EAT**
Community Gateway Association
The obligation of trust and confidence which each party has in a contract of employment is not suspended or put in abeyance because one party has broken that obligation. An employee who has committed a fundamental repudiatory breach of that implied term remains entitled to bring a claim of constructive dismissal based on a breach of contract by his employer provided that, for whatever reason, the breach by the employee has not already been accepted by the employer.

Woods v   **[1982] IRLR 413 CA**
W M Car Services (Peterborough) Ltd
There is no rule of law for determining whether a particular set of facts constitutes a repudiatory breach of contract by the employer entitling the employee to claim constructive dismissal. In cases of constructive dismissal, the EAT should only interfere with the decision of the employment tribunal if it is shown that the employment tribunal misdirected itself in law, or that the decision was such that no reasonable employment tribunal could reach it.

Spafax Ltd v   **[1980] IRLR 442 CA**
Harrison
Lawful conduct is not something which is capable of amounting to a repudiation. Therefore, conduct cannot be a repudiation unless it involves a breach of contract.

Kerry Foods Ltd v   **[2005] IRLR 680 EAT**
Lynch
An employer's service of a lawful notice of termination coupled with an offer of continuous employment on different terms cannot of itself amount to a repudiatory breach of contract. There is no present breach of the existing terms nor an anticipatory breach in indicating lawful termination of the contract on proper notice.

Lewis v   **[1985] IRLR 465 CA**
Motorworld Garages Ltd
Conduct is repudiatory if, viewed objectively, it evinces an intention no longer to be bound by the contract. Neither the intentions of the party nor their reasonable belief that their conduct would not be accepted as repudiatory are determinative.

Aparau v   **[1996] IRLR 119 EAT**
Iceland Frozen Foods plc
Where there is a unilateral alteration by the employer of the terms of employment which has no immediate practical effect, there is a need for great caution before implying that the employee has consented to the variation by continuing to work without objecting to it.

Brown v   **[1993] IRLR 568 EAT**
JBD Engineering Ltd
That an employer acted on a genuine though mistaken belief may be treated as a relevant factor in determining whether or not, in the circumstances, there has been a repudiatory breach, at least in cases in which the belief was reasonable and was brought about in whole or in part by the conduct of the employee. However, the fact that an employer acted on a genuine belief is not enough by itself to prevent his conduct from amounting to a repudiation and, therefore, is not per se an answer to a claim of constructive dismissal.

Bridgen v   **[1987] IRLR 58 CA**
Lancashire County Council
Per Sir John Donaldson MR: The mere fact that a party to a contract takes a view of its construction which is ultimately shown to be wrong does not of itself constitute repudiatory conduct. It has to be shown that he did not intend to be bound by the contract as properly construed.

Hilton International Hotels   **[1990] IRLR 316 EAT**
(UK) Ltd v
Protopapa
In order for conduct of a supervisor to be on the part of the "employer" within the meaning of [s.95(1)(c)], it does not have to be shown that the supervisor had the authority to dismiss. Whether the repudiatory conduct of a supervisory employee binds the employer is governed by the general principle of contract law that the employer is bound by acts done in the course of the employee's employment. If the supervisor is doing that which he is employed to do and in the course of doing it behaves in a way which, if done by the employer, would constitute a fundamental breach of contract between the employer and an employee, then the employer is bound by the supervisor's misdeeds.

Warnes and another v   **[1993] IRLR 58 EAT**
Trustees of Cheriton Oddfellows
  Social Club
An employer is not entitled to rely upon lack of power of one of its officers or organs in acting in a way which, if valid, would constitute a dismissal. Therefore, the fact that a resolution purporting to take away the appellant's duties was invalid did not prevent a finding of constructive dismissal in circumstances where the removal of the duties would have been a fundamental breach of contract.

Wadham Stringer Commercials   **[1983] IRLR 46 EAT**
(London) Ltd and Wadham
  Stringer Vehicles Ltd v
Brown
Neither the surrounding circumstances inducing a fundamental breach by the employer, nor the circumstances which led the employee to accept such repudiation are relevant for determining whether or not there has been a constructive dismissal.

Tolson v   **[2003] IRLR 842 EAT**
Governing Body of Mixenden
  Community School

When determining an issue as to constructive dismissal, the conduct to be considered is that of the employer. An alleged failure by the employee, for example regarding following or not following a grievance procedure, cannot be relevant.

Garner v   **[1977] IRLR 206 EAT**
Grange Furnishing Ltd

Conduct amounting to a repudiation can be a series of small incidents over a period of time. If the conduct of the employer is making it impossible for the employee to go on working, that is plainly a repudiation of the contract of employment.

Dryden v   **[1992] IRLR 469 EAT**
Greater Glasgow Health Board

An employer is entitled to make rules for the conduct of employees in their place of work within the scope of the contract. Where a rule, such as a no-smoking rule in this case, is introduced for a legitimate purpose, the fact that it bears hardly on a particular employee because he or she is unable to comply does not in itself justify an inference that the employer has acted in such a way as to repudiate the contract with that employee.

British Broadcasting   **[1983] IRLR 43 EAT**
  Corporation v
Beckett

The imposition of a punishment which is grossly out of proportion to the offence can amount to a repudiation of a contract of service.

Stanley Cole (Wainfleet) Ltd v   **[2003] IRLR 52 EAT**
Sheridan

Unjustified imposition of a final written warning can amount to a repudiatory breach of contract by the employer entitling the employee to resign and claim constructive dismissal.

Shaw v   **[2008] IRLR 284 EAT**
CCL Ltd

Unlawful discrimination can amount to a repudiatory breach of contract although a contention that any such act is a breach of the implied term of trust and confidence was characterised by Judge McMullen QC as putting it "too high".

Pay

Industrial Rubber Products v   **[1977] IRLR 389 EAT**
Gillon

A unilateral reduction in the basic rate of pay, even for good reasons and to a relatively small extent, is a material breach of a fundamental element in the contract of employment.

White v   **[1991] IRLR 331 EAT**
Reflecting Roadstuds Ltd

Where an employer acts within the contract of employment, the fact that that causes a loss of income to the employee does not render the employer's act a breach of contract.

R F Hill Ltd v   **[1981] IRLR 258 EAT**
Mooney

The obligation on the employer is to pay the contractual wages and he is not entitled to alter the formula whereby those wages are calculated. The obligation on an employer to pay remuneration is one of the fundamental terms of a contract. Although a mere alteration in the contractual provisions does not necessarily amount to a fundamental breach constituting repudiation, if an employer seeks to alter that contractual obligation in a fundamental way, such attempt is a breach going to the very root of the contract and is necessarily a repudiation.

Adams v   **[1978] IRLR 551 EAT**
Charles Zub Associates Ltd

Failure to pay an employee's salary on the due date may amount to conduct which constitutes a breach going to the root of the contract or which shows that the employer has no intention thereafter to honour the contract and thus justifies the employee in resigning. But the circumstances of each case must be looked at.

Reid v   **[1990] IRLR 268 EAT**
Camphill Engravers

Paying an employee a weekly sum in wages less than the required amount is a continuing breach of contract and even if the employee does not react to an initial breach, it is open to him to refer to that initial breach where the employer continues to commit further breaches.

Gillies v   **[1979] IRLR 457 EAT**
Richard Daniels & Co Ltd

Whether a unilateral reduction in additional pay or fringe benefits by the employer is of sufficient materiality as to entitle an employee to resign and claim constructive dismissal is a matter of degree.

Stokes v   **[1979] IRLR 298 EAT**
Hampstead Wine Co Ltd

A refusal to pay overtime payments for overtime hours worked was a breach going to the root of the contract of employment entitling the employee to claim constructive dismissal.

F C Gardner Ltd v   **[1978] IRLR 63 EAT**
Beresford

In most circumstances it would be reasonable to infer a contractual term along the lines that an employer will not treat his employees arbitrarily, capriciously or inequitably in matters of remuneration.

Clark v   **[2000] IRLR 766 HC**
Nomura International plc

An employer exercising a discretion which on the face of the contract of employment is unfettered or absolute, such as the award of a discretionary bonus which is not guaranteed in any way, will be in breach of contract if no reasonable employer would have exercised the discretion in that way.

Murco Petroleum Ltd v   [1987] IRLR 50 EAT
Forge
Where a contract of employment makes no reference whatsoever to pay increases it is impossible to say that there is an implied term in the contract that there will always be a pay rise.

Judge v   [2005] IRLR 823 CA
Crown Leisure Ltd
A promise to increase an employee's salary so as to achieve parity with other employees "in due course" does not amount to a binding contractual promise such as to justify the employee resigning and claiming constructive dismissal when that promise was not fulfilled. For there to be a legally binding and enforceable contractual commitment, there must be certainty as to the contractual commitment entered into, or alternatively facts from which certainty can be established. A promise to achieve parity within two years might well be sufficiently certain to be capable of enforcement, but a promise to achieve parity "eventually" or "in due course" is too vague ever to amount to a binding contractual commitment.

Job duties

Hilton v   [2001] IRLR 727 EAT
Shiner Ltd
Requiring an employee to cease doing what has been his principal job and to take up a new role will almost always be capable of being a repudiatory breach of contract. Whether in a particular case the breach is sufficiently material to be repudiatory has to be judged objectively by reference to its impact on the employee. The question whether the proposed change was justified is a different and distinct question. Once the breach is sufficiently material to be regarded as repudiatory, the motive underlying it becomes irrelevant. Thus, the presence of an allegation of dishonesty against the employee makes no difference.

Land Securities Trillium Ltd v   [2005] IRLR 765 EAT
Thornley
In determining what an employee's existing contractual duties were, the tribunal is entitled to look not only at how the duties were described in the employee's original job description but also at the actual work that the employee had been given. Job descriptions are not prescriptive documents.

Land Securities Trillium Ltd v   [2005] IRLR 765 EAT
Thornley
Changing the duties of an architect from a hands-on role to a mainly managerial one, which had the effect of de-skilling her, amounted to a repudiatory breach of contract entitling the employee to resign and complain of constructive dismissal.

A contractual clause requiring the employee to "perform to the best of your abilities all the duties of this post and ... any other duties which may reasonably be required of you", did not afford the employers carte blanche to require the employee to undertake any duties they wished, but expressly imposed a requirement of reasonableness on the employers' request. Once it was found that the duties required by the employers were unreasonably required of the employee, the fact that there may have been valid commercial grounds, as opposed to a wholly arbitrary basis, for the employers' requirement could not cure the unreasonableness of the requirement so far as the employee was concerned.

Coleman v   [1977] IRLR 342 EAT
S & W Baldwin
In removing an important part of the employee's functions and leaving him with residual duties of a humdrum character, the employers had unilaterally changed the whole nature of the employee's job and in so doing had repudiated the contract of employment.

Peter Carnie & Son Ltd v   [1979] IRLR 260 EAT
Paton
An employee who is engaged on general duties cannot insist upon doing only those duties which he likes most.

Milbrook Furnishing Industries Ltd v [1981] IRLR 309 EAT
McIntosh and others
If an employer, under the stresses of the requirements of his business, directs an employee to transfer to other suitable work on a purely temporary basis and at no diminution in wages, in the ordinary case that may not constitute a breach of contract. However, it must be clear that "temporary" means a period which is either defined as being a short fixed period, or which is in its nature one of limited duration.

McNeill v   [1984] IRLR 179 EAT
Messrs Charles Crimin (Electrical
  Contractors) Ltd
If the terms and conditions of employment require an employee to work in a certain capacity, it is a breach of those conditions for the employer to seek to insist that he should work in a different capacity, albeit on a temporary basis. For a breach of contract to constitute a material breach going to the root of the contract, it need not involve a substantial alteration to the terms of employment on a permanent basis. It is sufficient that it involves a substantial alteration to the terms of employment. In many cases, an employee may agree to a temporary alteration. However, he is not obliged to do so and, if he does, he will lose the opportunity of treating himself as having been constructively dismissed in view of the fact that he has acquiesced in the alteration.

British Broadcasting Corporation v   [1983] IRLR 43 EAT
Beckett
Downgrading following a disciplinary offence amounted to a repudiation of contract where the punishment was grossly out

of proportion to the offence notwithstanding that the disciplinary procedure expressly gave the contractual right to demote as a penalty for misconduct.

Location

Bass Leisure Ltd v   [1994] IRLR 104 EAT
Thomas
A breach of contract which consists of requiring an employee to work where she cannot be required to is obviously fundamental or repudiatory and entitles the employee to claim constructive dismissal.

Rank Xerox Ltd v   [1988] IRLR 280 EAT
Churchill and others
In determining where under a contract of employment an employee can be required to work, the correct approach to the analysis of the terms and conditions of employment is through contract and not through the overall superimposition of a test of reasonableness. Therefore, where a contract included a clear and unambiguous express mobility clause providing that "the company may require you to transfer to another location", it was an error of law for a tribunal to construe that clause on the basis of reasonableness as being restricted to a reasonable daily travelling distance.

Curling and others v   [1992] IRLR 549 EAT
Securicor Ltd
If an employer is going to rely on or avail himself of the benefit of a mobility clause in a situation of job or location changes, he must make his position clear in that respect. When a part of a business is to be closed down, an employer can take two different attitudes. He can invoke a contractual mobility clause and require the employee to go to a new location or job, if the clause entitles the employer so to do, whereupon the original employment continues and no question of redundancy will arise. Alternatively, the employer can decide not to invoke the mobility clause and rely instead on suitable offers of alternative employment as a defence to a claim to a redundancy payment. What the employer cannot do is dodge between the two attitudes and hope to be able to adopt the most profitable at the end of the day.

Courtaulds Northern Spinning Ltd v   [1988] IRLR 305 CA
Sibson and Transport & General
    Workers' Union
Where there is no express term in a contract of employment as to the employee's place of work or the employer's right to transfer, in order to give the contract business efficacy it is essential to imply into it that term which the parties if reasonable would probably have agreed on entering into the contract if they had directed their minds to the problem.

Aparau v   [1996] IRLR 119 EAT
Iceland Frozen Foods plc
Although there must necessarily be some term as to place of employment in a contract of employment, there is no neces-sity to have any implied clause about mobility, where the nature of the employee's work does not make such a clause necessary, nor is needed in order to give the contract business efficacy.

Courtaulds Northern Spinning Ltd v   [1988] IRLR 305 CA
Sibson and Transport & General
    Workers' Union
In the absence of any express contractual provision as to where an HGV driver was obliged to work, the correct term to imply was that the employer had a power to direct the employee for any reason to work at any place within reasonable daily travelling distance of his home. There was no need or justification to import into such an implied term a requirement that the employer's request that the employee work at another place must itself be "reasonable" or that a request could be reasonable only if made "for genuine operational reasons". Any such fetter on the employer's right to request the employee to move would have been potentially uncertain and difficult in operation and the employer reasonably could have objected to it.

Little v   [1980] IRLR 19 EAT
Charterhouse Magna Assurance
    Co Ltd
In the absence of any express contractual provision as to where a general manager was obliged to work, there was no basis for implying into the contract a geographical limitation on where over the five years of its duration the employee had to perform his duties.

Aparau v   [1996] IRLR 119 EAT
Iceland Frozen Foods plc
In the absence of any express contractual mobility clause, it was wrong to imply such a term in the contract of a shop assistant in a large chain of stores.

Prestwick Circuits Ltd v   [1990] IRLR 191 CS
McAndrew
An implied right to order an employee to transfer from one place of employment to another must be subject to the implied qualification that reasonable notice must be given. Whether the notice given in a particular case was reasonable is a question of fact and degree for the employment tribunal to determine.

United Bank Ltd v   [1989] IRLR 507 EAT
Akhtar
An employer's express discretion under a mobility clause whether to grant a relocation allowance was subject to an implied term that it would be exercised in such a way as not to render it impossible for an employee to comply with his contractual obligation to move. By signing a contract which expressly conferred discretion on the employer as to whether there would be a relocation allowance, the employee did not accept that the employer would not necessarily be under an obligation to exercise that

discretion in particular circumstances. Although it is impermissible to imply a term which negatives an express provision in a contract, it is permissible to imply a term which controls the exercise of a discretion which is expressly conferred in the contract.

White v   **[1991] IRLR 331 EAT**
Reflecting Roadstuds Ltd
The decision in *Akhtar* could not be understood as implying a term that an employer should act reasonably in exercising his discretion under a contractual mobility clause. To imply a term that a transfer in accordance with an express flexibility or mobility clause should be handled reasonably would be to introduce the reasonableness test into constructive dismissal cases by the back door and would fly in the face of *Western Excavating v Sharp*. However, if there were no reasonable or sufficient grounds for requiring the employee to move, there would be a breach of the term that a contractual discretion will not be exercised capriciously.

Hours of work

Dal and others v   **[1980] IRLR 413 EAT**
A S Orr
Where an employer had the contractual right to alter hours of work and shift systems, to alter hours of work without the employee's consent could not be regarded as a breach of contract.

Disciplinary procedure

The Post Office v   **[1981] IRLR 515 EAT**
Strange
A failure by the employers to perform the contract by properly observing their own disciplinary procedures, and the action they took against the employee as a result, amounted to a repudiation of the contract entitling the employee to treat the contract as at an end.

Grievance procedure

W A Goold (Pearmak) Ltd v   **[1995] IRLR 516 EAT**
McConnell and another
There is a fundamental implied term in a contract of employment that an employer will reasonably and promptly afford a reasonable opportunity to its employees to obtain redress of any grievance they may have.

Watson v   **[2011] IRLR 458 EAT**
University of Strathclyde
Actual, or apparent, bias in the constitution of an internal grievance appeal panel may amount to a fundamental breach of the implied term of trust and confidence because employees are entitled to a fair hearing of a grievance throughout, including at the appeal stage.

Lay off/suspension

D & J McKenzie Ltd v   **[1976] IRLR 345 CS**
Smith
An employer is not entitled unilaterally to suspend an employee unless there is some provision, express or implied, in the contract of employment permitting him to do so.

Kenneth MacRae & Co Ltd v   **[1984] IRLR 5 EAT**
Dawson
Where an employer has a contractual right to lay off an employee indefinitely, in the normal case he is not to be regarded as in breach of his obligation under the contract to supply work simply by virtue of the passage of time.

Waine v   **[1977] IRLR 434 EAT**
R Oliver (Plant Hire) Ltd
In the absence of an express contractual provision or a collective agreement, whether there is an implied right to lay off depends upon what the expectation would be, according to the customs in the particular trade, as to the terms upon which an employee in the position of the employee concerned was to be employed at the time his employment commenced.

Institute of the Motor Industry v   **[1992] IRLR 343 EAT**
Harvey
If a woman gives notice of intention to take maternity leave, her contract of employment is likely to continue when she goes on maternity leave unless it is terminated by agreement, resignation or dismissal. By implication, during maternity leave the contractual obligations for the employer to provide reasonable work and to make payment and for the employee to carry out that work are suspended.

Garden leave

Christie v   **[2010] IRLR 1016 EAT**
Johnston Carmichael
In the absence of a contractual garden leave clause, an employer would be in breach of contract in placing an employee on garden leave only if the contract of employment, on its true construction in the light of the surrounding circumstances, confers on the employee a "right to work". Relevant factors include whether the employee has specific and unique duties and whether his special skills require frequent exercise.

Trust and confidence

Woods v   **[1981] IRLR 347 EAT**
W M Car Services (Peterborough) Ltd
It is clearly established that there is implied in a contract of employment a term that the employers will not, without reasonable and proper cause, conduct themselves in a manner calculated or likely to destroy or seriously damage the relationship of confidence and trust between employer and employee. Any breach of this implied term is a fundamental

breach amounting to a repudiation since it necessarily goes to the root of the contract. To constitute a breach of this implied term, it is not necessary to show that the employer intended any repudiation of the contract. The employment tribunal's function is to look at the employer's conduct as a whole and determine whether it is such that its cumulative effect, judged reasonably and sensibly, is such that the employee cannot be expected to put up with it.

Eastwood v   **[2004] IRLR 733 HL**
Magnox Electric plc
McCabe v
Cornwall County Council
Per Lord Nicholls of Birkenhead: The trust and confidence implied term means that an employer must treat his employees fairly. In his conduct of his business and in his treatment of his employees, an employer must act responsibly and in good faith.

Horkulak v   **[2003] IRLR 756 HC**
Cantor Fitzgerald International
The obligation of mutual trust and confidence has emerged from the general duty of cooperation between contracting parties. In modern times, the "cooperation" required of an employer cannot be met simply by remuneration, nor is it affected by level of pay. An employer does not acquire a right to treat employees according to a different standard of conduct from that which might otherwise be required by paying substantial salaries.

United Bank Ltd v   **[1989] IRLR 507 EAT**
Akhtar
In the field of employment law, it is proper to imply an overriding obligation in the terms used in *Woods v W M Car Services (Peterborough) Ltd* which is independent of and in addition to the literal interpretation of the actions which are permitted to the employer under the terms of the contract. There may well be conduct which is calculated or likely to destroy or seriously damage the relationship of trust and confidence between employer and employee which a literal interpretation of the written words of the contract might appear to justify.

Reda v   **[2002] IRLR 747 PC**
Flag Ltd
The implied term of trust and confidence cannot sensibly be used to circumscribe an express power of dismissal without cause.

Kerry Foods Ltd v   **[2005] IRLR 680 EAT**
Lynch
The giving of lawful notice cannot of itself constitute a breach of the implied term of trust and confidence. Accordingly, there was no breach of the implied contractual term of trust and confidence where the employers had not unilaterally varied the claimant's contract but had given lawful notice of termination coupled with an offer of immediate re-engagement on new terms.

Lewis v   **[1985] IRLR 465 CA**
Motorworld Garages Ltd
Even if an employee has not treated a breach of an express contractual term as a wrongful repudiation, he is entitled to add such a breach to other actions which, taken together, may cumulatively amount to a breach of the implied obligation of trust and confidence.

London Borough of Waltham Forest v   **[2005] IRLR 35 CA**
Omilaju
In order to result in a breach of the implied term of trust and confidence, a "final straw", not itself a breach of contract, must be an act in a series of earlier acts which cumulatively amount to a breach of the implied term. The act does not have to be of the same character as the earlier acts. Its essential quality is that, when taken in conjunction with the earlier acts on which the employee relies, it amounts to a breach of the implied term of trust and confidence. It must contribute something to that breach, although what it adds may be relatively insignificant so long as it is not utterly trivial. The final straw, viewed in isolation, need not be unreasonable or blameworthy conduct. However, an entirely innocuous act on the part of the employer cannot be a final straw, even if the employee genuinely, but mistakenly, interprets the act as hurtful and destructive of his trust and confidence in the employer. The test of whether the employee's trust and confidence has been undermined is objective.

Brown v   **[1998] IRLR 682 NICA**
Merchant Ferries Ltd
In determining whether there has been a breach of the implied term of trust and confidence such as to amount to a constructive dismissal, the test to be applied is whether the employer's conduct so impacted on the employee that, viewed objectively, the employee could properly conclude that the employer was repudiating the contract. Although the correct approach to constructive dismissal is to ask whether the employer was in breach of contract and not did the employer act unreasonably, if the employer's conduct is seriously unreasonable that may provide sufficient evidence that there has been a breach of contract.

BG plc v   **[2001] IRLR 496 EAT**
O'Brien
In determining whether an employer is in breach of the implied contractual duty of trust and confidence, the question is whether, looked at objectively, the employer has acted in a manner likely to destroy or seriously damage the relationship of confidence and trust between the employer and employee. If the conduct has that effect, then the question of whether there was a reasonable and proper cause for the behaviour must be considered.

Hilton v   **[2001] IRLR 727 EAT**
Shiner Ltd
The implied term of trust and confidence is qualified by the requirement that the conduct of the employer about which

complaint is made must be engaged in without reasonable and proper cause. Thus, in order to determine whether there has been a breach of the implied term, two matters have to be determined. The first is whether, ignoring their cause, there have been acts which are likely on their face to seriously damage or destroy the relationship of trust and confidence between employer and employee. The second is whether there is no reasonable and proper cause for those acts. For example, any employer who proposes to suspend or discipline an employee for lack of capability or misconduct is doing an act which is capable of seriously damaging or destroying the relationship of trust and confidence, yet it could never be argued that the employer was in breach of the term of trust and confidence if he had reasonable and proper cause for taking the disciplinary action.

Bournemouth University Higher   **[2010] IRLR 445 CA**
  Education Corporation v
Buckland
The conduct of an employer who is said to have committed a repudiatory breach of the contract of employment is to be judged by an objective test rather than a range of reasonable responses test. Reasonableness may be one of the tools in the employment tribunal's factual analysis kit for deciding whether there has been a fundamental breach but it cannot be a legal requirement.

BCCI v   **[1999] IRLR 508 HC**
Ali (No.3)
To amount to a breach of the implied term of trust and confidence, misconduct on the part of an employer must be so serious as to amount to constructive dismissal, entitling the employee to leave immediately without notice on discovering it. The test is whether that conduct is such that the employee cannot reasonably be expected to tolerate it a moment longer after discovering it and can walk out of his job without prior notice.

Croft v   **[2002] IRLR 851 EAT**
Consignia plc
The implied term of trust and confidence is only breached by acts or omissions which seriously damage or destroy the necessary trust and confidence. Both sides are expected to absorb lesser blows. The gravity of a suggested breach of the implied term is very much left to the assessment of the tribunal as the "industrial jury".

The Post Office v   **[1980] IRLR 347 EAT**
Roberts
There does not have to be deliberate conduct or bad faith for the obligation of mutual trust and confidence to be destroyed. Whether the conduct of the party whose behaviour is challenged amounts to a repudiation of contract must be determined by whether it is such that its effect, judged reasonably and sensibly, is to disable the other party from properly carrying out his or her obligations.

Malik v   **[1997] IRLR 462 HL**
BCCI
In order to constitute a breach of the implied contractual term of mutual trust and confidence, the trust-destroying conduct need not be directed at the particular employee. The implied obligation extends to any conduct by the employer likely to destroy or seriously damage the relationship of trust and confidence between employer and employee. If conduct objectively considered is likely to cause damage to the relationship between employer and employee, a breach of the implied obligation may arise. The motives of the employer cannot be determinative or even relevant in judging the employee's claim that the implied term has been breached. Nor is it necessary that the employee's confidence is actually undermined. A breach occurs when the proscribed conduct takes place. Proof of a subjective loss of confidence in the employer is not an essential element of the breach.

BCCI v   **[1999] IRLR 508 HC**
Ali (No.3)
Where the misconduct was not directed at the employee or at employees generally, a high threshold is required to establish a breach of the implied term and the trust-destroying conduct may be required to be grave. The conduct must impinge on the relationship of employer and employee in the sense that, looked at objectively, it is likely to destroy or seriously damage the degree of trust and confidence the employee is entitled to have in his employer. The term "likely" requires a higher degree of certainty than a reasonable prospect or indeed a 51% probability and reflects what might colloquially be termed "a pretty good chance".

The Post Office v   **[1980] IRLR 347 EAT**
Roberts
There is no implied contractual term that an employer will treat an employee in a reasonable manner. Such a term would be too wide and too uncertain.

Cantor Fitzgerald International v   **[2002] IRLR 867 HC**
Bird
That an employee has lost confidence in management is not the same as conduct by the employer calculated to destroy or seriously damage trust and confidence between employer and employee in the sense of the implied term.

Johnson v   **[2001] IRLR 279 HL**
Unisys Ltd
The implied term of trust and confidence does not apply to dismissal or to the way in which the employment relationship was terminated. In this case, therefore, the claimant could not rely on the fact that he was dismissed without a fair hearing and in breach of the employer's disciplinary procedure in order to establish that his dismissal was a breach of the implied term of trust and confidence. An implied term cannot contradict an express term in the contract that the employer was entitled to dismiss without cause on giving due notice. In

the face of such an express provision, it was not possible to imply a term that the employer would not do so except for some good cause and after giving the employee a reasonable opportunity to demonstrate that no such cause existed.

Eastwood v   **[2002] IRLR 447 CA**
Magnox Electric plc
Johnson v Unisys precludes a claim for breach of the implied term of trust and confidence relating to the manner of dismissal, notwithstanding that the conduct complained of occurred before the act of dismissal.

Gebremariam v   **[2014] IRLR 354 EAT**
Ethiopian Airlines Enterprise
An unfair dismissal claim may be brought based on constructive dismissal as a result of a breach of the implied term of trust and confidence, for example, in the way that a redundancy process was handled. The *Johnson* exclusion zone does not apply to such a claim.

King v   **[2002] IRLR 252 CS**
University Court of the University of
   St Andrews
The duty of trust and confidence is to be implied throughout all aspects of the ongoing relationship of employer and employee and subsists, therefore, during the stage when an employer is investigating allegations against an employee and considering whether to dismiss him. Whilst the decision of the House of Lords in *Johnson v Unisys* makes it clear that there is no room for implication of the term once the decision to dismiss has been taken, it would be highly destructive and damaging to the employer/ employee relationship for the employers to act in breach of the implied duty during an assessment which had the potential either to reinforce or to terminate the contract of employment.

Malik v   **[1997] IRLR 462 HL**
BCCI
An employer which operates its business in a dishonest and corrupt manner is in breach of the implied contractual term of trust and confidence. In agreeing to work for the employer an employee, whatever his status, cannot be taken to have agreed to work in furtherance of a dishonest business.

BCCI v   **[1999] IRLR 508 HC**
Ali (No.3)
In determining whether there has been a breach of the trust and confidence term, it is not necessary that the employer's business or operations were exclusively, essentially or even predominantly fraudulent or dishonest. The test is to look at the degree of dishonesty, the size and number of the dishonest transactions, the level of employees involved and the importance and prevalence of the wrongdoing in the context of the employer's business as a whole, and to form a view whether the wrongdoing was so serious, substantial and systematic that the employer's business as a whole may fairly be characterised as tainted, and whether it amounted to unfair

or improper exploitation of the employees generally to require them to continue to be employed in such a business. In such a situation, the misconduct is a breach of the trust and confidence term in the contracts of all employees, irrespective of their individual status.

BCCI v   **[1999] IRLR 508 HC**
Ali (No.3)
Although carrying on a business in a corrupt and dishonest manner is an example of a breach of the implied term of trust and confidence, carrying on an insolvent business would not be enough to establish a breach, nor would fraudulent trading necessarily suffice.

Transco plc (formerly BG plc) v   **[2002] IRLR 444 CA**
O'Brien
Where an employer decides to offer the workforce a new contract on better terms, it is a breach of the implied term of trust and confidence to single out an employee on capricious grounds and refuse to offer him the same terms as are offered to the rest of the workforce. This is so even where the reason why the terms were not offered to that employee was the employers' genuine but erroneous belief that he did not qualify for the new terms.

Farrell, Matthews & Weir v   **[2005] IRLR 160 EAT**
Hansen
The imposition of conditions on the payment of a non-contractual discretionary bonus whereby an employee could be deprived of the balance of her bonus entitlement if her employment terminated for any reason, including redundancy, coupled with refusal to give her access to the accounts upon which the decision to impose the conditions was claimed to be based, amounted to a fundamental breach of the implied term of trust and confidence.

French v   **[1998] IRLR 646 CA**
Barclays Bank plc
To seek to invoke a change of policy or a change in the terms on which loans are made to employees required to relocate, which has been applied to other employees over many years and appeared in terms in the employer's staff manual at the time when the loan was made, is conduct on the part of the employer likely to destroy the confidence and trust between employers and their employees.

Transco plc (formerly BG plc) v   **[2002] IRLR 444 CA**
O'Brien
The implied term of trust and confidence is not restricted to regulating existing contractual terms. There may a breach of the implied term in a decision to refuse to offer an employee a new contract, just as in a decision to refuse to offer a variation.

Imperial Group Pension Trust Ltd   **[1991] IRLR 66 HC**
   and others v
Imperial Tobacco Ltd and others
An employer's implied obligation of good faith applies to the

employer's rights and powers under a pension scheme. In exercising its rights, an employer can have regard to the financial interests of the company, but only to the extent that in so doing the obligation of good faith to the employees is not breached.

University of Nottingham v   **[1999] IRLR 87 HC**
Eyett and the Pensions Ombudsman
The implied duty of mutual trust and confidence in a contract of employment does not include a positive obligation on the employer to warn an employee who is proposing to exercise important rights in connection with the contract of employment, such as pension rights, that the way in which he is proposing to exercise them may not be the most financially advantageous.

(1) Reed   **[1999] IRLR 299 EAT**
(2) Bull Information Systems Ltd v
Stedman
A course of unwanted and bullying behaviour by a manager, amounting to sexual harassment, is a breach of the duty of trust and confidence.

Bracebridge Engineering Ltd v   **[1990] IRLR 3 EAT**
Darby
Failure by the employer to treat an allegation of sexual harassment seriously was a breach of the implied contractual term relating to mutual trust and confidence which entitled the employee to resign and treat herself as having been constructively dismissed. The implied contractual term relating to mutual trust, confidence and support is an extremely important one for female staff.

Cantor Fitzgerald International v   **[2002] IRLR 867 HC**
Bird
Over-aggressive promotion of proposed changes to terms and conditions by a particular manager, including threatening and intimidating behaviour, can amount to conduct calculated or likely to seriously damage or destroy the relationship of trust and confidence between employer and employee.

McBride v   **[2012] IRLR 22 EAT**
Falkirk Football & Athletic Club
An employer cannot successfully defend a claim on the basis that he and others in his industry treat all employees badly and therefore treating an employee badly cannot amount to a breach of the duty to maintain trust and confidence.

Horkulak v   **[2003] IRLR 756 HC**
Cantor Fitzgerald International
The law has developed so as to recognise an employment contract as engaging obligations in connection with the self esteem and dignity of the employee. Whilst high standards of performance are legitimate requirements in an employment contract, these legitimate demands must be balanced by a fair system of enforcement which reflects the particular conditions affecting employment. The level of the rebuke

must be proportionate to the alleged failing on the part of the employee. Threats of dismissal should not be used to intimidate. Nor should they be issued in intemperate language. Frequent use of foul and abusive language does not sanitise its effect so as to remove its power to offend. Nor does the fact that a claimant himself was given to foul language deprive him of his entitlement to proper treatment in accordance with his contract.

Palmanor Ltd v   **[1978] IRLR 303 EAT**
Cedron
Where an employee resigns because of an employer's use of foul language, the employment tribunal should ask itself whether the employer's conduct was so unreasonable that it went beyond the limits of the contract. Although tribunals have to be careful not to attach too great importance to words used in the heat of the moment or in anger, there comes a time when the language is such that even if the person using it is in a state of anger, an employee cannot be expected to tolerate it.

Cantor Fitzgerald International v   **[2002] IRLR 267 HC**
Bird
Even in a working environment where it was accepted that bad language was commonplace, use of obscenities by a senior executive to a more junior employee may well on its own cross the threshold of conduct which repudiates of the contract of employment.

Isle of Wight Tourist Board v   **[1976] IRLR 413 EAT**
Coombes
The relationship between a director and his personal secretary must be one of complete confidence. In calling his secretary "a bitch" the employer's director had shattered that relationship, entitling the employee to terminate her contract and claim that she had been constructively dismissed.

Horkulak v   **[2003] IRLR 756 HC**
Cantor Fitzgerald International
The judgement of a senior manager cannot properly be subject to instant and dismissive conclusions which afford no respect to his viewpoint.

Courtaulds Northern Textiles Ltd v   **[1979] IRLR 84 EAT**
Andrew
Telling a manager that he could not do his job, when that was not a true expression of opinion, amounted to a breach of the implied contractual term that employers will not, without reasonable and proper cause, conduct themselves in a manner calculated or likely to destroy or seriously damage the relationship of confidence and trust between the parties.

Gogay v   **[2000] IRLR 703 CA**
Hertfordshire County Council
Suspending an employee without reasonable and proper cause pending a disciplinary investigation is a breach of the implied term of trust and confidence.

Walker v   **[1978] IRLR 105 EAT**
Josiah Wedgwood & Sons Ltd
Observed: The giving of an unjustified warning or series of warnings can be a matter of which legitimate complaint can be made by a person who claims constructive dismissal, particularly if he seeks to make a case that those warnings were not given with a view to improving his conduct and performance, but with a view to disheartening him and driving him out. In any case in which that sort of claim is made, nothing less than a full investigation by the employment tribunal of the merits of the warnings is required.

Hilton v   **[2001] IRLR 727 EAT**
Shiner Ltd
Merely to say that an employee is no longer trusted to handle money is not a breach of the implied term of trust and confidence in circumstances in which it is plain that the employer still has sufficient confidence in the employee to continue to employ him, and where there are fully justified suspicions of dishonesty and the alternative to retention in employment is dismissal.

TSB Bank plc v   **[2000] IRLR 157 EAT**
Harris
An employer who has undertaken to give a reference in respect of a current employee is under a contractual obligation to ensure that it is fair and reasonable and failure to do so may be a breach of the implied term of trust and confidence.

Visa International Service   **[2004] IRLR 42 EAT**
  Association v
Paul
Failure to notify a woman on maternity leave of a job vacancy which she would have applied for had she been aware of it, was a breach of the implied term of trust and confidence, entitling her to claim constructive dismissal, even though she did not in fact have the requisite experience to be shortlisted for the post. The point was that she believed that she was suitable for the post and the employers' failure to notify her of that opportunity fatally undermined her trust and confidence in them.

Blackburn v   **[2013] IRLR 846 EAT**
Aldi Stores
Failure to adhere to a grievance procedure is capable of amounting to or contributing to a breach of the implied term of trust and confidence. In particular, failure to hold a proper appeal in respect of a grievance may be a significant breach of the trust and confidence term entitling the employee to claim constructive dismissal, even where there is no issue as to the original grievance hearing.

Sita (GB) Ltd v   **[1997] IRLR 501 EAT**
Burton and others
The employer's implied duty of trust and confidence can only be breached by reason of the actions of third parties in the rarest of cases. The conduct of a potential transferee cannot be regarded as sufficiently affecting the employer's obligation of mutual trust and goodwill, where the employee's complaints or fears relate solely to the terms and conditions of the contract and where the substance of those complaints and fears are totally protected by the remedies available to the employee under TUPE.

Moores v   **[2000] IRLR 676 EAT**
Bude-Stratton Town Council
Individual local authority councillors are under a duty not to engage in conduct likely to undermine the trust and confidence required in employment contracts, and if that duty has been breached, then the council must be vicariously liable. It is an implied term of every contract that the employer will provide and maintain a working environment which is reasonably tolerable to all employees. Such term must apply to protect an employee from unacceptable treatment and behaviour and unauthorised interference in work duties.

BCCI v   **[1999] IRLR 226 HC**
Ali
The implied duty of mutual trust and confidence does not require either party to a contract of employment or to a compromise agreement to disclose to the other their own breaches of contract.

Duty to inform

Scally and others v   **[1991] IRLR 522 HL**
Southern Health and Social Services
  Board and others
There is an implied obligation on an employer to take reasonable steps to bring the term of a contract of employment to the employee's attention, so that he may be in a position to enjoy its benefit, where the terms of the contract have not been negotiated with the individual employee but result from negotiation with a representative body or are otherwise incorporated by reference; a particular term of the contract makes available to the employee a valuable right contingent upon action being taken by him to avail himself of its benefit; and the employee cannot, in all the circumstances, reasonably be expected to be aware of the term unless it is drawn to his attention. Accordingly, in the present case there was a contractual obligation on the employers of which they were in breach to take reasonable steps to bring the existence of the right to enhance their pension entitlement by the purchase of added years to the notice of the claimant employees.

Crossley v   **[2004] IRLR 377 CA**
Faithful & Gould Holdings Ltd
There is no duty on an employer to take reasonable care for an employee's economic well-being or to give an employee financial advice in relation to benefits accruing from his employment.

Ibekwe v   **[2003] IRLR 697 CA**
London General Transport
  Services Ltd
In principle, where a duty to inform is to be implied in accordance with the decision of the House of Lords in *Scal-*

ly v Southern Health and Social Services Board, the employer should give sufficient information to enable the employee to understand the options available to him at the time when he requires to have that information. The aim of the *Scally* implied term is to help ensure that the employee has effective access to information about benefits to which he is entitled. If the employer says to an employee that he is entitled at his option to a certain benefit but that no action needs to be taken at that stage and further information will be sent to him, the employee requires that information before he can "unlock" the benefit. In those circumstances, the duty to inform is not fulfilled until that further information is in fact sent to him. However, the employer does not have to ensure that the information was actually communicated to the employee. All the employer has to do is to take reasonable steps to inform the employee about his rights.

Crossley v   **[2004] IRLR 377 CA**
Faithful & Gould Holdings Ltd
Whether the implied duty to inform, as identified in *Scally*, does arise will always depend upon whether the employee can reasonably be expected to be aware of the existence of the relevant contractual provision unless it is brought to his attention by the employers. This criterion may be satisfied in relation to some, but not all, employees of the same employer, even if they were all subject to the same conditions of employment. Therefore, in deciding that the claimant in this case could reasonably have been expected to be aware of the provisions of the employers' long-term disability scheme even though they had not been brought to his attention by the employers, the judge was entitled to take account of the fact that he was a director and senior employee of the company.

Marlow v   **[2002] IRLR 798 HC**
East Thames Housing Group Ltd
The duty on an employer to give an employee information concerning pensions, as identified by the House of Lords in *Scally v Southern Health and Social Services Board*, depends upon the employee's ignorance. Thus, where the employee knew that she was not a member of the employers' pension scheme and had been told in clear terms of the need to approach the personnel department for an application form and details of the scheme, the employers were not under a duty to inform her of the steps she needed to take in order to join the pension scheme.

Co-operation

Associated Tyre Specialists   **[1976] IRLR 386 EAT**
   (Eastern) Ltd v
Waterhouse
It was a term of fundamental importance in a supervisor's contract that she should have her employer's support in her actions as supervisor and the employer's conduct in failing to back the supervisor up amounted to a constructive dismissal.

White v   **[1981] IRLR 261 EAT**
London Transport Executive
There is an implied term in the contracts of employment of probationary employees imposing an obligation on the employer to take reasonable steps to maintain an appraisal of a probationer during a trial period, giving guidance by advice or warning where necessary.

Health and safety

Marshall Specialist Vehicles Ltd v   **[2003] IRLR 672 EAT**
Osborne
There is an implied term in all contracts of employment that the employer should take reasonable care for the safety of employees. Where a breach of that term is said to justify a case of constructive dismissal, a fundamental breach must be established. The tribunal must therefore consider precisely what it is that the employer did wrong and whether what they did wrong was a repudiatory wrong.

Marshall Specialist Vehicles Ltd v   **[2003] IRLR 672 EAT**
Osborne
In determining whether there has been a breach of the implied health and safety term, an employment tribunal must consider separately the precise nature of the duty in the particular circumstances; the question of foreseeability of the harm; the nature and the extent of the breach; and the question of causation arising out of any breach established.

Walker v   **[1995] IRLR 35 HC**
Northumberland County Council
An employer owes a duty to his employees not to cause them psychiatric damage by the volume or character of the work which they are required to perform.

Dutton & Clark Ltd v   **[1985] IRLR 363 EAT**
Daly
The scope of the duty on an employer to provide a safe system of work must be assessed according to the band of reasonableness to be expected of a reasonable employer. The question for the tribunal is whether the reasonable employer could be expected to have done more or acted differently. If the answer is that no reasonable employer would have expected the employee to work in those conditions, then there was a fundamental breach of contract entitling the employee to treat it as a repudiation. But if it is possible that some reasonable employers might have done no more or less than the employer did in fact do, then there was not a fundamental breach of contract and the employee is not entitled to say that he was forced to resign.

British Aircraft Corporation Ltd v   **[1978] IRLR 332 EAT**
Austin
An employer's failure to investigate the employee's complaint about the protective eyewear provided amounted to conduct which entitled the employee to resign without notice. Employers are under a duty to take reasonable care for the

safety of their employees. As part and parcel of that general obligation, employers are also under an obligation under the terms of the contract of employment to act reasonably in dealing with matters of safety or complaints about lack of safety which are drawn to their attention by employees. Unless the matter drawn to their attention or the complaint is obviously not bona fide or is frivolous, it is only by investigating individual complaints promptly and sensibly that employers can discharge their general obligation to take reasonable care for the safety of their employees.

Graham Oxley Tool Steels Ltd v Firth [1980] IRLR 135 EAT

There is no principle that a breach of a statutory duty under the Factories Act or a breach of the common law duty to take reasonable care for the safety of his workpeople by providing them with a safe system of work and proper plant and materials by itself results in a fundamental breach of contract by the employer. What has to be done in every case is to look at the circumstances of the contract and the obligations under the contract, to determine whether there is a breach and whether the breach is of such a quality that it indicates that the employer no longer intends to be bound by his obligation under the contract.

Waltons & Morse v Dorrington [1997] IRLR 488 EAT

It is an implied term of every contract of employment that the employers will provide and monitor for employees, so far as is reasonably practicable, a working environment which is reasonably suitable for the performance by them of their contractual duties. It is a breach of that implied term to require an employee to work in an environment which is affected by the smoking habits of fellow employees.

Graham Oxley Tool Steels Ltd v Firth [1980] IRLR 135 EAT

That an employee had to endure working for several months in intolerably cold conditions constituted a breach by the employers of their implied contractual obligation to provide a proper working environment.

Anticipatory breach

Harrison v Norwest Holst Group Administration Ltd [1985] IRLR 240 CA

Where there is a contract already being performed between the parties but the relevant obligation remains either wholly or in part executory, the same rule applies as in the situation of an anticipatory breach, where the time for the performance of the contract has not yet arrived: the party in breach has an opportunity before the repudiation is accepted to cure the breach by withdrawing the threat not to perform the contract. Thus, there was no immediate repudiatory breach where the employers informed an employee that he would lose his directorship in a fortnight's time, since the obligation to continue the director-

ship was an obligation to be performed in the future so that there was sufficient anticipatory element in the breach to make the situation more in common with a pure anticipatory breach case, where all performance is still executory and the employers have a locus poenitentiae at any time before acceptance is communicated, than with a case of immediate breach.

Haseltine Lake & Co v Dowler [1981] IRLR 25 EAT

It was not an anticipatory breach of contract to tell an employee that if he did not find a job elsewhere his employment would eventually be terminated, since there was nothing to suggest that the employers did not intend ultimately to terminate the contract without proper notice. A contract of employment is not an agreement for perpetual servitude from which neither master nor servant can escape without committing a breach, and termination in accordance with the agreed terms does not itself constitute such a breach.

Greenaway Harrison Ltd v Wiles [1994] IRLR 380 EAT

There can be an anticipatory breach of contract giving rise to a dismissal under[s.95(1)(c)] where an employer tries to negotiate a new contract and threatens to determine the old contract by serving due notice if the employee does not agree.

Financial Techniques (Planning Services) Ltd v Hughes [1981] IRLR 32 CA

Where there is a genuine dispute between the parties about the terms of a contract of employment, it is not an anticipatory breach of the contract for one party to do no more than argue his point of view.

Per Lawton LJ: The mere fact that an employer is of the opinion, albeit mistakenly, that there is something to be discussed with his employee about the contract is a very long way from the employer taking up the attitude that he is not under any circumstances at all going to be bound by it.

Per Brandon LJ: As the employer genuinely believed there was a difference of opinion about the terms of the contract and did no more than insist on his view in the matter, he was not repudiating the contract. The dispute could have been litigated quite easily in an action to determine how much money was owed.

Per Templeman LJ: It could not be held that if any party to a contract has a plausible but mistaken view of his rights under that contract he may insist on that view, and his insistence cannot amount to repudiation. Whether or not there is a repudiation depends on the facts and consequences of each action by the party who holds mistaken views.

Acceptance of repudiation

Boyo v London Borough of Lambeth [1995] IRLR 50 CA

The decision of the Court of Appeal in *Gunton v London Borough of Richmond* is binding authority that a unilateral repudiation of the contract by the employers does not terminate the contract of employment until accepted by the employee.

Nottinghamshire County Council v Meikle
[2004] IRLR 703 CA

Once the repudiation of the contract by the employer has been established, the proper approach is to ask whether the employee has accepted that repudiation by treating the contract of employment as at an end. It must be in response to the repudiation, but the fact that the employee also objected to other actions or inactions of the employer, not amounting to a breach of contract, would not vitiate the acceptance of the repudiation. It is enough that the employee resigned in response, at least in part, to fundamental breaches by the employer.

Wright v North Ayrshire Council
[2014] IRLR 4 EAT

Where there is more than one reason why an employee leaves a job, the correct approach is to examine whether any of them is a response to the breach, not to see which amongst them is the effective cause. A repudiatory breach of contract can only be disregarded where it is plain that the resignation "was not in response to a breach, even though that occurred and even though it was serious, but for some other unconnected reason to the exclusion of a response to the breach". The issue is whether the breach played a part in the resignation.

White v Bristol Rugby Club Ltd
[2002] IRLR 204 HC

An acceptance of repudiation must be unequivocal. If a party says one thing and does another, his conduct is equivocal.

Edwards v Surrey Police
[1999] IRLR 456 EAT

An employee alleging constructive dismissal must communicate to the employer, whether by words or conduct, the fact that they are terminating their employment.

Western Excavating (ECC) Ltd v Sharp
[1978] IRLR 27 CA

The employee must make up his mind to leave soon after the conduct of which he complains. If he continues for any length of time without leaving, he will be regarded as having elected to affirm the contract and will lose his right to treat himself as discharged.

W E Cox Toner (International) Ltd v Crook
[1981] IRLR 443 EAT

The general principles of contract law applicable to a repudiation of contract are that if one party commits a repudiatory breach of the contract, the other party can choose either to affirm the contract and insist on its further performance or he can accept the repudiation, in which case the contract is at an end. The innocent party must at some stage elect between these two possible courses; if he once affirms the contract, his right to accept the repudiation is at an end. But he is not bound to elect within a reasonable or any other time. Mere delay by itself (unaccompanied by any express or implied affirmation of the contract) does not constitute affirmation of the contract; but if it is prolonged it may be evidence of an implied affirmation. Affirmation of the contract can be implied if the innocent party calls on the guilty party for further performance of the contract, since his conduct is only consistent with the continued existence of the contractual obligation. Moreover, if the innocent party himself does acts which are only consistent with the continued existence of the contract, such acts will normally show affirmation of the contract. Nevertheless, if the innocent party further performs the contract to a limited extent but reserving his rights to accept the repudiation or is only continuing so as to allow the guilty party to remedy the breach, such further performance does not prejudice his right subsequently to accept the repudiation.

An obvious difference between a contract of employment and most other contracts is that if an employee faced with a repudiation by his employer goes to work the next day, he will himself be doing an act which, in one sense, is only consistent with the continued existence of the contract, ie he might be said to be affirming the contract. When he accepts his next pay packet (ie further performance of the contract by the guilty party) the risk of being held to affirm the contract is very great. Therefore, if the ordinary principles of contract law were to apply to a contract of employment, delay might be very serious, not in its own right, but because any delay normally involves further performance of the contract by both parties. The Court of Appeal's decision in *Marriott v Oxford Co-operative Society* [1970] 1 QB 196, however, establishes that, provided the employee makes clear his objection to what is being done, he is not to be taken to have affirmed the contract by continuing to work and draw pay for a limited period of time, even if his purpose is merely to enable him to find another job. It was against this background that Lord Denning's summary of the law in *Western Excavating v Sharp* had to be read. The passage: "Moreover, he must make up his mind soon after the conduct of which he complains: for, if he continues for any length of time without leaving, he will lose his right to treat himself as discharged" was not intended to be a comprehensive statement of the whole law.

Henry v London General Transport Services Ltd
[2002] IRLR 472 CA

The principles to be applied in determining whether an employee affirmed a contract by his actions were correctly set out by the EAT in *W E Cox Toner (International) Ltd v Crook*.

Cantor Fitzgerald International v Bird
[2002] IRLR 267 HC

Affirmation is essentially the legal embodiment of the everyday concept of ""letting bygones be bygones". In this case, the employees had not affirmed their contracts by waiting more than two months before resigning with immediate effect. They had clearly indicated their discontent with the employment and given clear signs of their intention to leave.

Waltons & Morse v   **[1997] IRLR 488 EAT**
Dorrington
An employee does not affirm the contract by delaying a few weeks before acting upon the breach in order to find alternative employment.

Cockram v   **[2014] IRLR 672 EAT**
Air Products plc
It is possible for an employee to affirm his contract of employment even after he has resigned because of a repudiatory breach. Where he gives notice in excess of the notice required by his contract, he is offering additional performance of the contract to that which is required by it. That additional performance may be consistent only with affirmation of the contract. It is a question of fact and degree whether in such circumstances his conduct is properly to be regarded as affirmation of the contract.

Weathersfield Ltd v   **[1999] IRLR 94 CA**
Sargent
In order to establish a claim of constructive dismissal, there is no requirement as a matter of law that an employee must state that he is leaving because of the employer's repudiatory conduct. Whether there has been an acceptance of a repudiation of a contract of employment is for the tribunal to determine on the facts and evidence in each case, although where no reason is communicated to the employer at the time, the tribunal may readily conclude that the repudiatory conduct was not the reason for the employee leaving.

Harrison v   **[1985] IRLR 240 CA**
Norwest Holst Group
   Administration Ltd
An employee's letter headed "without prejudice" could not be regarded as an unequivocal communication of acceptance of a repudiatory threat of the employers, since the effect of this heading was to communicate to the recipient that the letter was to be regarded as the commencement of a process of negotiation or compromise. That was a different stance from taking up an unequivocal position upon which the writer seeks to establish his legal rights.

L Lipton Ltd v   **[1979] IRLR 179 EAT**
Marlborough
An employee whose resignation letter stated "I wish to terminate my employment and would request that in view of my future employment I be released at your earliest convenience" could not claim that he had been constructively dismissed by reason of the employer's conduct. The difference between a termination by mutual agreement and a constructive dismissal is that in the first case the employee says "Please may I go?" and the employer says "Yes"; in the case of constructive dismissal, the employee says "You have treated me in such a way as I'm going without a 'by your leave'."

Seligman & Latz Ltd v   **[1979] IRLR 130 EAT**
McHugh
Once there has been a fundamental breach by the employer going to the root of the contract, the employee is entitled as a matter of law to treat the contract as at an end. There is no duty on the employee to use the employer's grievance procedure in order to try to solve the difficulty that had arisen.

Bournemouth University Higher   **[2010] IRLR 445 CA**
   Education Corporation v
Buckland
Once there has been a repudiatory breach, it is not open to the employer, by curing it, to preclude the employee from accepting the breach as terminating the contract. Once a repudiatory breach has been committed all the cards are in the hand of the wronged party: the defaulting party cannot choose to retreat. What it can do is invite affirmation by making amends.

Hunt v   **[1979] IRLR 379 EAT**
British Railways Board
An employee who continues to report for duty with his employer after issuing a claim claiming unfair dismissal cannot maintain that he had been constructively dismissed, since his behaviour is not consistent with his position that he had treated the contract as at an end by reason of the employer's conduct. Although in a constructive dismissal situation issuing a claim is a good way of the employee saying that he has made up his mind to treat the contract as at an end by reason of the employer's conduct, the law does not allow the employee to have his cake and eat it. He must not go on acting as if he was employed when what he is trying to say is that he was not.

Wilkins and others v   **[1978] IRLR 483 EAT**
Cantrell and Cochrane (GB) Ltd
Where an employer is in fundamental breach of contract, the act of going out on strike is not sufficient indication by an employee that he is treating the contract as at an end.

Frustration

General principles

Notcutt v   **[1986] IRLR 218 CA**
Universal Equipment Co (London) Ltd
There is no reason in principle why a periodic contract of employment determinable by short or relatively short notice should not in appropriate circumstances be held to have been terminated without notice by frustration, according to the accepted and long-established doctrine of frustration in the law of contract.

Notcutt v   **[1986] IRLR 218 CA**
Universal Equipment Co (London) Ltd

The principles which govern frustration are set out in the speeches of Lord Reid and Lord Radcliffe in *Davis Contractors Ltd v Fareham Urban District Council.* Per Lord Reid: ". . . the proper approach . . . is to take . . . all the facts which throw light on the nature of the contract, or which can properly be held to be extrinsic evidence relevant to assist in its construction and then, as a matter of law, to construe the contract and to determine whether the ultimate situation . . . is or is not within the scope of the contract so construed." Per Lord Radcliffe: ". . . frustration occurs whenever the law recognises that without default of either party a contractual obligation has become incapable of being performed because the circumstances in which performance is called for would render it a thing radically different from that which was undertaken by the contract." For it to be said that a contract has been terminated by frustration, it need not also be shown that it would be unjust to hold the parties to the literal terms of their contract. There is no need to introduce a separate factor of injustice since if the unexpected event produced a situation which, as a matter of construction, is not within the scope of the contract or would render performance impossible or something radically different from that which was undertaken by the contract, then it is unjust that the contracting party should be still bound by the contract in those altered circumstances.

Four Seasons Healthcare Ltd v   **[2005] IRLR 324 EAT**
Maughan

Frustration requires that there should be some outside event or extraneous change of situation, not foreseen or provided for by the parties within the contract. That the employee could have been summarily dismissed in accordance with a contractual disciplinary procedure inhibited a finding in favour of frustration.

G F Sharp & Co Ltd v   **[1998] IRLR 632 EAT**
McMillan

A contract of employment which has come to an end by reason of frustration cannot be treated by the parties as subsisting and, therefore, as not terminating until brought to an end by either side giving formal notice. There is nothing to prevent the parties entering into a new contract, but they must do so with the clear intention to achieve that result. However, after a contract has become frustrated, there can be in existence an arrangement falling short of a contract of employment, albeit under the umbrella of "employment", as was contemplated by Sir John Donaldson in *Marshall v Harland & Wolff Ltd* in relation to the practice of keeping sick employees "on the books".

Williams v   **[1990] IRLR 164 EAT**
Watsons Luxury Coaches Ltd

The doctrine of frustration when applied to employment contracts is one which, unless severely limited in its scope, can do harm to good industrial relations since it provides an easy escape from the obligations of investigation which should be carried out by a conscientious employer.

Illness

Marshall v   **[1972] IRLR 90 NIRC**
Harland & Wolff Ltd and the
   Secretary of State for Employment

A contract comes to an end through frustration and ceases to bind the parties if, through no fault of either of them, unprovided for circumstances arise in which a contractual obligation becomes impossible of performance or in which performance of the obligation would be rendered a thing radically different from that which was undertaken by the contract. In the context of incapacity due to sickness, the tribunal must ask itself: "Was the employee's incapacity of such a nature, or did it appear likely to continue for such a period, that further performance of his obligations in the future would either be impossible or would be a thing radically different from that undertaken by him and agreed to be accepted by the employer under the agreed terms of his employment?" In considering the answer to this question, the tribunal should take account of:

   1. the terms of the contract, including the provisions as to sick pay;

   2. how long the employment was likely to last in the absence of sickness;

   3. the nature of the employment – whether the employee is one of many in the same category or whether he occupies a key post;

   4. the nature of the illness or injury and how long it has already continued and the prospects for recovery;

   5. the period of past employment.

The onus of proof is on the employer to show that a contract has been frustrated.

The Egg Stores (Stamford Hill) Ltd v   **[1976] IRLR 376 EAT**
Leibovici

In deciding whether a contract of employment has been frustrated, a similar question has to be considered as when deciding whether a dismissal in such circumstances is unfair: has the time come when the employer can no longer reasonably be expected to keep the absent employee's post open for him. Often it will be extremely relevant to note that the employer has not thought it right to dismiss the absent employee. The reason may be that he does not think that a sufficient length of time has elapsed to make it a proper course to take. If so, that will be one (but not the only) fact to be taken into consideration in deciding whether the contract has been frustrated. In addition to the questions set out in *Marshall v Harland & Wolff*, one needs to know in what kind of circumstances it can be said that further performance of the employee's obligations in the future will be impossible. Where an event such as an illness or accident, the course and outcome of which is uncertain, is relied upon as bringing about frustration, it may be a long process before one is able to say whether the event is such as to bring about the frustration of the contract. But there will have been frustration of the contract, even though at the time of the event the outcome was uncertain, if the time arrives when, looking back, one can say that at some point matters had gone on so long and the prospects for future employment were so poor, that it was no longer practical to regard the contract as still subsisting. Among the matters to be taken into account in such a case are:

1. the length of the previous employment;

2. how long it had been expected that the employment would continue;

3. the nature of the job;

4. the nature, length and effect of the illness or disabling event;

5. the need of the employer for the work to be done, and the need for a replacement to do it;

6. the risk to the employer of acquiring obligations in respect of redundancy payments or compensation for unfair dismissal to the replacement employee;

7. whether wages have continued to be paid;

8. the acts and the statements of the employer in relation to the employment, including the dismissal of or failure to dismiss the employee; and

9. whether in all the circumstances a reasonable employer could have been expected to wait any longer.

Williams v [1990] IRLR 164 EAT
Watsons Luxury Coaches Ltd
The following principles are relevant to the application of the doctrine of frustration to contracts of employment in the event of illness. First, the tribunal must guard against too easy an application of frustration, especially when redundancy occurs and also when the true situation may be a dismissal by reason of disability. Second, although it is not necessary to decide that frustration occurred on a particular date, an attempt to decide the relevant date is far from a useless exercise since it may help to determine whether there was a true frustration situation. Third, to the factors set out in *Egg Stores (Stamford Hill) Ltd v Leibovici* (see above) should be added the terms of the contract as to the provisions for sick pay, if any, and a consideration of the prospects for recovery. Fourth, as was made clear in *F C Shepherd & Co Ltd v Jerrom* (see below), the party alleging frustration should not be allowed to rely upon a frustrating event which was caused by the fault of that party.

Villella v [1999] IRLR 468 HC
MFI Furniture Centres Ltd
An occurrence which is both foreseen and provided for by the contract is incapable of amounting to frustration. Therefore, where a contract expressly foresees and provides for long-term incapacity due to illness by means of a permanent health insurance scheme, the later occurrence of such long-term incapacity cannot frustrate the contract.

Hart v [1977] IRLR 51 EAT
A R Marshall & Sons (Bulwell) Ltd
In applying the tests of whether a short-term periodic contract has come to an end through frustration as set out in *Marshall v Harland & Wolff* and *The Egg Stores (Stamford Hill) v Leibovici*, considerable importance attaches to the failure of an employer to dismiss the employee. But it is not conclusive, since to say that unless the employee is dismissed the contract must always be taken to continue is tantamount to saying

that frustration can never occur in the case of a short-term periodic contract of employment. The important question is to determine what was the reason for the failure to dismiss. If it was due to the fact that the employer did not think that the time had arrived when he could not reasonably wait any longer, it is a piece of evidence of the greatest value in indicating that the contract had not been frustrated. On the other hand, failure to dismiss may be attributable to the simple fact that the employer never applied his mind to the question at all.

Converfoam (Darwen) Ltd v [1981] IRLR 195 EAT
Bell
A contract of employment cannot be frustrated by the risk of an employee's health deteriorating. Frustration is a doctrine which puts an end to a contract where performance of the whole or a substantial part of it is prevented by a supervening event. A contract which is still capable of being performed but becomes subject to an unforeseen risk is not frustrated. Frustration results from events happening, not by risk of such events.

Imprisonment

F C Shepherd & Co Ltd v [1986] IRLR 358 CA
Jerrom
The imposition of a custodial sentence on an employee is capable in law of frustrating a contract of employment, notwithstanding that it may arise as a result of fault on the employee's part. For a contract to come to an end through frustration two essential factors must be present. First, there must be some event capable of rendering performance of the contract impossible or something radically different from what the parties contemplated when they entered into it. Second, that event must occur without the fault or default of either party. A party who was at fault cannot rely on frustration due to his own act. Thus the party who asserts that the performance of a contract has been frustrated must prove that the frustrating event was not caused by any fault or default on his part. And the party against whom frustration is asserted cannot rely on his own misconduct by way of an answer. To permit an employee to improve his position by asserting that an event which would otherwise bring about a mutual discharge by frustration did not do so because it was caused by his own fault, would be an affront to common sense and an infringement of the fundamental legal and moral rule that a man should not be allowed to take advantage of his own wrong.

Other circumstances

Four Seasons Healthcare Ltd v [2005] IRLR 324 EAT
Maughan
A period of bail, even if it prevents an employee from attending work, cannot be considered as a frustrating event.

Effective date of termination

97. *(1) Subject to the following provisions of this section, in this Part "the effective date of termination" –*

   (a) in relation to an employee whose contract of employment is terminated by notice, whether given by his employer or by the employee, means the date on which the notice expires;

   (b) in relation to an employee whose contract of employment is terminated without notice, means the date on which the termination takes effect; and

   (c) in relation to an employee who is employed under a limited-term contract which terminates by virtue of the limiting event without being renewed under the same contract, means the date on which the termination takes effect.

(2) Where –

   (a) the contract of employment is terminated by the employer, and

   (b) the notice required by s.86 to be given by an employer would, if duly given on the material date, expire on a date later than the effective date of termination (as defined by subsection (1)),

for the purposes of ss.108(1), 119(1) and 227(3) the later date is the effective date of termination.

(3) In subsection (2)(b) "the material date" means –

   (a) the date when notice of termination was given by the employer, or

   (b) where no notice was given, the date when the contract of employment was terminated by the employer.

(4) Where –

   (a) the contract of employment is terminated by the employee,

   (b) the material date does not fall during a period of notice given by the employer to terminate that contract, and

   (c) had the contract been terminated not by the employee but by notice given on the material date by the employer, that notice would have been required by s.86 to expire on a date later than the effective date of termination (as defined by subsection (1)),

for the purposes of ss.108(1), 119(1) and 227(3) the later date is the effective date of termination.

(5) In subsection (4) "the material date" means –

   (a) the date when notice of termination was given by the employee, or

   (b) where no notice was given, the date when the contract of employment was terminated by the employee.

EMPLOYMENT RIGHTS ACT 1996 (as amended)

General principles

Fitzgerald v   **[2004] IRLR 300 CA**
University of Kent at Canterbury

The effective date of termination, which by law sets time running for lodging a claim in the employment tribunal, is to be objectively determined and cannot be fixed by agreement between employer and employee. The effective date of ter-mination is a statutory construct which depends upon what has happened between the parties over time and not on what they may agree to treat as having happened.

Brindle v   **[1972] IRLR 125 CA**
H W Smith (Cabinets) Ltd

The date of dismissal is the date when the notice of dismissal expires or is due to expire and not the date when it is given.

West v   **[1986] IRLR 430 EAT**
Kneels Ltd

When notice of termination is given orally, the notice period excludes any day on which work has been done.

Wang v   **[2011] IRLR 542 EAT**
University of Keele

Where an employer gives written notice of termination of employment: (1) unless (a) there is an express term in the employment contract dealing with when the notice period starts, or (b) the agreement that notice is to start immediately can be construed from the wording of the contract and the wording of the notice letter set in the factual matrix of the case, the period of notice will start to run on the day after written notice is communicated to the employee; and (2) in this regard, construction of the wording of the contract and the wording of the notice letter should be to the advantage of the employee (ie the "contra proferentem" rule applies).

TBA Industrial Products Ltd v   **[1982] IRLR 331 CA**
Morland

[Section 97(1)(a)], which provides that the effective date of termination "in relation to an employee whose contract of employment is terminated by notice, whether given by his employer or by the employee, means the date on which that notice expires", requires that the notice should be causative of the termination.

Thompson v   **[1991] IRLR 488 EAT**
GEC Avionics Ltd

Where an employee under notice from the employer gives counter-notice to terminate the employment before the employer's notice expires, the effective date of termination is the date on which that counter-notice expires.

London Borough of Newham v   **[1985] IRLR 509 CA**
Ward

The date on which an employee receives his P45 from his employers has nothing whatever to do with the date on which employment terminates.

McMaster v   **[1998] IRLR 112 EAT**
Manchester Airport plc

The effective date of termination of a contract of employment cannot be earlier than the date on which an employee receives knowledge that he is being dismissed. The doctrine of constructive or presumed knowledge has no place in questions as to whether a dismissal has been communicated or not, save only in the evidential sense that an employment tribunal will be likely to assume that letters usually arrive in the normal course of post and that people are to be taken, normally, as opening their letters promptly after they have arrived.

GISDA Cyf v   **[2010] IRLR 1073 SC**
Barratt
The construction and application of ERA 1996 s.97 should be guided principally by the underlying purpose of the statute, the protection of the employee's rights, and not by the conventional principles of contract law. Following the decision in *Brown v Southall & Knight* [1980] IRLR 130 EAT, where dismissal is communicated by letter the effective date of termination is the date when the employee reads it (or has had a reasonable opportunity of reading it) rather than the date when the letter was posted or delivered, or the date when the employer has decided to dismiss the employee. In determining whether the employee had a reasonable opportunity to find out about the dismissal, the correct test is to take into account the reasonableness of the employee's behaviour rather than concentrating entirely on what is practically feasible.

Palfrey v   **[2004] IRLR 916 EAT**
Transco plc
A notice of dismissal may be varied by agreement so as to bring forward the date of termination. There is no need for the original notice to be withdrawn and a new notice issued. Account must be taken of what has happened between the parties over time. Where there is a variation of the notice, the notice expires on the new date, as does the contract of employment. This means that the effective date of termination is brought forward, and hence the time limit for presenting an unfair dismissal complaint begins to run.

BMK Ltd and another v   **[1993] IRLR 477 EAT**
Logue
In determining the effective date of termination in a constructive dismissal case, the question to be asked is "When did the termination take effect?" That turns on the legal relationship between the parties on the date in question, not on when acceptance of the constructive dismissal occurred or on whether the contract subsisted or upon the employee's intellectual understanding of what had happened.

Dismissal without notice

Octavius Atkinson & Sons Ltd v   **[1989] IRLR 158 CA**
Morris
Dismissal is either with or without notice. Where an employee is summarily dismissed during the course of a working day, and no question arises as to whether that dismissal constitutes a repudiation by the employer which the employee has not

accepted, both the contract of employment and status of employee cease at the moment when the dismissal is communicated to the employee. To say that notwithstanding a summary dismissal, the employment in fact lasted after dismissal is to say that the dismissal is not summary but on short notice. Therefore, in the present case, the employee's contractual right to pay for the whole day or for travelling time was no indication that the contract was intended to continue after the time when it was expressly terminated. The entitlement to such pay was only a right to damages for breach of contract in the same way as an entitlement to pay in lieu of notice where there is a summary dismissal in breach of contract.

Stapp v   **[1982] IRLR 326 CA**
The Shaftesbury Society
The "effective date of termination" means the actual date of termination of the employment, whether the employee was wrongfully dismissed or rightfully dismissed. If there are no reasons to justify summary dismissal, and if by summary dismissal the employee is deprived of his right to allege unfair dismissal, the employee may have a remedy by claiming damages for wrongful dismissal at common law. Such damages might include the loss of the right to complain of unfair dismissal which the employee would have had had he not been summarily dismissed.

Batchelor v   **[1987] IRLR 136 CA**
British Railways Board
The effect of a clear notice of immediate dismissal cannot be altered by the fact that the employers had not operated the disciplinary procedure properly. If there was a breach of contract and the employee was wrongfully dismissed, he may have an action at law in respect of it but that cannot alter the date on which the actual determination of the contract took place.

Dedman v   **[1973] IRLR 379 CA**
British Building and Engineering
   Appliances Ltd
Per Lord Denning MR: Where the employment is terminated immediately but a "salary" is paid in respect of a subsequent period, the payment of salary should be regarded as compensation for immediate dismissal and not by way of continuation of the employee's employment, so that the effective date of termination is the date on which the immediate dismissal took place.

Robert Cort & Son Ltd v   **[1981] IRLR 437 EAT**
Charman
Where an employer dismisses an employee summarily and without giving the period of notice required by the contract, for the purposes of [s.97(1)] the effective date of termination is the date of the summary dismissal whether or not the employer makes a payment in lieu of notice. This principle applies even assuming that where an employee is dismissed without due notice, the contract itself is not thereby determined but will only be so when the employee accepts the repudiation.

Pay in lieu

Adams v   [1980] IRLR 416 EAT
GKN Sankey Ltd
There is a distinction between a case where an employee is dismissed with notice but is given payment in lieu of working out that notice, and a case where no notice of dismissal is given but a payment is made in lieu of notice. Where notice of termination is given, as the Court of Appeal made plain in *Brindle v H W Smith (Cabinets) Ltd,* the effective date of termination is the date when the notice expires and the fact that a person is not required to work during the period of notice does not mean that the employment terminated earlier than the date specified. However, if the date of termination of employment is immediate but salaries or monies are paid in respect of a subsequent period, per Lord Denning in the Court of Appeal in *Dedman v British Building and Engineering Appliances Ltd,* they are to be taken as compensation for immediate dismissal and not by way of continuation of the employment.

Chapman v   [1981] IRLR 440 EAT
Letheby & Christopher Ltd
There is no binding authority forcing the conclusion that where the employer gives notice of dismissal as from a future date and offers to pay wages in lieu of notice, the employee is summarily dismissed. Whether in a particular case a dismissal letter evinces on the one hand an intention on the part of the employer to terminate the contract at once, wages being paid in lieu of proper notice, or on the other hand, an intention only to terminate the contract at a future date with wages being paid notwithstanding that the employee is not called upon to work out his notice, depends upon the construction of the letter itself. The construction to be put on the letter should not be a technical one, but should reflect what an ordinary, reasonable employee would understand by the words used. It should be construed in the light of the facts known to the employee on the date he received the letter. Moreover, where an employer relies on a notice served by him as having a particular meaning, he should be required to demonstrate that it unambiguously has that meaning. If an employer can rely on ambiguities being resolved in his favour, the employee may be left in doubt as to where he stands and may lose his statutory rights.

Leech v   [1985] IRLR 337 EAT
Preston Borough Council
To determine the effective date of termination where there has been an oral notification of dismissal, followed by a confirmatory letter, the oral and written words have to be read and construed together. The question to be answered is how would any reasonable employee in the employee's position have interpreted the terms of his dismissal when those terms were regarded as a whole, looking to the spoken words of dismissal and the confirmatory language of the subsequent letter?

Effect of internal appeal

Savage v   [1980] IRLR 109 CA
J Sainsbury Ltd
Where an employee is dismissed on the terms that he ceases to have the right to work under the contract of employment and the employer ceases likewise to be under an obligation to pay him, the contract of employment is at an end unless a provision giving the employee the right to appeal can be read as saving the contract in all the circumstances pending conclusion of the appeal. In the absence of such a provision, the effective date of termination is the date on which the employee is dismissed and not the date on which he is informed that his appeal against dismissal failed. (Approved by the House of Lords in *West Midlands Co-operative Society Ltd v Tipton* [1986] IRLR 112.)

Drage v   [2000] IRLR 314 CA
Governors of Greenford High School
In determining the effective date of termination of employment in a case where contractual provision is made for an internal appeal against the employer's decision to dismiss an employee, the critical question is whether during the period between the initial notification of dismissal and the outcome of the appeal, the employee stands (a) dismissed with the possibility of reinstatement, or (b) suspended with the possibility of the proposed dismissal not being confirmed and the suspension thus ended. In the latter circumstances, the dismissal does not actually take place until the appeal is decided. Although the terms of the initial notification are likely to be of great importance in deciding whether the case is one of suspension or of possible reinstatement, they are not necessarily determinative. The effect of the initial notification must be considered in its contractual context and in the light of subsequent events.

McMaster v   [2011] IRLR 235 NICA
Antrim Borough Council
Where an employee appeals under a contractual right of appeal to an independent third party and is successful but the employer refuses to reinstate the employee, the original date of dismissal is not the effective date of dismissal because the contract must be regarded as reinstated at the date of the successful appeal.

Statutory extension

Fox Maintenance Ltd v   [1977] IRLR 306 EAT
Jackson
[Section 97(2)] provides for the effective date of termination of an employee dismissed without notice or with inadequate notice to be extended for the purpose of an unfair dismissal complaint by the statutory minimum notice to which the

employee would be entitled rather than by any contractual notice to which the employee was entitled.

Secretary of State for Employment v   [1989] IRLR 117 CA
Staffordshire County Council

[Section 97(2)] applies to the determination of the effective date of termination even where, as provided for in [s.86(3)], the employee has waived his entitlement to a period of notice complying with [s.86(1)]. [Section 97(2)] refers to the notice "required" to be given under [s.86(1)]. Notwithstanding any waiver, [s.86(1)] still requires notice of a specified length to be given and [s.97(2)] continues to apply.

Per Glidewell LJ: The fact that an employee has waived his right to notice or accepted payment in lieu of notice under [s.86(3)], is relevant only to his rights in contract. It has no relevance to his right [to claim unfair dismissal]. The reference in [s.97(2)] to the notice required under [s.86(1)] is merely a way of describing the period of notice. It does not import any part of [s.86] into the [unfair dismissal] apparatus.

Lanton Leisure Ltd v   [1987] IRLR 119 EAT
White and another

An employer's designation of the reason for summary dismissal as "gross misconduct" is not of itself sufficient to preclude an employee from relying on [s.97(2)] to extend the effective date of termination by his statutory notice entitlement. It is necessary first to find out by means of an inquiry on the merits whether there was in fact such conduct as would enable the employer to terminate without notice. Were that not so, an employer could avoid [s.97(2)] simply by defining a dismissal as gross misconduct.

3. REASON FOR DISMISSAL

Designated reasons

98. *(1) In determining for the purposes of this Part whether the dismissal of an employee is fair or unfair, it is for the employer to show –*

> *(a) the reason (or, if more than one, the principal reason) for the dismissal, and*
>
> *(b) that it is either a reason falling within subsection (2) or some other substantial reason of a kind such as to justify the dismissal of an employee holding the position which the employee held.*

(2) A reason falls within this subsection if it –

> *(a) relates to the capability or qualifications of the employee for performing work of the kind which he was employed by the employer to do,*
>
> *(b) relates to the conduct of the employee,*
>
> *(ba) ...*
>
> *(c) is that the employee was redundant, or*
>
> *(d) is that the employee could not continue to work in the position which he held without contravention (either on his part or on that of his employer) of a duty or restriction imposed by or under an enactment.*

(2A) ...

EMPLOYMENT RIGHTS ACT 1996 (as amended)

General principles

Standard of proof

Abernethy v   **[1974] IRLR 213 CA**
Mott, Hay and Anderson
A reason for dismissal is a set of facts known to the employer or beliefs held by him which cause him to dismiss the employee.

Wilson v   **[2000] IRLR 834 CA**
Post Office
Determining under which part of s.98 the reason in fact given by the employer falls is a question of legal analysis. Wrong characterisation of the reason by an employment tribunal is therefore an error of law.

McCrory v   **[1983] IRLR 414 NICA**
Magee
Although an employment tribunal cannot pick out and substitute a reason for dismissal which was neither given nor entertained by the employer merely because the tribunal thinks it a better reason or one which would justify dismissal when the employer's stated reason would not, a tribunal may properly find that the reason proffered by the employer is not the real reason or the principal reason, provided it is satisfied on adequate evidence that the reason it selects was the employer's reason at the time of the dismissal.

Union of Construction and Allied   **[1981] IRLR 224 CA**
Trades and Technicians v
Brain
Per Donaldson LJ: The employer has to show why *in fact* he dismissed the employee. The Act does not concern itself with possible justifications which occur to the employer later or which did not move him at the time. This is no great burden upon the employer since he must know why he dismissed the employee. Next the employer has to show that this reason falls into one of the four categories of reasons set out in [s.98(2)] or that it was "some other substantial reason of a kind such as to justify the dismissal of an employee holding the position which that employee held". This is not an exercise in elaborate legal classification. All that is required is that the tribunal shall consider whether, looking at the matter broadly and giving the words their ordinary meaning, the reason for the dismissal falls within one or other of these five descriptions.

Parkinson v   **[1997] IRLR 308 CA**
March Consulting Ltd
When a dismissal is by notice, the employers' reason for the dismissal has to be determined both by reference to the reason for giving the notice to terminate and by reference to the reason when the dismissal occurs. Dismissal cannot be for a justified reason if that reason did not exist when notice of termination was given.

British Railways Board v   **[1994] IRLR 235 CA**
Jackson
An employment tribunal should state the reason found for dismissal.

Adams v   **[1986] IRLR 163 EAT**
Derby City Council
It is an error of law for a tribunal simply to consider whether there was a dismissible offence without first having been satisfied by the employer as to the reason for dismissal.

Burden of proof

Maund v   **[1984] IRLR 24 CA**
Penwith District Council
If the employer produces evidence to the tribunal that appears to show the reason for the dismissal, then the burden passes to the employee to show that there is a real issue as to whether that was the true reason. But this burden is a lighter one than the legal burden placed upon the employer of showing the reason for the dismissal. The burden on the employee is not to prove the reason for his dismissal; it is an evidential burden to produce some evidence that casts doubt upon the employer's reason. The burden cannot be discharged, however, by the employee merely asserting in argument that that was not the true reason. He must produce evidence that raises some doubt about the reason for the dismissal. Once this evidential burden is discharged, the onus

remains on the employer to prove the reason for the dismissal.

Trusthouse Forte Leisure Ltd v   **[1976] IRLR 251 EAT**
Aquilar
Whilst the employer's description of the reason for dismissal is by no means conclusive and the employment tribunal must look into the matter and determine what was the real reason, there is no burden on the employer to prove that the reason was well judged and justified – for example, by establishing that a man dismissed for drunkenness was in fact a victim of drink.

Abernethy v   **[1974] IRLR 213 CA**
Mott, Hay and Anderson
The reason for dismissal does not have to be correctly labelled at the time of the dismissal.

Hotson v   **[1984] IRLR 422 EAT**
Wisbech Conservative Club
Where there is a change in the label given to the reason for dismissal, great care must be taken to ensure that the employee is not placed at a procedural or evidential disadvantage as a result.

Clarke v   **[1993] IRLR 148 EAT**
Trimoco Group Ltd and another
Where there is a discrepancy between the reason given at the time of dismissal and the real reason, the critical question is whether the employee was aware of the real reason and, therefore, whether the facts in relation to that real reason were available to him to challenge in the employment tribunal proceedings.

Ely v   **[1993] IRLR 500 CA**
YKK Fasteners (UK) Ltd
An employment tribunal is entitled to find that a set of facts known to an employer is capable of constituting a "reason for dismissal" in a case where the employer is not in his own mind purporting to act by way of dismissal but insists, albeit in error, that the employee has already terminated the contract by resignation. The principle in *Abernethy* can justifiably be extended so as to permit resort to a state of facts known to and relied on by the employer not only for the purpose of substituting a valid reason for any invalid or misdescribed reason given by the employer through misapprehension or mistake, but also for the purpose of supplying him with a reason for dismissal which, as a consequence of his misapprehension of the true nature of the circumstances, he was disabled from treating as such at the time.

Delabole Slate Ltd v   **[1985] IRLR 305 CA**
Berriman
The only way in which the statutory requirements of the [1996] Act can be made to fit in a case of constructive dismissal is to read [s.98(1)] as requiring the employer to show the reasons for his conduct which entitled the employee

to terminate the contract thereby giving rise to a deemed dismissal by the employer.

Kwik Save Stores Ltd v   **[1998] IRLR 245 CA**
Greaves
Crees v
Royal London Mutual Insurance
It is not a justification for dismissal that the employer got the law wrong. Thus, the fact that the employers reasonably believed, in accordance with their understanding of the law, that a woman who was unable to work on the notified day of her return from extended maternity leave had not been dismissed by them, was not a ground for fair dismissal.

Multiple reasons

Patterson v   **[1977] IRLR 137 EAT**
Messrs Bracketts
"The reason" for dismissal is frequently made up of all sorts of reasons and sub-reasons. Therefore, the correct practice is to consider all the reasons which form part of "the reason" for dismissal when determining whether the dismissal is fair or unfair.

Associated Society of Locomotive   **[2006] IRLR 576 EAT**
   Engineers and Firemen v
Brady
Dismissal may be for an unfair reason even where a fair reason, such as misconduct, exists. If the employer treats the fair reason as an excuse to dismiss an employee in circumstances in which he would not have treated others in a similar way, then the principal reason for dismissal will not be the fair reason at all. The question is whether the employer has proved that the fair reason was the principal reason for the dismissal.

Bates Farms and Dairy Ltd v   **[1976] IRLR 214 EAT**
Scott
The onus on the employer to show the reason, or if more than one, the principal reason for dismissal does not require the employment tribunal, or the employer, to dissect the reason or reasons in excessive analytical detail. It is not necessary for the employer to be required to go into every sub-reason since in practice a reason and even a principal reason may be compounded of several elements which do not necessarily each in themselves constitute a separate reason.

Carlin v   **[1974] IRLR 188 NIRC**
St Cuthbert's Co-operative
   Association Ltd
If an employer gives two reasons for dismissing an employee and one only is established by the evidence led before the tribunal and there is no evidence as to which reason, if either, was subordinate to the other, the employer's defence may fail upon the view that what was in fact the principal reason for dismissal has not been proved.

Changing the reason

Monie v   **[1980] IRLR 464 CA**
Coral Racing Ltd
Where there has been a dismissal followed by an internal appeal in which the dismissal was confirmed, the employer cannot justify the dismissal by a reason that was not the reason for the original dismissal but was the reason for which it was affirmed. It is not open to an employer to substitute another reason for the reason which was in his mind at the time of dismissal. The general rule is that laid down by the House of Lords in *Devis v Atkins* that the only reason that can be relied on is one that operated at the time of dismissal.

Hotson v   **[1984] IRLR 422 EAT**
Wisbech Conservative Club
Although the authorities on the employer's duty to state the ground of dismissal have the effect that an employer is not tied to the label he happens to put on the particular facts relied on, where the original reason given for dismissal is lack of capability, the substitution or addition of suspected dishonesty as a reason, even though precisely the same facts may be relied upon by the employer, goes beyond a mere change of label. Suspected dishonesty is a grave and serious ground for dismissal which should be stated at the outset by the employer or not stated at all.

Nelson v   **[1977] IRLR 148 CA**
BBC
Where the only reason given by the employers for a dismissal is the wrong reason, they fail to show a potentially valid reason for dismissal and the dismissal is automatically unfair. Facts found in relation to [s.98(4)] cannot be applied to a possible but unpleaded defence under [s.98(1)] and then treated as applicable to [s.98(4)].

Church v   **[1998] IRLR 492 EAT**
West Lancashire NHS Trust (No.2)
On remission of a case following a successful appeal, it is not open to the employers to seek to justify the dismissal on a different ground from that which had previously been argued.

Capability

Abernethy v   **[1974] IRLR 213 CA**
Mott, Hay and Anderson
An employee's inflexibility and lack of adaptability come within his "aptitude" and "mental qualities" and therefore within the statutory definition of "capability".

Sutton & Gates (Luton) Ltd v   **[1978] IRLR 486 EAT**
Boxall
In approaching a case involving dismissal on grounds of lack of capability, the employment tribunal should clearly distinguish in their own minds whether the case in point is one of sheer incapability due to an inherent incapacity to function or one of failure to exercise to the full such talent as is possessed. Cases where a person has not come up to standard through his own carelessness, negligence or idleness are much more appropriately dealt with as cases of misconduct rather than of capability.

Ill health

Leonard v   **[1979] IRLR 235 CS**
Fergus & Haynes Civil Engineering Ltd
An employer is entitled to rely upon ill health as the reason for dismissal in accordance with a clause in the contract providing for dismissal of an employee frequently absent on medical grounds, notwithstanding that not all his absences are due to ill health. It is enough that the dismissal followed absences on medical grounds which could properly be described as frequent. It did not matter that the employee had also been absent without explanation before the absences on medical grounds began.

Lynock v   **[1988] IRLR 510 EAT**
Cereal Packaging Ltd
The mere fact that an employee is fit at the time of dismissal does not make the dismissal unfair.

McAdie v   **[2007] IRLR 895 CA**
Royal Bank of Scotland
Where an employer is responsible for an employee's incapacity, that may be relevant to whether, and if so when, it is reasonable to dismiss him for that incapacity. It may, for example, be necessary in such a case to go the extra mile in finding alternative employment for such an employee, or to put up with a longer period of sickness absence than would otherwise be reasonable. However, the fact that an employer has caused the incapacity in question, however culpably, cannot preclude him forever from effecting a fair dismissal.

Shook v   **[1986] IRLR 46 EAT**
London Borough of Ealing
In cases of dismissal for lack of capability, the reason must *relate* to the capability for performing work of the relevant kind. It is not necessary to show that the employee was incapacitated from performing every task which the employers are entitled by law to call upon him to discharge.

East Lindsey District Council v   **[1977] IRLR 181 EAT**
Daubney
The decision to dismiss or not is not a medical question but one to be answered by employers in the light of available medical evidence. It is not the function of employers, any more than it is of employment tribunals, to turn themselves into some sort of medical appeal tribunal to review the opinions and advice received from their medical advisers.

Liverpool Area Health Authority   **[1977] IRLR 471 EAT**
  (Teaching) Central & Southern District v
Edwards

An employer, faced with a medical opinion, is not required to evaluate it as a layman in terms of medical expertise, unless it is plainly erroneous as to the facts in some way, or plainly contains an indication that no proper examination of any sort has taken place.

Ford Motor Co Ltd v   **[1987] IRLR 163 EAT**
Nawaz

The fact that they are entitled to act on the say so of their medical advisers does not wholly absolve management from carrying out, through their medical agent, the proper investigation which is required in any dismissal case. What has to be determined is whether the medical expert had sufficient material before him upon which to advise management to take the decision they did. If the medical expert employed by the company fails to investigate the matter properly, the company is saddled with that lack of investigation.

Hutchinson v   **[1981] IRLR 318 EAT**
Enfield Rolling Mills

Employers are entitled to challenge the fact that an employee was off work ill even where that fact was certified by a doctor.

Converfoam (Darwen) Ltd v   **[1981] IRLR 195 EAT**
Bell

Risk of illness cannot amount to a ground for fair dismissal unless the nature of the employment is such that the risk is of such importance as to make it unsafe for the employee to continue in his job. The present case of a works manager in a factory with a heart condition was quite different, for example, from the case of a sole wireless operator on a sea-going ship who has the risk of a heart attack.

Marshall v   **[1981] IRLR 264 EAT**
Alexander Sloan & Co Ltd

An employee's obligations under the contract are not all suspended when he is off work ill. Although a term has to be implied into a contract limiting the employee's obligation to perform all the terms of his contract whilst he is off work sick, such a term should be no wider than is necessary to give the contract business effect. Business common sense requires only that when an employee is off work sick, he is relieved of the obligation to perform such services as his sickness prevents him from carrying out.

Qualifications

Blue Star Ship Management Ltd v   **[1979] IRLR 16 EAT**
Williams

"Qualification" as defined by the statute has in mind matters relating to aptitude or ability. A mere licence, permit or authorisation is not such a qualification unless it is substantially concerned with the aptitude or ability of the person to do the job.

Blackman v   **[1974] IRLR 46 NIRC**
The Post Office

"Qualifications" has to be construed in the light of the particular position which the employee held. Therefore, in certain circumstances, failure to pass a required aptitude test can be a reason for dismissal relating to the qualifications for the job.

Singh v   **[1976] IRLR 176 EAT**
London Country Bus Services Ltd

"Trustworthiness" in regard to the handling of money does not fall within the meaning of "qualifications" as defined by the statute.

Conduct

Thomson v   **[1983] IRLR 403 EAT**
Alloa Motor Co Ltd

Conduct within the meaning of [s.98(2)(b)] means actions of such a nature, whether done in the course of employment or outwith it, that reflect in some way upon the employer-employee relationship.

Perkin v   **[2005] IRLR 934 CA**
St George's Healthcare NHS Trust

An employee's "personality" of itself cannot be a ground for dismissal. However, an employee's personality may manifest itself in such a way as to bring the actions of the employee within s.98. Whether, on the facts of a particular case, the manifestations of an individual's personality result in conduct which can fairly give rise to the employee's dismissal, or whether they give rise to some other substantial reason of a kind such as to justify the dismissal of an employee holding the position which the employee held, the employer has to establish the facts which justify the reason or principal reason for the dismissal.

Neary v   **[1999] IRLR 288**
Dean of Westminster   **(Special Commissioner)**

Conduct amounting to gross misconduct justifying summary dismissal must so undermine the trust and confidence which is inherent in the particular contract of employment that the employer should no longer be required to retain the employee in his employment. Whether particular misconduct justifies summary dismissal is a question of fact. The character of the institutional employer, the role played by the employee in that institution and the degree of trust required of the employee vis-à-vis the employer must all be considered in determining the extent of the duty of trust and the seriousness of any breach thereof.

West London Mental Health   **[2014] IRLR 227 SC**
  NHS Trust v
Chhabra

Gross misconduct justifying dismissal is unlikely to extend to conduct which was not a wilful or deliberate breach of rule.

Hamilton v   **[1993] IRLR 99 EAT**
Argyll & Clyde Health Board
Willingness by an employer to offer re-employment in a suitable capacity is not inconsistent with a conclusion that an employee has been guilty of gross misconduct. What is gross misconduct must be considered in relation to the particular employment and the particular employee.

Sarkar v   **[2010] IRLR 508 CA**
West London Mental Health NHS Trust
In considering whether dismissal was within the range of reasonable responses to an act of misconduct a tribunal is entitled to consider the fact that the employer had earlier agreed, in respect of that misconduct, to use an informal conflict resolution procedure which could not have led to dismissal.

Trevillion v   **[1973] IRLR 176 NIRC**
The Hospital of St John &
  St Elizabeth
Because an employee had agreed from time to time to vary his contract does not mean that he is under an obligation to continue to vary it at the employer's request.

Robinson v   **[2008] IRLR 408 EAT**
Tescom Corporation
A failure to observe terms and conditions of employment which have been varied may amount to misconduct justifying dismissal, even if an employee only agreed to work those terms under protest.

Nova Plastics Ltd v   **[1982] IRLR 146 EAT**
Froggatt
There is no general implied term that an employee is expected to work loyally for an employer and that any work for a competitor is to be regarded as being in breach of trust or a failure to give loyal service. There is no implication in any contract of employment other than that an employee is expected to give loyal service and not to do anything which can create substantial harm to his employer. If it can be shown that what an employee is doing in his spare time can cause great harm to the employer then that will be a breach of trust or of an implied term that an employee shall loyally serve his employer. However, per Lord Greene MR in *Hivac Ltd v Park Royal Scientific Instruments Ltd* (1946) 1 Ch 169, it would be wrong for any court to support a contention that a workman cannot usefully and profitably employ himself in his free time in some other capacity for some other employer.

Laughton and Hawley v   **[1986] IRLR 245 EAT**
Bapp Industrial Supplies Ltd
An employee does not breach the implied contractual duty of loyalty to the employer merely be indicating his intention to set up in competition with his employer in the future.

Adamson v   **[1995] IRLR 193 EAT**
B & L Cleaning Services Ltd
An employee is in breach of the implied contractual duty to give faithful service by tendering for the future business of

the employer's customers in competition with the employer. Competing with the employer for contracts while still employed is different from indicating an intention to set up in competition with the employer in the future, or seeking employment with a competitor.

Statutory restriction

Bouchaala v   **[1980] IRLR 382 EAT**
Trusthouse Forte Hotels Ltd
[Section 98(2)(d)] of the Act does not apply where the employer genuinely believes that continued employment would be unlawful although, in fact, he was mistaken in that belief. There is no justification for expanding the clear words of subsection (d) to include the concept of genuine but erroneous belief on the part of an employer.

Sandhu v   **[1978] IRLR 208 EAT**
1. Department of Education and
  Science and
2. London Borough of Hillingdon
That the employers could not have lawfully continued to employ an employee without contravening a duty or restriction imposed by or under an enactment does not inevitably lead to the conclusion that a dismissal for a reason falling within [s.98(2)(d)] is fair.

Some other substantial reason for dismissal

Dobie v   **[1984] IRLR 329 CA**
Burns International Security
  Services (UK) Ltd
[Section 98(1)(b)] requires the employment tribunal to consider the reason established by the employer and to decide whether it falls within the category of reasons which could justify the dismissal of an employee – not that employee but an employee – holding the position which that employee held. Thus different types of reasons could justify the dismissal of the office boy from those which could justify dismissal of the managing director.

Cobley v   **[2003] IRLR 706 EAT**
Forward Technology Industries plc
The reasons available to an employer under s.98(1)(b) are not limited to reasons of the same kind as those spelt out in s.98(2), nor do they require consideration of the fairness of the dismissal, which falls to be considered under s.98(4) rather than at the prior stage of identifying the reason for dismissal.

Kent County Council v   **[1985] IRLR 18 CA**
Gilham and others
In obiter: The burden on the employer of showing a substantial reason for dismissal is designed to deter employers from

dismissing for some trivial or unworthy reason. If, on the face of it, the reason *could* justify the dismissal, then it passes as a substantial reason and the enquiry moves to [s.98(4)] and the question of reasonableness.

Saunders v   **[1980] IRLR 174 EAT**
Scottish National Camps Association
In order to clear the first hurdle under [s.98(1)], the employer need only show, on a balance of probabilities, that the reason for the dismissal was one of those expressly specified or if not, was one which he considered to be substantial and of a kind such as to justify the dismissal.

Harper v   **[1980] IRLR 260 EAT**
National Coal Board
Although an employer cannot claim that a reason for dismissal is substantial if it is a whimsical or capricious reason which no person of ordinary sense would entertain, if he can show that he had a fair reason in his mind at the time when he decided on dismissal and that he genuinely believed it to be fair, this would bring the case within the category of some other substantial reason. Where the belief is one which is genuinely held, and particularly is one which most employers would be expected to adopt, it may be a substantial reason even where modern sophisticated opinion can be adduced to show that it has no specific foundation.

Nelson v   **[1977] IRLR 148 CA**
BBC
It is not open to the EAT to use the findings of an employment tribunal in connection with a finding that a dismissal on grounds of redundancy was fair to support an unpleaded defence that if not on grounds of redundancy, the dismissal was for some other substantial reason such as to justify the dismissal of the employee from the position which he held.

Gorman v   **[1978] IRLR 22 EAT**
London Computer Training Centre
If for technical reasons an employer fails to establish that the reason for an employee's dismissal was redundancy, it is open to the employer to argue that the same reason constituted some other substantial reason for dismissal. The Court of Appeal's decision in *Nelson v BBC* was not intended to equate the somewhat primitive "pleadings" which exist in employment tribunals to the sort of pleadings which exist in the High Court. What the Court of Appeal had in mind was that every case must proceed in such a way that if issues are taken which have not been noted before the case came on, the employment tribunal must take care to see that the parties are not prejudiced.

Murphy v   **[1984] IRLR 271 CA**
Epsom College
Although it is not necessary to "plead" in the full technical sense of the word some other substantial reason for dismissal, in the light of the Court of Appeal's decision in *Nelson v BBC*,

before an employment tribunal reaches a decision on whether a dismissal was for some other substantial reason, where the employers never sought to justify the dismissal on that ground, the matter should be expressly ventilated in the employment tribunal so that the parties can have a full and proper opportunity to deploy their case on that matter.

Hannan v   **[1986] IRLR 165 EAT**
TNT-IPEC (UK) Ltd
Although a tribunal is not entitled to find a dismissal fair on a ground not pleaded or argued where the difference in grounds goes to facts and substance and there would or might have been some substantial or significant difference in the way the case was conducted so that the employee was thereby prejudiced, where the different grounds are really different labels and nothing more, the late introduction, even without pleading or argument, is not a ground for interference on appeal. There are three stages where a party complains that a tribunal has found a dismissal fair on a ground not pleaded or investigated: the appellant must show some ground for thinking that there had been prejudice; the respondent must then demonstrate prima facie that it would in fact have made no difference had the matters which the tribunal relied upon in fact been canvassed before them; the appellant must then show what he would in fact have wished to do which would have materially affected the outcome of the case.

Willow Oak Developments Ltd   **[2006] IRLR 607 CA**
  t/a Windsor Recruitment v
Silverwood and others
An employee's refusal to accept covenants proposed by the employer for the protection of his legitimate interests could amount to some other substantial reason justifying dismissal even if those covenants were found to be unreasonably wide. It would then be a question under s.98(4) of whether the employer had acted reasonably or unreasonably in treating that reason as sufficient to dismiss the employee.

Reorganisation/redundancy

Hollister v   **[1979] IRLR 238 CA**
National Farmers' Union
Where there is a sound good business reason for a reorganisation and the only sensible way to deal with it is to terminate the existing contracts offering the employees reasonable new ones, and an employee refuses to accept the new agreement, that is a substantial reason such as to justify his dismissal within the meaning of [s.98(1)(b)].

Robinson v   **[1977] IRLR 477 EAT**
British Island Airways Ltd
Where there is a genuine reorganisation which has dislodged an employee who cannot be fitted in to the reorganisation, it must be open to the employer to dismiss him and in such circumstances the dismissal will be for some other substantial reason.

Ladbroke Courage Holidays Ltd v   **[1981] IRLR 59 EAT**
Asten

If an employer seeks to rely on business reorganisation or economic necessity as a reason for dismissal, he should produce some evidence to show that there was a reorganisation or that there was some need for economy and it is material for the tribunal to know whether the company was making profits or losses.

Kerry Foods Ltd v   **[2005] IRLR 680 EAT**
Lynch

An employer passes the low hurdle of showing that dismissal of an employee for refusing to agree to proposed changes in terms and conditions of employment was for some other substantial reason for dismissal where some advantage to the business can be shown. It is not necessary to show the quantum of improvement achieved.

Copsey v   **[2005] IRLR 811 CA**
WWB Devon Clays Ltd

Dismissal of an employee for refusing, because of his religious beliefs, to agree to a contractual variation in his working hours which meant that he could be required to work on Sundays was fair and reasonable, where the employers had compelling economic reasons for requiring the change in hours, they had done everything that they reasonably could to accommodate the claimant's wish not to work on Sundays and all alternatives to dismissal had been fully explored.

Genower v   **[1980] IRLR 297 EAT**
Ealing, Hammersmith & Hounslow
  Area Health Authority

A breach of contract by the employer, such as a change in the place of work, which justifies the employee resigning and claiming constructive dismissal, can nonetheless be a dismissal for some other substantial reason.

Replacements

106. *(1) Where this section applies to an employee he shall be regarded for the purposes of section 98(1)(b) as having been dismissed for a substantial reason of a kind such as to justify the dismissal of an employee holding the position which the employee held.*

  (2) This section applies to an employee where –

    (a) on engaging him the employer informs him in writing that his employment will be terminated on the resumption of work by another employee who is, or will be, absent wholly or partly because of pregnancy or childbirth, or on adoption leave or shared parental leave, and

    (b) the employer dismisses him in order to make it possible to give work to the other employee.

  (3) This section also applies to an employee where –

    (a) on engaging him the employer informs him in writing that his employment will be terminated on the end of a suspension of another employee from work on medical grounds or maternity grounds (within the meaning of Part VII), and

    (b) the employer dismisses him in order to make it possible to allow the resumption of work by the other employee.

  (4) Subsection (1) does not affect the operation of section 98(4) in a case to which this section applies.

        EMPLOYMENT RIGHTS ACT 1996 (as amended)

Victoria and Albert Museum v   **[2011] IRLR 290 EAT**
Durrant

ERA 1996 s.106 provides that where an employee is dismissed in order to make it possible for the employer to give work to an employee who is resuming work after maternity leave, the replacement is to be regarded as having been dismissed for some other substantial reason if on engaging him the employer has informed him in writing that his employment will be terminated on the resumption of work by the returning employee. However, if the language of the written information does not convey the simple message required by the subsection, there is nothing in the statute to suggest that the information can be conveyed by a combination of the text of the written document as supplemented by inferences drawn from the surrounding circumstances.

Further examples

Perkin v   **[2005] IRLR 934 CA**
St George's Healthcare NHS Trust

A breakdown in confidence between an employer and a senior executive for which the latter was responsible and which actually or potentially damaged the operation of the employer's organisation, or which rendered it impossible for senior executives to work together as a team, can amount to some other substantial reason for dismissal. Provided the terms of s.98(4) are satisfied, it must be possible for an employer fairly to dismiss an employee in such circumstances.

Ezsias v   **[2011] IRLR 550 EAT**
North Glamorgan NHS Trust

Where a fundamental and irretrievable breakdown of working relations between an employee and his colleagues has occurred, and the employee is dismissed because of the fact that the breakdown has occurred and not because he was to blame for causing it, the reason for dismissal is "some other substantial reason" rather than conduct, and therefore the employer need not follow its own conduct dismissal procedures.

North Yorkshire County Council v   **[1985] IRLR 247 CA**
Fay

Dismissal of an employee whose fixed term contract expires and is not renewed because the post that he had been employed to fill on a temporary basis is permanently filled by someone else can be for some other substantial reason. Merely to say that there was a contract for a specific period and that that period has expired does not by itself establish that there was a substantial reason for dismissal within the meaning of [s.98(1)(b)]. But if it is shown that the fixed term contract was adopted for a genuine purpose and that fact was known to the employee, and it is also shown that the specific purpose for which the contract was adopted has ceased to be applicable, then those facts are capable of constituting some other substantial reason. The approach adopted by the EAT in *Terry v East Sussex County Council* was correct.

Terry v   **[1976] IRLR 332 EAT**
East Sussex County Council
Whether the expiry and non-renewal of a fixed term contract constitutes some other substantial reason for dismissal depends upon whether the case is a genuine one where the employee has to his own knowledge been employed for a particular period, or a particular job, on a temporary basis. The employment tribunal should draw a balance between the need for protection for employers who have a genuine need for fixed term employment, which can be seen from the outset not to be ongoing, and the need for protection for employees against being deprived of their rights through ordinary employments being dressed up in the form of temporary fixed-term contracts.

Scott Packing & Warehousing Ltd v   **[1978] IRLR 166 EAT**
Paterson
Dismissal of an employee because the company's best customer was not willing to accept him doing their work can be a substantial reason for dismissal.

Grootcon (UK) Ltd v   **[1984] IRLR 302 EAT**
Keld
If an employer wishes to establish that his reason for dismissing an employee is that a valuable customer has threatened to withdraw his custom if he fails to do so, he must lead sufficient evidence to discharge the onus which rests upon him.

Henderson v   **[2010] IRLR 466 EAT**
Connect (South Tyneside) Ltd
If a client exercises a contractual right to veto an individual's employment and the employer does everything that he reasonably can to avoid or mitigate the injustice brought about by the stance of the client – most obviously by trying to get the client to change his mind and, if that is impossible, by trying to find alternative work for the employee – but fails, any eventual dismissal will be fair.

Kingston v   **[1984] IRLR 146 CA**
British Railways Board
A sentence of three months' imprisonment, involving an absence of two months from work, is capable of being some other substantial reason for dismissal.

Singh v   **[1976] IRLR 176 EAT**
London Country Bus Services Ltd
Where an employee is found guilty of theft, unconnected with his work, that may constitute some other substantial reason for dismissal.

Cobley v   **[2003] IRLR 706 EAT**
Forward Technology Industries plc
Dismissal of a company's chief executive following a hostile takeover of the business may be for "some other substantial reason". Although, in general, a change in the ownership of the shares of a company or in the control of it does not have a necessary effect on employment relationships between the company and its staff, it is always necessary to consider the facts of the particular dismissal. Section 98(1)(b) focuses on the sufficiency of the reason to justify dismissal of an employee "holding the position which the employee held". In deciding whether there was a substantial reason for dismissing the chief executive on a successful takeover, different consideration would apply than in the case of a secretary or a storeman.

Pregnancy and family leave

99. *(1) An employee who is dismissed shall be regarded for the purposes of this Part as unfairly dismissed if –*

    (a) the reason or principal reason for the dismissal is of a prescribed kind, or,

    (b) the dismissal takes place in prescribed circumstances.

  (2) In this section "prescribed" means prescribed by regulations made by the Secretary of State.

  (3) A reason or set of circumstances prescribed under this section must relate to –

    (a) pregnancy, childbirth or maternity,

    (aa) time off under section 57ZE,

    (ab) time off under section 57ZJ or 57ZL,

    (b) ordinary, compulsory or additional maternity leave,

    (ba) ordinary or additional adoption leave,

    (bb) shared parental leave,

    (c) parental leave,

    (ca) ordinary or additional paternity leave, or

    (d) time off under s.57A;

and it may also relate to redundancy or other factors.

  (4) A reason or set of circumstances prescribed under subsection (1) satisfies subsection (3)(c) or (d) if it relates to action which an employee –

    (a) takes,

    (b) agrees to take, or

    (c) refuses to take,

under or in respect of a collective or workforce agreement which deals with parental leave.

  (5) Regulations under this section may –

    (a) make different provision for different cases or circumstances;

    (b) apply any enactment, in such circumstances as may be specified and subject to any conditions specified, in relation to persons regarded as unfairly dismissed by reason of this section.

EMPLOYMENT RIGHTS ACT 1996 (as amended)

20. *(1) An employee who is dismissed is entitled under s.99 of the 1996 Act to be regarded for the purposes of Part X of that Act as unfairly dismissed if –*

    (a) the reason or principal reason for the dismissal is of a kind specified in para. (3), or,

    (b) the reason or principal reason for the dismissal is that the employee is redundant, and reg. 10 has not been complied with.

  (2) An employee who is dismissed shall also be regarded for the purposes of Part X of the 1996 Act as unfairly dismissed if –

    (a) the reason (or, if more than one, the principal reason) for the dismissal is that the employee was redundant, or,

    (b) it is shown that the circumstances constituting the redundancy applied equally to one or more employees in the same undertaking who held positions similar to that held by the employee and who have not been dismissed by the employer, and

    (c) it is shown that the reason (or, if more than one, the principal reason) for which the employee was selected for dismissal was a reason of a kind specified in para. (3).

  (3) The kinds of reason referred to in paras. (1) and (2) are reasons connected with –

    (a) the pregnancy of the employee;

    (b) the fact that the employee has given birth to a child;

    (c) the application of a relevant requirement, or a relevant recommendation, as defined by s.66(2) of the 1996 Act;

    (d) the fact that she took, sought to take or availed herself of the benefits of, ordinary maternity leave or additional maternity leave;

    (e) the fact that she took or sought to take –

      (i) ...;

      (ii) parental leave, or

      (iii) time off under s.57A of the 1996 Act;

    (ee) the fact that she failed to return after a period of ordinary or additional maternity leave in a case where –

      (i) the employer did not notify her, in accordance with reg. 7(6) and (7) or otherwise, of the date on which the period in question would end, and she reasonably believed that that period had not ended, or

      (ii) the employer gave her less than 28 days' notice of the date on which the period in question would end, and it was not reasonably practicable for her to return on that date;

    (eee) the fact that she undertook, considered undertaking or refused to undertake work in accordance with reg. 12A;

    (f) the fact that she declined to sign a workforce agreement for the purposes of these Regulations; or

    (g) the fact that the employee, being –

      (i) a representative of members of the workforce for the purposes of Schedule 1, or

      (ii) a candidate in an election in which any person elected will, on being elected, become such a representative,

    performed (or proposed to perform) any functions or activities as such a representative or candidate.

  (4) Paragraphs (1)(b) and (3)(b) only apply where the dismissal ends the employee's ordinary or additional maternity leave period

  (5) Paragraphs (3) and (3A) of reg. 19 apply for the purposes of para. (3)(d) as they apply for the purposes of para. (2)(d) of that regulation.

  (7) Paragraph (1) does not apply in relation to an employee if –

    (a) it is not reasonably practicable for a reason other than redundancy for the employer (who may be the same employer or a successor of his) to permit her to return to a job which is both suitable for her and appropriate for her to do in the circumstances;

    (b) an associated employer offers her a job of that kind, and

    (c) she accepts or unreasonably refuses that offer.

  (8) Where on a complaint of unfair dismissal any question arises as to whether the operation of para. (1) is excluded by the provisions of para. (7), it is for the employer to show that the provisions in question were satisfied in relation to the complainant.

MATERNITY AND PARENTAL LEAVE
REGULATIONS 1999 (as amended)

29 Unfair dismissal

(1) An employee who is dismissed is entitled under s.99 of the 1996 Act to be regarded for the purpose of Part 10 of that Act as unfairly dismissed if –

    (a) the reason or principal reason for the dismissal is of a kind specified in paragraph (3), or

(b)   the reason or principal reason for the dismissal is that the employee is redundant, and reg. 23 has not been complied with.

(2) An employee who is dismissed shall also be regarded for the purposes of Part 10 of the 1996 Act as unfairly dismissed if –

(a)   the reason (or, if more than one, the principal reason) for the dismissal is that the employee was redundant;

(b)   it is shown that the circumstances constituting the redundancy applied equally to one or more employees in the same undertaking who had positions similar to that held by the employee and who have not been dismissed by the employer, and

(c)   it is shown that the reason (or, if more than one, the principal reason) for which the employee was selected for dismissal was a reason of a kind specified in paragraph (3).

(3) The kinds of reason referred to in paragraph (1) and (2) are reasons connected with the fact that –

(a)   the employee took, or sought to take, paternity or adoption leave;

(za) the employee took or sought to take time off under section 57ZE of the 1996 Act;

(zb) the employer believed that the employee was likely to take time off under section 57ZE of the 1996 Act;

(b)   the employer believed that the employee was likely to take ordinary or additional adoption leave, ...

[(bb) the employee undertook, considered undertaking or refused to undertake work in accordance with reg. 21A; or]

(c)   the employee failed to return after a period of additional adoption leave in a case where –

(i) the employer did not notify him, in accordance with reg. 17(7) and (8) or otherwise, of the date on which that period would end, and he reasonably believed that the period had not ended, or

(ii) the employer gave him less than 28 days' notice of the date on which the period would end, and it was not reasonably practicable for him to return on that date.

(4) ...

(5) Paragraph (1) does not apply in relation to an employee if –

(a)   it is not reasonably practicable for a reason other than redundancy for the employer (who may be the same employer or a successor of his) to permit the employee to return to a job which is both suitable for the employee and appropriate for him to do in the circumstances;

(b)   an associated employer offers the employee a job of that kind; and

(c)   the employee accepts or unreasonably refuses that offer.

(6) Where, on a complaint of unfair dismissal, any question arises as to whether the operation of paragraph (1) is excluded by the provisions of paragraph ... (5), it is for the employer to show that the provisions in question were satisfied in relation to the complainant.

**PATERNITY AND ADOPTION LEAVE
REGULATIONS 2002 (as amended)**

Brown v   **[1988] IRLR 263 HL**
Stockton-on-Tees Borough Council

[Section 99] must be seen as a part of social legislation passed for the specific protection of women and to put them on an equal footing with men. Although it is often a considerable inconvenience to an employer to have to make the necessary arrangements to keep a woman's job open for her whilst she is absent from work in order to have a baby, that is a price that has to be paid as a part of the social and legal recognition of the equal status of women in the workplace.

Clayton v   **[1990] IRLR 177 EAT**
Vigers

In accordance with the decision of the House of Lords in *Brown v Stockton-on-Tees Borough Council*, the words "any other reason connected with her pregnancy" (in s.60(1) EP(C)A 1978, now s.20 MAPLE 1999) ought to be read widely so as to give full effect to the mischief at which the statute was aimed. Accordingly, the submission on behalf of the appellant that the words must mean "causally connected with" her pregnancy rather than "associated with" could not be accepted. Therefore, where a woman who intended to take maternity leave was dismissed because the employer was unable to find a temporary replacement for her, there was a dismissal for a reason connected with pregnancy.

Atkins v   **[2008] IRLR 420 EAT**
Coyle Personnel plc

Obiter: the reason for a dismissal must be causally connected to paternity leave, and not merely "associated" with it, in order to establish automatically unfair dismissal. In reg. 29(3) PAL 2002, "connected with" means causally connected with rather than some vaguer, less stringent connection. Therefore, a man who was dismissed because of a heated argument with his line manager while he was on paternity leave was dismissed fairly because the dismissal was not because he had taken paternity leave.

Del Monte Foods Ltd v   **[1980] IRLR 224 EAT**
Mundon

For there to be a finding of unfair dismissal on grounds of a woman's pregnancy or for some other reason connected with her pregnancy in accordance with the provisions of [s.99] of the Act, it must be shown that the employers knew or believed either that the woman was pregnant or that they were dismissing her for a reason connected with her pregnancy. If they did not know of the pregnancy, or did not believe that the pregnancy existed, it is not possible for them to have as their reason for dismissal that the woman was pregnant. In a case where it is said that the reason for dismissal is another reason connected with her pregnancy, not the pregnancy itself, the employers have to know the facts alleged by the employee as grounding the reason and also to know or believe that those facts relied upon are connected with the woman's pregnancy.

Brown v   **[1988] IRLR 263 HL**
Stockton-on-Tees Borough Council

Selection of a woman for redundancy because she is pregnant and will require maternity leave is dismissal for a "reason connected with her pregnancy" and is therefore deemed to be unfair. It cannot have been intended that an employer should be able to take advantage of a redundancy situation to weed out his pregnant employees.

Caledonia Bureau Investment   **[1998] IRLR 110 EAT**
    & Property v
Caffrey

Section 99 of the Employment Rights Act covers the position where a pregnancy-related illness arises during the period of maternity leave, and that illness is the direct cause of dismissal in due course. It is not limited to dismissals occurring during the period of pregnancy and maternity leave. It applies after maternity leave has expired, so long as the contract of employment has been expressly extended. Therefore, dismissal of the claimant when she failed to return to work after the expiration of her maternity leave due to post-natal depression was for a reason connected with her pregnancy within the meaning of s.99, and thus automatically unfair.

Qua v   **[2003] IRLR 184 EAT**
John Ford Morrison Solicitors

An employment tribunal determining whether the reason for an employee's dismissal was that she had taken, or had sought to take, time off under s.57A should ask themselves the following questions:

(1) Did the claimant take time off or seek to take time off from work during her working hours? If so, on how many occasions and when?

(2) If so, on each of those occasions did the claimant (a) as soon as reasonably practicable inform her employer of the reason for her absence; and (b) inform him how long she expected to be absent; (c) if not, were the circumstances such that she could not inform him of the reason until after she had returned to work?

If the tribunal finds that the claimant had not complied with the requirements of s.57A(2), then the right to take time off work under subsection (1) does not apply. The absences would be unauthorised and the dismissal would not be automatically unfair.

(3) If the claimant had complied with these requirements then the following questions arise:

(a) Did she take or seek to take time off work in order to take action which was necessary to deal with one or more of the five situations listed at paragraphs (a) to (e) of subsection (1)?

(b) If so, was the amount of time off taken or sought to be taken reasonable in the circumstances?

(4) If the claimant satisfied questions (3)(a) and (b), was the reason or principal reason for her dismissal that she had taken/sought to take that time off work?

If the tribunal answers that final question in the affirmative, then the claimant is entitled to a finding of automatic unfair dismissal.

Health and safety cases

100. *(1) An employee who is dismissed shall be regarded for the purposes of this Part as unfairly dismissed if the reason (or, if more than one, the principal reason) for the dismissal is that –*

(a) having been designated by the employer to carry out activities in connection with preventing or reducing risks to health and safety at work, the employee carried out (or proposed to carry out) any such activities,

(b) being a representative of workers on matters of health and safety at work or member of a safety committee –

(i) in accordance with arrangements established under or by virtue of any enactment, or

(ii) by reason of being acknowledged as such by the employer,

the employee performed (or proposed to perform) any functions as such a representative or a member of such a committee,

(ba) the employee took part (or proposed to take part) in consultation with the employer pursuant to the Health and Safety (Consultation with Employees) Regulations 1996 or in an election of representatives of employee safety within the meaning of those Regulations (whether as a candidate or otherwise),

(c) being an employee at a place where –

(i) there was no such representative or safety committee, or

(ii) there was such a representative or safety committee but it was not reasonably practicable for the employee to raise the matter by those means,

he brought to his employer's attention, by reasonable means, circumstances connected with his work which he reasonably believed were harmful or potentially harmful to health or safety,

(d) in circumstances of danger which the employee reasonably believed to be serious and imminent and which he could not reasonably have been expected to avert, he left (or proposed to leave) or (while the danger persisted) refused to return to his place of work or any dangerous part of his place of work, or

(e) in circumstances of danger which the employee reasonably believed to be serious and imminent, he took (or proposed to take) appropriate steps to protect himself or other persons from the danger.

(2) For the purposes of subsection (1)(e), whether steps which an employee took (or proposed to take) were appropriate is to be judged by reference to all the circumstances including, in particular, his knowledge and the facilities and advice available to him at the time.

(3) Where the reason (or, if more than one, the principal reason) for the dismissal of an employee is that specified in subsection (1)(e), he shall not be regarded as unfairly dismissed if the employer shows that it was (or would have been) so negligent for the employee to take the steps which he took (or proposed to take) that a reasonable employer might have dismissed him for taking (or proposing to take) them.

EMPLOYMENT RIGHTS ACT 1996 (as amended)

Goodwin v   **[1997] IRLR 665 EAT**
Cabletel UK Ltd

The protection against dismissal afforded to a "designated employee" by s.100(1)(a) includes the manner in which he carried out his health and safety activities as well as the actual doing of them. A similar approach is appropriate to that taken by the courts to the protection afforded where an employee is dismissed for taking part in trade union activities. The protection afforded to a designated employee must not be diluted by too easily finding acts done for the purpose of carrying out health and safety activities to be a justification for dismissal. On the other hand, not every act, however malicious and irrelevant to the task in hand, must necessarily be treated as a protected act in circumstances where dismissal would be justified on legitimate grounds.

Balfour Kilpatrick Ltd v Acheson   [2003] IRLR 683 EAT

In order for s.100(1)(c) to come into play, it is first necessary to show that it was not reasonably practicable for the employee to raise the health and safety matters through the safety representative or safety committee. Secondly, the employee must have brought to the employer's attention by reasonable means the circumstances that he reasonably believes are harmful or potentially harmful to health or safety. Thirdly, the reason for dismissal, or at least the principal reason if there is more than one, must be the fact that the employee was exercising his rights.

Balfour Kilpatrick Ltd v Acheson   [2003] IRLR 683 EAT

Although, on its face, s.100(1)(c) requires an employment tribunal to ask whether it was reasonably practicable to use a safety representative rather than asking whether it was reasonable for the employee to use some other means of communicating with the employer, the important thing is that the message is communicated quickly and succinctly. Article 13(2)(d) of the EC Framework Directive on Health and Safety provides in terms that workers must "immediately inform the employer" of serious and immediate dangers to health and safety. It is clear that an employee exercising his obligations under Article 13 of the Directive cannot conceivably be lawfully dismissed under English law on that account. Section 100(1)(c) could be construed compatibly with the Directive by inserting the words "or to communicate these circumstances by any appropriate means to the employer" in s.100(1)(e), which would in turn restrict the scope of s.100(1)(c).

Balfour Kilpatrick Ltd v Acheson   [2003] IRLR 683 EAT

Taking industrial action is not "reasonable means" of bringing health and safety concerns to the employer's attention. Although, in exceptional circumstances, communication can be by action rather than words, the concept of informing the employer cannot extend to taking industrial action to impress upon the employer the gravity of the issue as perceived by the employees.

Harvest Press Ltd v McCaffrey   [1999] IRLR 778 EAT

Dangers caused by the behaviour of fellow employees are within the wide scope of s.100(1)(d). The word "danger" is used in the section without any limitation and was intended to cover any danger however originating.

Oudahar v Esporta Group Ltd   [2011] IRLR 730 EAT

Section 100(1)(e) should be applied in two stages: first, the tribunal should consider whether the criteria set out in that provision have been met, as a matter of fact. Were there circumstances of danger which the employee reasonably believed to be serious and imminent? Did he take or propose to take appropriate steps to protect himself or other persons from the danger? Or did he take appropriate steps to communicate these circumstances to his employer by appropriate means? If these criteria are not satisfied, s.100(1)(e) is not engaged. If the criteria are made out, the tribunal should then ask whether the employer's sole or principal reason for dismissal was that the employee took or proposed to take such steps. If it was, then the dismissal must be regarded as unfair. The mere fact that an employer disagreed with an employee as to whether there were (for example) circumstances of danger, or whether the steps were appropriate, is irrelevant. The employee's belief that there is a serious and imminent danger must be objectively reasonable and not fanciful, but so long as that is the case, the employee will be protected regardless of the employer's assessment of the level of risk.

Masiak v City Restaurants (UK) Ltd   [1999] IRLR 780 EAT

The expression "other persons" in s.100(1)(e) extends to protection of members of the public from danger. Neither that section nor the provisions of the EC Directive to which it gives effect seek to limit the class of persons at risk of danger to those employed by the employer.

Working time cases

101A. *(1) An employee who is dismissed shall be regarded for the purposes of this Part as unfairly dismissed if the reason (or, if more than one, the principal reason) for the dismissal is that the employee –*

    (a) refused (or proposed to refuse) to comply with a requirement which the employer imposed (or proposed to impose) in contravention of the Working Time Regulations 1998,

    (b) refused (or proposed to refuse) to forgo a right conferred on him by those Regulations,

    (c) failed to sign a workforce agreement for the purposes of those Regulations, or to enter into, or agree to vary or extend, any other agreement with his employer which is provided for in those Regulations, or

    (d) being –

        (i) a representative of members of the workforce for the purposes of Schedule 1 to those Regulations, or

        (ii) a candidate in an election in which any person elected will, on being elected, be such a representative,

    performed (or proposed to perform) any functions or activities as such a representative or candidate.

(2) A reference in this section to the Working Time Regulations 1998 includes a reference to –

    (a) the Merchant Shipping (Working Time: Inland Waterways) Regulations 2003;

    (b) the Fishing Vessels (Working Time: Sea-fishermen) Regulations 2004;

    (c) the Cross-border Railway Services (Working Time) Regulations 2008;

    (d) the Merchant Shipping (Hours of Work) Regulations 2002.

EMPLOYMENT RIGHTS ACT 1996 (as amended)

McLean v   **[2007] IRLR 14 EAT**
Rainbow Homes Ltd

If an employee is dismissed because they refused to comply with a requirement that the employer proposed to impose which as a matter of fact would have contravened the Working Time Regulations it is irrelevant that the refusal was not for that reason. The dismissal would still be automatically unfair.

Protected disclosures

103A. *An employee who is dismissed shall be regarded for the purposes of this Part as unfairly dismissed if the reason (or, if more than one, the principal reason) for the dismissal is that the employee made a protected disclosure.*

43A. *In this Act a "protected disclosure" means a qualifying disclosure (as defined by s.43B) which is made by a worker in accordance with any ss.43C to 43H.*

43B. *(1) In this Part a "qualifying disclosure" means any disclosure of information which, in the reasonable belief of the worker making the disclosure, is made in the public interest and tends to show one or more of the following –*

    (a) that a criminal offence has been committed, is being committed or is likely to be committed,

    (b) that a person has failed, is failing or is likely to fail to comply with any legal obligation to which he is subject,

    (c) that a miscarriage of justice has occurred, is occurring or is likely to occur,

    (d) that the health or safety of any individual has been, is being or is likely to be endangered,

    (e) that the environment has been, is being or is likely to be damaged, or

    (f) that information tending to show any matter falling within any one of the preceding paragraphs has been, or is likely to be deliberately concealed.

(2) For the purposes of subsection (1), it is immaterial whether the relevant failure occurred, occurs or would occur in the United Kingdom or elsewhere, and whether the law applying to it is that of the United Kingdom or of any other country or territory.

(3) A disclosure of information is not a qualifying disclosure if the person making the disclosure commits an offence by making it.

(4) A disclosure of information in respect of which a claim to legal professional privilege (or, in Scotland, to confidentiality as between client and professional legal adviser) could be maintained in legal proceedings is not a qualifying disclosure if it is made by a person to whom the information had been disclosed in the course of obtaining legal advice.

(5) In this Part "the relevant failure", in relation to a qualifying disclosure, means the matter falling within paragraphs (a) to (f) of subsection (1).

43C. *(1) A qualifying disclosure is made in accordance with this section if the worker makes the disclosure –*

    (a) to his employer, or

    (b) where the worker reasonably believes that the relevant failure relates solely or mainly to –

        (i) the conduct of a person other than his employer, or

        (ii) any other matter for which a person other than his employer has legal responsibility,

    to that other person.

(2) A worker who, in accordance with a procedure whose use by him is authorised by his employer, makes a qualifying disclosure to a person other than his employer, is to be treated for the purposes of this Part as making the qualifying disclosure to his employer.

43D. *A qualifying disclosure is made in accordance with this section if it is made in the course of obtaining legal advice.*

43E. *A qualifying disclosure is made in accordance with this section if –*

    (a) the worker's employer is –

        (i) an individual appointed under any enactment (including any enactment comprised in, or in an instrument made under, an Act of the Scottish Parliament) by a Minister of the Crown or a member of the Scottish Executive, or

        (ii) a body any of whose members are so appointed, and

    (b) the disclosure is made to a Minister of the Crown or a member of the Scottish Executive.

43F. *(1) A qualifying disclosure is made in accordance with this section if the worker –*

    (a) makes the disclosure to a person prescribed by an order made by the Secretary of State for the purposes of this section, and

    (b) reasonably believes –

        (i) that the relevant failure falls within any description of matters in respect of which that person is so prescribed, and

        (ii) that the information disclosed, and any allegation contained in it, are substantially true.

  (2) An order prescribing persons for the purposes of this section may specify persons or descriptions of persons, and shall specify the descriptions of matters in respect of which each person, or persons of each description, is or are prescribed.

43G. *(1) A qualifying disclosure is made in accordance with this section if –*

    (a) ...

    (b) the worker reasonably believes that the information disclosed, and any allegation contained in it, are substantially true,

    (c) he does not make the disclosure for purposes of personal gain,

    (d) any of the conditions in subsection (2) is met, and

    (e) in all the circumstances of the case, it is reasonable for him to make the disclosure.

  (2) The conditions referred to in subsection (1)(d) are –

    (a) that, at the time he makes the disclosure, the worker reasonably believes that he will be subjected to a detriment by his employer if he makes a disclosure to his employer or in accordance with s.43F,

    (b) that, in a case where no person is prescribed for the purposes of s.43F in relation to the relevant failure, the worker reasonably believes that it is likely that evidence relating to the relevant failure will be concealed or destroyed if he makes a disclosure to his employer, or

    (c) that the worker has previously made a disclosure of substantially the same information –

        (i) to his employer, or

        (ii) in accordance with s.43F.

  (3) In determining for the purposes of subsection (1)(e) whether it is reasonable for the worker to make the disclosure, regard shall be had, in particular, to –

    (a) the identity of the person to whom the disclosure is made,

    (b) the seriousness of the relevant failure,

    (c) whether the relevant failure is continuing or is likely to occur in the future,

    (d) whether the disclosure is made in breach of a duty of confidentiality owed by the employer to any other person,

    (e) in a case falling within subsection (2)(c)(i) or (ii), any action which the employer or the person to whom the previous disclosure in accordance with s.43F was made has taken or might reasonably be expected to have taken as a result of the previous disclosure, and

    (f) in a case falling within subsection (2)(c)(i), whether in making the disclosure to the employer the worker complied with any procedure whose use by him was authorised by the employer.

  (4) For the purposes of this section a subsequent disclosure may be regarded as a disclosure of substantially the same information as that disclosed by a previous disclosure as mentioned in subsection (2)(c) even though the subsequent disclosure extends to information about action taken or not taken by any person as a result of the previous disclosure.

43H. *(1) A qualifying disclosure is made in accordance with this section if –*

    (a) ...

    (b) the worker reasonably believes that the information disclosed, and any allegation contained in it, are substantially true,

    (c) he does not make the disclosure for purposes of personal gain,

    (d) the relevant failure is of an exceptionally serious nature, and

    (e) in all the circumstances of the case, it is reasonable for him to make the disclosure.

  (2) In determining for the purposes of subsection (1)(e) whether it is reasonable for the worker to make the disclosure, regard shall be had, in particular, to the identity of the person to whom the disclosure is made.

EMPLOYMENT RIGHTS ACT 1996 (as amended)

Miklaszewicz v   **[2002] IRLR 344 CS**
Stolt Offshore Ltd

Whether an employee is protected depends upon the date of dismissal, not the date of disclosure. It is the dismissal which triggers the employee's entitlement to invoke the statutory remedies. The making of the disclosure requires to be considered at that point of time and it is then that the criteria for treating it as a protected disclosure are applicable. Thus, a disclosure made prior to the legislation coming into force on 2 July 1999 acquires the status of a protected disclosure if a dismissal is effected by reason of it after the legislation came into force.

ALM Medical Services Ltd v   **[2002] IRLR 807 CA**
Bladon

In a protected disclosure case, where the employee has not served the qualifying period needed to acquire the general right not to be unfairly dismissed, the critical issue is not substantive or procedural unfairness but whether all the requirements of the protected disclosure provisions have been satisfied on the evidence.

Darnton v   **[2003] IRLR 133 EAT**
University of Surrey

There can be a qualifying disclosure in terms of s.43B(1) even if the worker was wrong in what he alleged. A "qualifying disclosure" means any disclosure of information which in the reasonable belief of the worker making it tends to show a relevant failure. For there to be a "qualifying disclosure", it must have been reasonable for the worker to believe that the factual basis of what was disclosed was true and that it tends to show a relevant failure, even if the worker was wrong, but reasonably mistaken. The determination of the factual accuracy of the allegations may be an important tool in determining whether the worker held the reasonable belief that is required by s.43B(1), in that it is extremely difficult to see how a worker can reasonably believe that an allegation tends to show that there has been a relevant failure if he knew or believed that the factual basis was false. However, reasonable belief must be based on facts as understood by the worker, not as actually found to be the case.

Parkins v [2002] IRLR 109 EAT
Sodexho Ltd
Disclosure of an alleged breach of a contract of employment can amount to a protected disclosure. A legal obligation which arises from a contract of employment falls within the definition of a "qualifying disclosure" in s.43B(1)(b). That provision is drawn very broadly and there is no reason to distinguish a legal obligation which arises from a contract of employment from any other form of legal obligation. For the purposes of s.43B, however, it is not sufficient that there has simply been a breach of the contract. What has to be shown is, first, that the breach of the employment contract was a breach of a legal obligation under that contact. Secondly, there must be a reasonable belief on the part of the worker that such a breach has, is or is likely to happen. Thirdly, the reason for dismissal must be that the worker has complained that his employer has broken the contract of employment.

Kraus v [2004] IRLR 260 EAT
Penna plc
The word "likely" in s.43B(1)(b) requires more than a possibility or a risk that an employer might fail to comply with a relevant legal obligation. The information disclosed should, in the reasonable belief of the worker at the time it is disclosed, tend to show that it is probable or more probable than not that the employer will fail to comply with the relevant obligation.

Babula v [2007] IRLR 346 CA
Waltham Forest College
In order to bring a claim in respect of a protected disclosure, it is sufficient that the employee reasonably believes that the matters he relies upon amount to a criminal act, or found a legal obligation, even if it turns out that this belief is wrong.

Street v [2004] IRLR 687 CA
Derbyshire Unemployed
  Workers' Centre
In the context of s.43C and s.43G, "in good faith" means more than a reasonable belief in the truth of the information disclosed. Where a statement is made without reasonable belief

in its truth, that fact would be highly relevant as to whether it was made in good faith. But where a statement is made in that belief, it does not necessarily follow that it is made in good faith. A disclosure will not be made in good faith if an ulterior motive was the dominant or predominant purpose of making it. Thus, the disclosures made by the employee in this case could not be regarded as having been made in good faith because her dominant, if not her sole purpose in making them was her personal antagonism towards her manager.

Bolton School v [2007] IRLR 140 CA
Evans
The term "disclosure" should be given its ordinary meaning, and does not protect a course of conduct leading up to the disclosure. This affirms the EAT decision in this case reported at [2006] IRLR 500 that actions by an employee designed to establish or confirm a reasonable belief in wrongdoing by an employer have no protection (as part of a protected disclosure) from detriment or dismissal as a result, even if they do provide evidence of wrongdoing.

Kuzel v [2008] IRLR 530 CA
Roche Products Ltd
It is for the employer to prove a fair reason for dismissal. There is no burden on the employee either to disprove the reason put forward by the employer, or to positively prove a different reason, even where the employee is asserting that the dismissal was for an inadmissible reason. However, the employee who positively asserts that there was a different and inadmissible reason for dismissal, such as making protected disclosures (as in this case), must produce "some evidence" supporting the case that there was an inadmissible reason and challenging the evidence produced by the employer. The employer can defeat a claim of an inadmissible reason for dismissal either by proving a different reason or by successfully contesting the reason put forward by the employee. If the tribunal is not satisfied that the reason for dismissal is the reason asserted by the employer, it is open to it to find that it is the reason asserted by the employee, but it does not have to so find.

Assertion of statutory rights

104. *(1) An employee who is dismissed shall be regarded for the purposes of this Part as unfairly dismissed if the reason (or, if more than one, the principal reason) for the dismissal is that the employee –*

(a) brought proceedings against the employer to enforce a right of his which is a relevant statutory right, or

(b) alleged that the employer had infringed a right of his which is a relevant statutory right.

(2) It is immaterial for the purposes of subsection (1) –

(a) whether or not the employee has the right, or

(b) whether or not the right has been infringed;

but, for that subsection to apply, the claim to the right and that it has been infringed must be made in good faith.

(3) It is sufficient for subsection (1) to apply that the employee, without specifying the right, made it reasonably clear to the employer what the right claimed to have been infringed was.

(4) The following are relevant statutory rights for the purposes of this section –

(a) any right conferred by this Act for which the remedy for its infringement is by way of a complaint or reference to an employment tribunal,

(b) the right conferred by s.86 of this Act,

(c) the rights conferred by ss.68, 86, 145A, 145B, 146, 168, 168A, 169 and 170 of the Trade Union and Labour Relations (Consolidation) Act 1992 (deductions from pay, union activities and time off),

(d) the rights conferred by the Working Time Regulations 1998, the Merchant Shipping (Hours of Work) Regulations 2002, the Merchant Shipping (Working Time: Inland Waterways) Regulations 2003, the Fishing Vessels (Working Time: Sea-fishermen) Regulations 2004 or the Cross-border Railway Services (Working Time) Regulations 2008.

EMPLOYMENT RIGHTS ACT 1996 (as amended)

Mennell v [1997] IRLR 519 CA
Newell & Wright (Transport Contractors) Ltd

Section 104 is not confined to cases where a statutory right has actually been infringed. It is sufficient if the employee has alleged that the employer has infringed the statutory right and that the making of that allegation was the reason or principal reason for dismissal. The allegation need not be specific, provided it was made reasonably clear to the employer what right was claimed to have been infringed. The allegation need not be correct, either as to the entitlement to the right or as to its infringement, provided that the claim was made in good faith. The important point is that the employee must have made an allegation of the kind protected by s.104: if he did not, the making of the allegation could not have been the reason for dismissal.

Elizabeth Claire Care Management [2005] IRLR 858 EAT
Ltd v
Francis

Failure by an employer to pay any or all of an employee's wages on time amounts to an unlawful deduction from wages under s.13(1) of the Employment Rights Act and is therefore a breach of a relevant statutory right for the purposes of s.104. Accordingly, if the reason for dismissal is that an employee has alleged in good faith that the employer has delayed paying wages, the employee will be regarded as having been unfairly dismissed.

Selection for redundancy

105. *(1) An employee who is dismissed shall be regarded for the purposes of this Part as unfairly dismissed if –*

    (a) the reason (or, if more than one, the principal reason) for the dismissal is that the employee was redundant,

    (b) it is shown that the circumstances constituting the redundancy applied equally to one or more other employees in the same undertaking who held positions similar to that held by the employee and who have not been dismissed by the employer, and

    (c) it is shown that any of subsections (2A) to (7N) applies.

(2) . . .

(2A) This subsection applies if the reason (or, if more than one, the principal reason) for which the employee was selected for dismissal was one of those specified in subsection (1) of s.98B (unless the case is one to which subsection (2) of that section applies).

(3) This subsection applies if the reason (or, if more than one, the principal reason) for which the employee was selected for dismissal was one of those specified in subsection (1) of s.100 (read with subsections (2) and (3) of that section).

(4) This subsection applies if either –

    (a) the employee was a protected shop worker or an opted-out shop worker, or a protected betting worker or an opted-out betting worker, and the reason (or, if more than one, the principal reason) for which the employee was selected for dismissal was that specified in subsection (1) of s.101 (read with subsection (2) of that section), or

    (b) the employee was a shop worker or a betting worker and the reason (or, if more than one, the principal reason) for which the employee was selected for dismissal was that specified in subsection (3) of that section.

(4A) This subsection applies if the reason (or, if more than one, the principal reason) for which the employee was selected for dismissal was one of those specified in s.101A.

(5) This subsection applies if the reason (or, if more than one, the principal reason) for which the employee was selected for dismissal was that specified in s.102(1).

(6) This subsection applies if the reason (or, if more than one, the principal reason) for which the employee was selected for dismissal was that specified in s.103.

(6A) This subsection applies if the reason (or, if more than one, the principal reason) for which the employee was selected for dismissal was that specified in s.103A.

(7) This subsection applies if the reason (or, if more than one, the principal reason) for which the employee was selected for dismissal was one of those specified in subsection (1) of s.104 (read with subsections (2) and (3) of that section).

(7A) This subsection applies if the reason (or, if more than one, the principal reason) for which the employee was selected for dismissal was one of those specified in subsection (1) of s.104A (read with subsection (2) of that section).

(7B) This subsection applies if the reason (or, if more than one, the principal reason) for which the employee was selected for dismissal was one of those specified in subsection (1) of s.104B (read with subsection (2) of that section).

(7BA) This subsection applies if the reason (or, if more than one, the principal reason) for which the employee was selected for dismissal was one of those specified in s.104C.

(7BB) This subsection applies if the reason (or, if more than one, the principal reason) for which the employee was selected for dismissal was one of those specified in s.104E.

(7C) This subsection applies if –

    (a) the reason (or, if more than one, the principal reason) for which the employee was selected for dismissal was the reason mentioned in s.238A(2) of the Trade Union and Labour Relations (Consolidation) Act 1992 (participation in official industrial action), and

    (b) subsection (3), (4) or (5) of that section applies to the dismissal.

(7D) This subsection applies if the reason (or, if more than one, the principal reason) for which the employee was selected for dismissal was one specified in paras. (3) or (6) of reg. 28 of the Transnational Information and Consultation of Employees Regulations 1999 (read with paras. (4) and (7) of that regulation).

(7E) This subsection applies if the reason (or, if more than one, the principal reason) for which the employee was selected for dismissal was one specified in para. (3) of reg. 7 of the Part-Time Workers (Prevention of Less Favourable Treatment) Regulations 2000 (unless the case is one to which para. (4) of that regulation applies).

(7F) This subsection applies if the reason (or, if more than one, the principal reason) for which the employee was selected for dismissal was one specified in para. 3 of reg. 6 of the Fixed-term Employees (Prevention of Less Favourable Treatment) Regulations 2002 (unless the case is one to which para. (4) of that regulation applies).

(7G) This subsection applies if the reason (or, if more than one, the principal reason) for which the employee was selected for redundancy was one specified in para. (3) or (6) of reg. 42 of the European Public Limited-Liability Company Regulations 2004 (read with paras. (4) and (7) of that regulation.

(7H) This subsection applies if the reason (or, if more than one, the principal reason) for which the employee was selected for dismissal was one specified in para. (3) or (6) of reg. 30 of the Information and Consultation of Employees Regulations 2004 (read with paras. (4) and (7) of that regulation).

(7I) This subsection applies if the reason (or, if more than one, the principal reason) for which the employee was selected for dismissal was one specified in para. 5(3) or (5) of the Schedule to the Occupational and Personal Pension Schemes (Consultation by Employers and Miscellaneous Amendment) Regulations 2006 (read with para. 5(6) of that Schedule).

(7IA) . . .

(7J) This subsection applies if the reason (or, if more than one, the principal reason) for which the employee was selected for dismissal was one specified in para. (3) or (6) of reg. 31 of the European Cooperative Society (Involvement of Employees) Regulations 2006 (read with paras. (4) and (7) of that regulation).

(7JA) This subsection applies if the reason (or, if more than one, the principal reason) for which the employee was selected for dismissal was one of those specified in subsection (1) of section 104D (read with subsection (2) of that section).

(7K) This subsection applies if the reason (or, if more than one, the principal reason) for which the employee was selected for dismissal was one specified in –

    (a) paragraph (2) of reg. 46 of the Companies (Cross-Border Mergers) Regulations 2007 (read with paras. (3) and (4) of that regulation); or

(b) paragraph (2) of reg. 47 of the Companies (Cross-Border Mergers) Regulations 2007 (read with para. (3) of that regulation).

(7L) This subsection applies if the reason (or, if more than one, the principal reason) for which the employee was selected for dismissal was one specified in paragraph (3) or (6) of reg. 29 of the European Public Limited-Liability Company (Employee Involvement) (Great Britain) Regulations 2009 (SI 2009/2401) (read with paragraphs (4) and (7) of that regulation).

(7M) This subsection applies if –

(a) the reason (or, if more than one, the principal reason) for which the employee was selected for dismissal was the one specified in the opening words of section 104F(1), and

(b) the condition in paragraph (a) or (b) of that subsection was met.

(7N) This subsection applies if the reason (or, if more than one, the principal reason) for which the employee was selected for dismissal was one specified in paragraph (3) of regulation 17 of the Agency Workers Regulations 2010 (unless the case is one to which paragraph (4) of that regulation applies).

(8) For the purposes of s.36(2)(b) or 41(1)(b), the appropriate date in relation to this section is the effective date of termination.

(9) In this Part "redundancy case" means a case where paras. (a) and (b) of subsection (1) of this section are satisfied.

EMPLOYMENT RIGHTS ACT 1996 (as amended)

Powers and Villiers v   **[1981] IRLR 483 EAT**
A Clarke & Co (Smethwick) Ltd
In determining whether two groups of employees hold similar positions, that employees in one group can do the work of the other group is not sufficient. The flexibility must work both ways.

Transfer of undertakings

4. *(1) Except where objection is made under para. (7), a relevant transfer shall not operate so as to terminate the contract of employment of any person employed by the transferor and assigned to the organised grouping of resources or employees that is subject to the relevant transfer, which would otherwise be terminated by the transfer, but any such contract shall have effect after the transfer as if originally made between the person so employed and the transferee.*
...

(3) Any reference in para. (1) to a person employed by the transferor and assigned to the organised grouping of resources or employees that is subject to a relevant transfer, is a reference to a person so employed immediately before the transfer, or who would have been so employed if he had not been dismissed in the circumstances described in reg. 7(1), including, where the transfer is effected by a series of two or more transactions, a person so employed and assigned or who would have been so employed and assigned immediately before any of those transactions.
...

(7) Paragraphs (1) and (2) shall not operate to transfer the contract of employment and the rights, powers, duties and liabilities under or in connection with it of an employee who informs the transferor or the transferee that he objects to becoming employed by the transferee.

(8) Subject to paras. (9) and (11), where an employee so objects, the relevant transfer shall operate so as to terminate his contract of employment with the transferor but he shall not be treated, for any purpose, as having been dismissed by the transferor.

(9) Subject to reg. 9, where a relevant transfer involves or would involve a substantial change in working conditions to the material detriment of a person whose contract of employment is or would be transferred under para. (1), such an employee may treat the contract of employment as having been terminated, and the employee shall be treated for any purpose as having been dismissed by the employer.
...

(11) Paragraphs (1), (7), (8) and (9) are without prejudice to any right of an employee arising apart from these Regulations to terminate his contract of employment without notice in acceptance of a repudiatory breach of contract by his employer.

7. *(1) Where either before or after a relevant transfer, any employee of the transferor or transferee is dismissed, that employee is to be treated for the purposes of Part 10 of the 1996 Act (unfair dismissal) as unfairly dismissed if the sole or principal reason for the dismissal is the transfer.*

(2) This paragraph applies where the sole or principal reason for the dismissal is an economic, technical or organisational reason entailing changes in the workforce of either the transferor or the transferee before or after a relevant transfer.

(3) Where paragraph (2) applies –

(a) paragraph (1) does not apply;

(b) without prejudice to the application of section 98(4) of the 1996 Act (test of fair dismissal), for the purposes of sections 98(1) and 135 of that Act (reason for dismissal) –

(i) the dismissal is regarded as having been for redundancy where section 98(2)(c) of that Act applies; or

(ii) in any other case, the dismissal is regarded as having been for a substantial reason of a kind such as to justify the dismissal of an employee holding the position which that employee held.

(3A) In paragraph (2), the expression "changes in the workforce" includes a change to the place where employees are employed by the employer to carry on the business of the employer or to carry out work of a particular kind for the employer (and the reference to such a place has the same meaning as in section 139 of the 1996 Act).

(4) The provisions of this regulation apply irrespective of whether the employee in question is assigned to the organised grouping of resources or employees that is, or will be, transferred.

(5) Paragraph (1) shall not apply in relation to the dismissal of any employee which was required by reason of the application of s.5 of the Aliens Restriction (Amendment) Act 1919 to his employment.

(6) Paragraph (1) shall not apply in relation to a dismissal of an employee if the application of s.94 of the 1996 Act to the dismissal of the employee is excluded by or under any provision of the 1996 Act, the 1996 Tribunals Act or the 1992 Act.

TRANSFER OF UNDERTAKINGS (PROTECTION OF EMPLOYMENT) REGULATIONS 2006

The following cases, most of which were decided before the Transfer of Undertakings (Protection of Employment) Regulations 2006 came into effect on 6 April 2006, refer to the similar provisions to those above which existed under regs. 5 and 8 of the Transfer of Undertakings (Protection of Employment) Regulations 1981 (as amended). References to those regulations in the case notes have been amended to reflect this.

Wilson and others v   **[1998] IRLR 706 HL**
St Helens Borough Council
British Fuels Ltd v
Baxendale and Meade
A dismissal for a reason connected with the transfer of an undertaking is legally effective and not a nullity. A dismissed employee cannot compel the transferee to employ him.

Litster and others v   **[1989] IRLR 161 HL**
Forth Dry Dock & Engineering Co Ltd
Where an employee has been unfairly dismissed before a transfer for a reason connected with the transfer, he is to be deemed to have been employed in the undertaking "immediately before the transfer" and the employment is statutorily continued with the transferee.

Wilson and others v   **[1998] IRLR 706 HL**
St Helens Borough Council
British Fuels Ltd v
Baxendale and Meade
Where the transferee does not take on the transferor's employees, because they have already been dismissed by the transferor, or because the transferee itself dismissed the employees on the transfer, then the transferee must meet all the transferor's contractual and statutory obligations unless either the employee objects to being employed by

the transferee or there is an economic, technical or organisational reason for the dismissal entailing changes in the workforce.

Kerry Foods Ltd v   **[2000] IRLR 10 EAT**
Creber
In applying [regs. 7(1), 7(2) and 7(3)] the following principles of law may be formulated:
(1) Every dismissal is effective to terminate the employment relationship.
(2) A dismissal by the transferor by reason of the impending transfer will be automatically unfair.
(3) The employees concerned will enforce their remedies in relation to that dismissal against the transferee, in accordance with the *Litster* principle.
(4) If the main reason for the dismissal by the transferor is an economic, technical or organisational reason, neither [reg. 7(1)] nor the *Litster* principle will apply.
(5) If the reason for the dismissal is an economic, technical or organisational reason but the dismissal is nonetheless unfair, the principle in point (4) remains true and the employee may recover only from the transferor. It is only when [reg. 7(1)] applies that the *Litster* principle operates.
(6) If the dismissal is effected by the transferee, either by reason of the transfer or for an economic, technical or organisational reason, then the employee's remedy lies against the transferee.

Spaceright Europe Ltd v   **[2012] IRLR 111 CA**
Baillavoine
The natural and ordinary meaning of the language of reg. 7(1) does not require a particular transfer or transferee to be in existence or in contemplation at the time of the dismissal.

Morris v   **[1998] IRLR 499 EAT**
John Grose Group Ltd
A dismissal falls within [reg. 7(1)] if a transfer to any transferee who might appear is the reason or principal reason for dismissal. In order for [reg. 7(1)] to apply, there must have been a relevant transfer, which means that the identity of the transferee, the date of the transfer and the terms of the actual transfer have all been decided by the time that the matter comes before an employment tribunal. The words "the transfer" in [reg. 7(1)], however, do not have to refer to the relevant particular transfer which has actually taken place. The view expressed by the EAT in *Ibex Trading Co Ltd v Walton* could not be agreed with.

BSG Property Services v   **[1996] IRLR 134 EAT**
Tuck and others
Where an employee is dismissed with notice by the transferor which expires after the date of transfer, it is the transferor who dismisses and it is the transferor's reason for the dismissal notice which is relevant, even though liability in connection with the notice to terminate is transferred to the transferee. Accordingly, the notice of termination given by the transferor for the reason of the transferor is deemed to have been a notice given by the transferee for that reason.

Longden and Paisley v   **[1994] IRLR 157 EAT**
Ferrari Ltd and Kennedy
  International Ltd

The transfer was not the principal reason for dismissal where a prospective purchaser identified those employees whom it was essential to retain, and the other employees were dismissed by receivers because of financial constraints.

Hazel v   **[2014] IRLR 392 CA**
Manchester College

Where, following a TUPE transfer, a dismissal takes place because the transferee wishes to harmonise the terms of employees inherited as a result of the transfer with those of their existing workforce, it is the reason for the particular employee's dismissal that must be considered; it is irrelevant that the harmonisation of terms is part of an overall package of proposals which includes proposed redundancies.

Warner v   **[1998] IRLR 394 CA**
Adnet Ltd

Regulations [7(1), 7(2) and 7(3)] must be read as a whole rather than as mutually exclusive. Although [reg. 7(1)] covers a dismissal which will be automatically unfair, [reg. 7(3)] expressly contemplates circumstances in which [reg. 7(1)] will be disapplied and that the view formed by a tribunal under [reg. 7(1)] is a provisional or prima facie finding.

Whitehouse v   **[1999] IRLR 492 CA**
Chas A Blatchford & Sons Ltd

If an employee is dismissed solely by reason of a transfer, he must be taken to be unfairly dismissed. But if, in addition, there is an economic, technical or organisational reason, the tribunal has to determine whether that is the principal reason within the meaning of [reg. 7(2)].

Thompson v   **[2001] IRLR 802 EAT**
SCS Consulting Ltd

Whether an ETO reason was or was not the reason or the principal reason for dismissal is a factual decision for the employment tribunal. In making that decision, the tribunal must consider whether the reason was connected with the future conduct of the business as a going concern. It is entitled to take into account as relevant factual material whether there was any collusion between transferor and transferee and whether the transferor or those acting on its behalf had any funds to carry on the business at the time of the decision to dismiss.

Delabole Slate Ltd v   **[1985] IRLR 305 CA**
Berriman

In order to come within [reg. 7(2)], it must be shown that a change in the workforce is part of the economic, technical or organisational reason for dismissal. It must be an objective of the employer's plan to achieve changes in the workforce, not just a possible consequence of it. Thus where an employee resigned following a transfer because the transferees proposed to reduce his wages to that of their existing employees, the reason for the employer's ultimatum was to produce standard rates of pay and was not in any way to reduce the number in the workforce.

Delabole Slate Ltd v   **[1985] IRLR 305 CA**
Berriman

The dismissal of one employee followed by the engagement of another in his place does not constitute a change in the "workforce" within the meaning of [reg. 7(2)]. Changes in the identity of the individuals who make up the workforce do not constitute changes in the workforce itself so long as the overall numbers and functions of the employees looked at as a whole remain unchanged. The word "workforce" connotes the whole body of employees as an entity: it corresponds to the "strength" or the "establishment".

Crawford v   **[1990] IRLR 42 EAT**
Swinton Insurance Brokers Ltd

There can be a "change in a workforce" for the purpose of [reg. 7(2)] if the same people are kept on but they are given entirely different jobs to do. As, in accordance with the decision in *Delabole Slate Ltd v Berriman*, the "workforce" connotes the whole body of employees as an entity, what has to be looked at is the workforce as a whole, separate from the individuals who make it up. It then has to be determined whether the reason in question is one which involves a change in that workforce, strength or establishment. If, as a result of an organisational change on a relevant transfer, a workforce is engaged in a different occupation, there is a change in the workforce for the purpose of [reg. 7(2)].

Meter U v   **[2012] IRLR 367 EAT**
Ackroyd
Meter U v
Hardy

When considering whether dismissals following a TUPE transfer were for an economic, technical or organisational reason entailing changes in the workforce, the term "workforce" does not include limited companies that are franchisees of the transferee, even if each of those companies is a vehicle through which one individual provides his services, provided that the arrangement is not a sham.

Porter and Nanayakkara v   **[1993] IRLR 486 HC**
Queen's Medical Centre

A change in the method of providing services required can amount to a reorganisation entailing changes in the workforce in that the reorganisation can require that the employers should be free to make an uninhibited choice in filling new posts.

Trafford v   **[1994] IRLR 325 EAT**
Sharpe & Fisher
  (Building Supplies) Ltd

There is no decision of the European Court which supports the suggestion by the Advocate-General in the *D'Urso* case that "only dismissals which would have been made in any case" fall within the exclusion permitted by Article 4(1) of the EC Business Transfers Directive. Therefore, the EAT could not accept the submission that to make [reg. 7(3)(a)] comply with the obligations contained in the Directive requires the insertion in the regulation of the words "provided that the dismissal would have been made in any case".

Anderson and McAlonie v　　　　　**[1984] IRLR 429 EAT**
Dalkeith Engineering Ltd　(in receivership)
The three reasons entailing changes in the workforce specified in [reg. 7(2)] – economic, technical or organisational – are not mutually exclusive.

Whitehouse v　　　　　　　　　　　**[1999] IRLR 492 CA**
Chas A Blatchford & Sons Ltd
The words, "economic, technical or organisational reason entailing changes in the workforce" clearly mean that the reason must be connected with the future conduct of the business as a going concern. Where a transferor has no intention of continuing the business, a reason for dismissal cannot be related to the future conduct of the business.

Spaceright Europe Ltd v　　　　　**[2012] IRLR 111 CA**
Baillavoine
An economic, technical or organisational reason is not available as a defence in the case of dismissing an employee to enable administrators "to make the business of the company a more attractive proposition to prospective transferees of a going concern". Instead, "there must be an intention to change the workforce and to continue to conduct the business, as distinct from the purpose of selling it."

Crystal Palace FC (2000) Ltd v　　　**[2014] IRLR 139 CA**
Kavanagh
The fact that an administrator needs to reduce the wage bill in order to continue running the business and to avoid liquidation may amount to an economic, technical or organisational reason for dismissal. A distinction may be drawn between the administrator's reason for particular dismissals and his ultimate objective of selling the business.

Wheeler v　　　　　　　　　　　　**[1987] IRLR 211 EAT**
Patel and J Goulding Group
An "economic reason" for dismissal, to fall within [reg. 7(2)], must be a reason which relates to the conduct of the business. A desire to obtain an enhanced price for the business or to achieve a sale is not a reason which relates to the conduct of the business and is therefore not an "economic" reason. The view expressed in *Anderson v Dalkeith Engineering Ltd* that where an employee is dismissed by the transferor at the insistence of the transferee the reason is "economic" within the meaning of [reg. 7(2)] could not be agreed with. On such a broad literal construction, the transferor's reason would always be an economic reason.

Nationwide Building Society v　　　**[2010] IRLR 922 EAT**
Benn
To establish an economic, technical or organisational reason for a dismissal which occurs as a result of changes in terms

and conditions of employment on a transfer of an undertaking, (a) it is not necessary that that reason affect the entirety of the workforce, and (b) such a reason may be established even where the only persons affected are those that transferred.

Whitehouse v　　　　　　　　　　**[1999] IRLR 492 CA**
Chas A Blatchford & Sons Ltd
A dismissal which took place because the grant of a contract was made conditional upon a reduction in the employer's workforce was for an economic or organisational reason, and not by reason of the transfer of the undertaking. The transfer was the occasion for the reduction in the requirement of the employers, but it was not the cause or reason for that reduction. A dismissal which was in order to get a contract is in no way analogous to the position of the vendor of a business who dismissed employees solely for the purpose of achieving the best price for the business.

Crawford v　　　　　　　　　　　**[1990] IRLR 42 EAT**
Swinton Insurance Brokers Ltd
Where there is a case of constructive dismissal following a transfer, the employment tribunal must identify the principal reason for the conduct of the employer which entitled the employee to terminate the contract and then determine whether that reason is an economic, technical or organisational one entailing changes in the workforce.

Hynd v　　　　　　　　　　　　　**[2007] IRLR 338 CS**
Armstrong
A transferor employer cannot rely on the transferee's reason for dismissal in order to establish an "economic, technical or organisational reason" so as to provide a potential defence under TUPE. A transferor can only rely on a reason of its own.

Tapere v　　　　　　　　　　　　**[2009] IRLR 972 EAT**
South London and Maudsley NHS Trust
In reg. 4(9) "working conditions" applies to contractual terms and conditions as well as physical conditions and whether or not there is a "substantial change in working conditions" is a question of fact looking at both the nature and the degree of the change. Whether it is to "the material detriment" of the claimant is to be determined in accordance with the approach of the House of Lords (per Lord Scott) to "detriment" in *Shamoon v Chief Constable of the Royal Ulster Constabulary* [2003] IRLR 285, which is that "what has to be considered is the impact of the proposed change from the employee's point of view". It is not an issue to be objectively determined. Therefore, a change will be to the employee's material detriment if she regards it as detrimental and if that was "a reasonable position for the employee to adopt".

Rehabilitation of offenders

4. *(1) Subject to ss.7 and 8 below, a person who has become a rehabilitated person for the purposes of this Act in respect of a conviction shall be treated for all purposes in law as a person who has not committed or been charged with or prosecuted for or convicted of or sentenced for the offence or offences which were the subject of that conviction; and, notwithstanding the provisions of any other enactment or rule of law to the contrary, but subject as aforesaid –*

(a) *no evidence shall be admissible in any proceedings before a judicial authority exercising its jurisdiction or functions in England, Wales or Scotland to prove that any such person has committed or been charged with or prosecuted for or convicted of or sentenced for any offence which was the subject of a spent conviction; and*

(b) *a person shall not, in any such proceedings, be asked, and, if asked, shall not be required to answer, any question relating to his past which cannot be answered without acknowledging or referring to a spent conviction or spent convictions or any circumstances ancillary thereto.*

(2) Subject to the provisions of any order made under subsection (4) below, where a question seeking information with respect to a person's previous convictions, offences, conduct or circumstances is put to him or to any other person otherwise than in proceedings before a judicial authority –

(a) *the question shall be treated as not relating to spent convictions or to any circumstances ancillary to spent convictions, and the answer thereto may be framed accordingly; and*

(b) *the person questioned shall not be subjected to any liability or otherwise prejudiced in law by reason of any failure to acknowledge or disclose a spent conviction or any circumstances ancillary to a spent conviction in his answer to the question.*

(3) Subject to the provisions of any order made under subsection (4) below –

(a) *any obligation imposed on any person by any rule of law or by the provisions of any agreement or arrangement to disclose any matters to any other person shall not extend to requiring him to disclose a spent conviction or any circumstances ancillary to a spent conviction (whether the conviction is his own or another's); and*

(b) *a conviction which has become spent or any circumstances ancillary thereto, or any failure to disclose a spent conviction or any such circumstances, shall not be a proper ground for dismissing or excluding a person from any office, profession, occupation or employment, or for prejudicing him in any way in any occupation or employment.*

(4) The Secretary of State may by order –

(a) *make such provision as seems to him appropriate for excluding or modifying the application of either or both of paras. (a) and (b) of subsection (2) above in relation to questions put in such circumstances as may be specified in the order;*

(b) *provide for such exceptions from the provisions of subsection (3) above as seem to him appropriate, in such cases or classes of case, and in relation to convictions of such a description, as may be specified in the order.*

(5) For the purposes of this section and s.7 below any of the following are circumstances ancillary to a conviction, that is to say –

(a) *the offence or offences which were the subject of that conviction;*

(b) *the conduct constituting that offence or those offences; and*

(c) *any process or proceedings preliminary to that conviction, any sentence imposed in respect of that conviction, any proceedings (whether by way of appeal or otherwise) for reviewing that conviction or any such sentence, and anything done in pursuance of or undergone in compliance with any such sentence.*

(6) For the purposes of this section and s.7 below "proceedings before a judicial authority" includes, in addition to proceedings before any of the ordinary courts of law, proceedings before any tribunal, body or person having power –

(a) *by virtue of any enactment, law, custom or practice;*

(b) *under the rules governing any association, institution, profession, occupation or employment; or*

(c) *under any provision of any agreement providing for arbitration with respect to questions arising thereunder;*

to determine any question affecting the rights, privileges, obligations or liabilities of any person, or to receive evidence affecting the determination of any such question.

REHABILITATION OF OFFENDERS ACT 1974

Property Guards Ltd v   **[1982] IRLR 175 EAT**
Taylor and Kershaw

Since s.4(3)(b) of the Rehabilitation of Offenders Act provides in terms that a dismissal for failure to disclose a spent conviction is not a proper ground for dismissal, an employment tribunal was entitled to conclude that where there was no obligation to answer a question so as to make any reference to a spent conviction, dismissal based upon a conviction that was spent must be unfair.

Torr v   **[1977] IRLR 184 EAT**
British Railways Board

There is no rule of law that employers must extend the social philosophy found in the Rehabilitation of Offenders Act so as to make it unfair to dismiss a person solely because he has a previous conviction. Where the Rehabilitation of Offenders Act did not apply and the terms of appointment expressly provided that the employers could dismiss without notice if unsatisfactory references were received, the employers were entitled to dismiss an employee as soon as it was appreciated that he had obtained employment by dishonest concealment of a past criminal conviction. It is of the utmost importance that an employer seeking an employee to hold a position of responsibility and trust should be able to select for employment a candidate in whom he can have confidence. It is fundamental to that confidence that the employee should truthfully disclose his history so far as it is sought by the intending employer.

Trade union membership and activities

152. *(1) For purposes of Part X of the Employment Rights Act 1996 (unfair dismissal) the dismissal of an employee shall be regarded as unfair if the reason for it (or, if more than one, the principal reason) was that the employee –*

    (a) was, or proposed to become, a member of an independent trade union,

    (b) had taken part, or proposed to take part, in the activities of an independent trade union at an appropriate time,

    (ba) had made use, or proposed to make use, of trade union services at an appropriate time,

    (bb) had failed to accept an offer made in contravention of s.145A or 145B, or

    (c) was not a member of any trade union, or of a particular trade union, or of one of a number of particular trade unions, or had refused or proposed to refuse to become or remain a member.

(2) In subsection (1) "an appropriate time" means –

    (a) a time outside the employee's working hours; or

    (b) a time within his working hours at which, in accordance with arrangements agreed with or consent given by his employer, it is permissible for him to take part in the activities of a trade union or (as the case may be) make use of trade union services;

and for this purpose "working hours", in relation to an employee, means any time when, in accordance with his contract of employment, he is required to be at work.

(2A) In this section –

    a) "trade union services" means services made available to the employee by an independent trade union by virtue of his membership of that union, and

    (b) references to an employee's "making use" of trade union services include his consent to the raising of a matter on his behalf by an independent trade union of which he is a member.

(2B) Where the reason or one of the reasons for the dismissal was that an independent trade union (with or without the employee's consent) raised a matter on behalf of the employee as one of its members, the reason shall be treated as a reason falling within subsection (1)(ba).

(3) Where the reason, or one of the reasons, for the dismissal was –

    (a) the employee's refusal, or proposed refusal, to comply with a requirement (whether or not imposed by his contract of employment or in writing) that, in the event of his not being a member of any trade union, or of a particular trade union, or of one of a number of particular trade unions, he must make one or more payments; or

    (b) his objection, or proposed objection (however expressed) to the operation of a provision (whether or not forming part of his contract of employment or in writing) under which, in the event mentioned in para. (a), his employer is entitled to deduct one or more sums from the remuneration payable to him in respect of his employment,

the reason shall be treated as falling within subsection (1)(c).

(4) References in this section to being, becoming or ceasing to remain a member of a trade union include references to being, becoming or ceasing to remain a member of a particular branch or section of that union or of one of a number of particular branches or sections of that trade union.

(5) References in this section –

    (a) to taking part in the activities of a trade union, and

    (b) to services made available by a trade union by virtue of membership of the union,

shall be construed in accordance with subsection (4).

153. *Where the reason or principal reason for the dismissal of an employee was that he was redundant, but it is shown –*

    (a) that the circumstances constituting the redundancy applied equally to one or more other employees in the same undertaking who held positions similar to that held by him and who have not been dismissed by the employer; and

    (b) that the reason (or, if more than one, the principal reason) why he was selected for dismissal was one of those specified in s.152(1);

the dismissal shall be regarded as unfair for the purposes of Part X of the Employment Rights Act 1996 (unfair dismissal).

154. *Sections 108(1) and 109(1) of the Employment Rights Act 1996 (qualifying period and upper age limit for unfair dismissal protection) do not apply to a dismissal which by virtue of s.152 or 153 is to be regarded as unfair for the purposes of Part 10 of that Act.*

               **TRADE UNION AND LABOUR RELATIONS
(CONSOLIDATION) ACT 1992 (as amended)**

Onus of proof

Smith v   **[1978] IRLR 413 CA**
The Chairman and other
   Councillors of Hayle Town Council
Where an employee does not have the requisite period of continuous employment for making a complaint of unfair dismissal, he has the burden of proving that the reason for his dismissal was an inadmissible reason within the meaning of [s.152].

Shannon v   **[1981] IRLR 505 NICA**
Michelin (Belfast) Ltd
Where the employee has adequate service to complain of unfair dismissal, there is no onus on him to prove that the reason for his dismissal related to his trade union membership or activities.

Maund v   **[1984] IRLR 24 CA**
Penwith District Council
Where the employee has adequate service to complain of unfair dismissal, the legal burden of proving the reason for dismissal is on the employer. Where the employer produces evidence that appears to show the reason for the dismissal, but the employee alleges that the real reason related to his union membership or activities, there is an evidential burden on the employee to

produce evidence that casts doubt upon the employer's reason. Once this evidential burden is discharged, the onus remains on the employer to prove the reason for the dismissal.

Maund v   **[1982] IRLR 399 EAT**
Penwith District Council
If an admissible reason is engineered in order to effect dismissal because the true reason would not be admissible, the true view must be that the employer fails because the underlying principal reason for the dismissal is not within [s.98(2)].

Dismissal on grounds of union membership

CGB Publishing v   **[1993] IRLR 520 EAT**
Killey
A "but for" test for determining whether an employee has been dismissed by reason of his trade union membership is wrong in principle because it does not introduce any question as to the state of mind of the employer and does not adequately approach the notion of causation.

Ridgway and another v   **[1987] IRLR 80 CA**
National Coal Board
[Section 152(1)(a)] is not restricted to cases where the reason for dismissal was that the employer objected to the employee being a member of any trade union whatsoever. The phrase "an independent trade union" refers to a particular union as well as to any union. If the organisation of which the employee is, or proposes to become, a member is an independent trade union [s.152(1)(a)] applies and the employee has the stated statutory protection in respect of his membership of that union.

Dismissal on grounds of union activities

The Marley Tile Co Ltd v   **[1980] IRLR 25 CA**
Shaw
In determining whether an employee was dismissed on grounds of trade union activities, what has to be established is:
1. For what reason or reasons did the company dismiss the employee and, if more than one, what was the principal reason?
2. Was the employee's conduct, which formed the only or the principal reason for dismissal, trade union activities?
3. If so, was it with the consent, express or implied, of the company?

Port of London Authority v   **[1992] IRLR 447 EAT**
Payne and others
Whether an employee's activities fall within the phrase "the activities of an independent trade union" must be judged objectively.

Therm A Stor Ltd v   **[1983] IRLR 78 CA**
Atkins and others
[S.152] is not concerned with an employer's reactions to a trade union's activities but with his reaction to an individual employee's activities in a trade union context.

Fitzpatrick v   **[1991] IRLR 376 CA**
British Railways Board
An employer is in clear breach of [s.152(1)(b)] if he dismisses an employee because of union activities in previous employment, when the only rational basis for doing so is the fear that those activities will be repeated in the present employment. Although the activities referred to in [s.152(1)(b)] are activities in the employment from which the employee alleges unfair dismissal, what happened in previous employment may form the reason for that dismissal and may, therefore, be highly relevant in determining whether the dismissal fell within [s.152(1)(b)]. The decision of the EAT in *City of Birmingham District Council v Beyer* [1977] IRLR 211 could not be regarded as meaning that what happened in previous employment can have no relevance to whether or not an employee has been unfairly dismissed from subsequent employment in accordance with [s.152(1)(b)]. The effect of *Beyer* is to make clear that if the employee obtained employment by deceit and the employer dismisses for that deceit [s.152(1)(b)] does not apply albeit that the deceit concerned previous union activities.

Fitzpatrick v   **[1991] IRLR 376 CA**
British Railways Board
To fall within [s.152(1)(b)], the activity need not be sufficiently precise to be identifiable. The purpose of [s.152(1)(b)] is to protect those who engage in union activities and there is no reason why that should not apply irrespective of whether the precise activities can be identified.

Brennan and Ging v   **[1976] IRLR 378 EAT**
Ellward (Lancs) Ltd
In order to determine whether an employee was dismissed for taking part in union activities within the meaning of [s.152], it is necessary for the employment tribunal to summarise carefully all the acts and facts relied upon as constituting "activities", including as an element (but not the only element) whether the employee is a trade union representative, and then to decide as a matter of common sense whether such acts taken together constitute the activities of an independent trade union. It is not necessarily fatal to that conclusion that the employee is also acting for his own benefit.

Lyon and Scherk v   **[1976] IRLR 215 EAT**
St James Press Ltd
While the special protection afforded by [s.152] to trade union activities must not be allowed to operate as a cloak or an excuse for conduct which ordinarily would justify dismissal and wholly unreasonable, extraneous or malicious acts done in support of trade union activities might be a ground for dismissal which would not be unfair, the right to take part in the

affairs of a union must not be obstructed by too easily finding acts for that purpose to be a justification for dismissal.

British Airways Engine Overhaul Ltd v   **[1981] IRLR 9 EAT**
Francis
Discussion of matters with which an independent trade union is concerned is capable of being an activity of an independent trade union within the meaning of the statute.

Drew v   **[1980] IRLR 459 EAT**
St Edmundsbury Borough Council
Taking part in industrial action does not constitute taking part in the activities of an independent trade union within the meaning of [s.152]. It is impossible, therefore, for a person to fall at the same time under [s.152], which deals with dismissal for an inadmissible reason, and [s.238], which deals with dismissal in connection with industrial action.

Britool Ltd v   **[1993] IRLR 481 EAT**
Roberts and others
Participating in the preliminary planning and organising of industrial action can amount to taking part in trade union activities within the meaning of [s.152(1)(b)].

Drew v   **[1980] IRLR 459 EAT**
St Edmundsbury Borough Council
The personal activities of a union member are not the activities of a trade union within the meaning of [s.152].

Appropriate time

Post Office v   **[1974] IRLR 22 HL**
UPW
The right of employees to take part in trade union activities includes the right to take part in those activities while they are on the employer's premises in accordance with their contracts of employment but not actually working.

The Marley Tile Co Ltd v   **[1980] IRLR 25 CA**
Shaw
In a proper case, consent of the employer to a trade union activity taking place during working hours can be implied. However, the employer's consent could not be implied from his silence when an announcement that the activity was going to take place was made.

The Marley Tile Co Ltd v   **[1978] IRLR 238 EAT**
Shaw
Taking part in union activities at an appropriate time within the meaning of [s.152(2)(b)] is not restricted to cases where express arrangements have been agreed or express consent given for union activities to take place during an employee's normal working hours. Such consent can be implied from the general relationship between management and the unions. Were that not the case, it would be tantamount to saying that there could be an appropriate time within working hours only where the union was fully recognised by the employer since it is likely to

be only in such cases that there are express arrangements or consent. The words "appropriate time" must be construed against the background of industry as it is organised in practice. It is common practice within industry to have satisfactory working relations where a union is not formally recognised. It would be strange if, in such circumstances, employees had no protection against dismissal or victimisation for taking part in the activities of an independent trade union.

Bass Taverns Ltd v   **[1995] IRLR 596 CA**
Burgess
An employer's consent for a shop steward to use a company-organised course as a union recruitment forum was not subject to an implied limitation that he should say nothing to criticise or undermine the company, such as to mean that his dismissal for making disparaging remarks about the company fell outside the scope of s.152. A consent to recruit must include a consent to underline the services which the union can provide and that may reasonably involve a submission to prospective members that, in some respects, the union will provide a service which the company does not.

Zucker v   **[1978] IRLR 385 EAT**
Astrid Jewels Ltd
In determining whether an employee was taking part in trade union activities at an appropriate time within the meaning of [s.152(2)], the House of Lords' decision in *Post Office v Union of Post Office Workers* makes clear that an employee is entitled to take part in union activities whilst he is on the employer's premises but not actually working. Merely because an employee is on the premises during a time in respect of which he is being paid does not mean that the employee is necessarily required to be at work and, therefore, that the time is within working hours, so that a paid meal break is not a time within working hours so as to require the employer's consent to take part in union activities.

Zucker v   **[1978] IRLR 385 EAT**
Astrid Jewels Ltd
If employees while working are permitted to converse upon anything they feel like with fellow employees nearby to the extent that it does not cause disruption, there is no reason why an employment tribunal cannot come to the conclusion that there was implied consent or implied arrangements to converse upon trade union activities.

Dismissal on grounds of non-membership

Crosville Motor Services Ltd v   **[1986] IRLR 475 EAT**
Ashfield
For the purposes of [s.152(1)(c)], a proposal to refuse to remain a member of a union need not be unqualified. It may be conditional or contingent upon something occurring or not occurring.

Selection for redundancy

Dundon v   **[1995] IRLR 403 EAT**
GPT Ltd

An employer does not have to be motivated by malice or a deliberate desire to be rid of a trade union activist in order to fall within s.153.

O'Dea v   **[1995] IRLR 599 CA**
ISC Chemicals Ltd

Anything that an employee did or had a contractual right to do as an official of a trade union must be left out of account in determining whether the circumstances of the redundancy applied equally to one or more other employees in the undertaking who held similar positions to him and who were not dismissed. It cannot be right that, for the purposes of s.153, the trade union activities of an employee shop steward should distinguish his position from that of other employees.

Port of London Authority v   **[1992] IRLR 447 EAT**
Payne and others

Selection of shop stewards for redundancy because the employers believed that they would engage in disruptive activities in the future was dismissal on grounds of trade union activities and, therefore, automatically unfair. The employers' belief was based on the shop stewards' activities in the past. Since in the main they were the activities of an independent trade union, the only conclusion that could be reached was that any similar future activities would also be trade union activities.

Driver v   **[1994] IRLR 636 EAT**
Cleveland Structural Engineering
  Co Ltd

In determining whether selection for redundancy was on grounds related to an employee's trade union membership or activities, it is relevant to look at the reason why the employee was not offered available alternative employment.

Pressure to dismiss

107. *(1) This section applies where there falls to be determined for the purposes of this Part a question –*

    (a) as to the reason, or principal reason, for which an employee was dismissed,

    (b) whether the reason or principal reason for which an employee was dismissed was a reason fulfilling the requirement of s.98(1)(b), or

    (c) whether an employer acted reasonably in treating the reason or principal reason for which an employee was dismissed as a sufficient reason for dismissing him.

    (2) In determining the question no account shall be taken of any pressure which, by calling, organising, procuring or financing a strike or other industrial action, or threatening to do so, was

exercised on the employer to dismiss the employee; and the question shall be determined as if no such pressure had been exercised.

EMPLOYMENT RIGHTS ACT 1996

Ford Motor Co Ltd v   **[1978] IRLR 66 EAT**
Hudson

It is not necessary for a case to fall within [s.107] that those exerting the pressure on the employer explicitly sought the dismissal of the employee. The test to be applied is: Was the pressure exerted on the employers such that it could be foreseen that it would be likely to result in the dismissal of those employees in respect of whom the pressure was being brought?

Dismissal and industrial action

237. *(1) An employee has no right to complain of unfair dismissal if at the time of dismissal he was taking part in an unofficial strike or other unofficial industrial action.*

(1A) Subsection (1) does not apply to the dismissal of the employee if it is shown that the reason (or, if more than one, the principal reason) for the dismissal or, in a redundancy case, for selecting the employee for dismissal was one of those specified in or under –

> *(a) section 98B, 99, 100, 101A(d), 103, 103A, 104C, 104D or 104E of the Employment Rights Act 1996 (dismissal in jury service, family, health and safety, working time, employee representative, protected disclosure, flexible working, pension scheme membership, and study and training cases),*
>
> *(b) section 104 of that Act in its application in relation to time off under s.57A of that Act (dependants).*

In this subsection "redundancy case" has the meaning given in s.105(9) of that Act; and a reference to a specified reason for dismissal includes a reference to specified circumstances of dismissal.

(2) A strike or other industrial action is unofficial in relation to an employee unless –

> *(a) he is a member of a trade union and the action is authorised or endorsed by that union; or*
>
> *(b) he is not a member of a trade union but there are among those taking part in the industrial action members of a trade union by which the action has been authorised or endorsed.*

Provided that a strike or other industrial action shall not be regarded as unofficial if none of those taking part in it are members of a trade union.

(3) The provisions of s.20(2) apply for the purposes of determining whether industrial action is to be taken to have been authorised or endorsed by a trade union.

(4) The question whether industrial action is to be so taken in any case shall be determined by reference to the facts as at the time of dismissal.

Provided that, where an act is repudiated as mentioned in s.21, industrial action shall not thereby be treated as unofficial before the end of the next working day after the day on which the repudiation takes place.

(5) In this section the "time of dismissal" means –

> *(a) where the employee's contract of employment is terminated by notice, when the notice is given;*
>
> *(b) where the employee's contract of employment is terminated without notice, when the termination takes effect; and*
>
> *(c) where the employee is employed under a contract for a fixed term which expires without being renewed under the same contract, when that term expires;*

and a "working day" means any day which is not a Saturday or Sunday, Christmas Day, Good Friday or a bank holiday under the Banking and Financial Dealings Act 1971.

(6) For the purposes of this section membership of a trade union for purposes unconnected with the employment in question shall be disregarded; but an employee who was a member of a trade union when he began to take part in industrial action shall continue to be treated as a member for the purpose of determining whether that action is unofficial in relation to him or another notwithstanding that he may in fact have ceased to be a member.

238. *(1) This section applies in relation to an employee who has a right to complain of unfair dismissal (the "complainant") and who claims to have been unfairly dismissed, where at the date of the dismissal –*

> *(a) the employer was conducting or instituting a lock-out; or*
>
> *(b) the complainant was taking part in a strike or other industrial action.*

(2) In such a case an employment tribunal shall not determine whether the dismissal was fair or unfair unless it is shown –

> *(a) that one or more relevant employees of the same employer have not been dismissed; or*
>
> *(b) that a relevant employee has before the expiry of the period of three months beginning with the date of his dismissal been offered re-engagement and that the complainant has not been offered re-engagement.*

(2A) Subsection (2) does not apply to the dismissal of the employee if it is shown that the reason (or, if more than one, the principal reason) for the dismissal or, in a redundancy case, for selecting the employee for dismissal was one of those specified in or under –

> *(a) section 98B, 99, 100, 101A(d), 103A, 104C, 104D or 104E of the Employment Rights Act 1996 (dismissal in jury service, family, health and safety, working time, employee representative, and flexible working, pension scheme membership, and study and training cases),*
>
> *(b) section 104 of that Act in its application in relation to time off under s.57A of the Act (dependants).*

In this section "redundancy case" has the meaning given in s.105(9) of that Act; and a reference to a specified reason for dismissal includes a reference to specified circumstances of dismissal.

(2B) Subsection (2) does not apply in relation to an employee who is regarded as unfairly dismissed by virtue of s.238A below.

(3) For this purpose "relevant employees" means –

> *(a) in relation to a lock-out, employees who were directly interested in the dispute in contemplation or furtherance of which the lock-out occurred; and*
>
> *(b) in relation to a strike or other industrial action, those employees at the establishment of the employer at or from which the complainant works who at the date of his dismissal were taking part in the action.*

Nothing in s.237 (dismissal of those taking part in unofficial industrial action) affects the question who are relevant employees for the purposes of this section.

(4) An offer of re-engagement means an offer (made either by the original employer or by a successor of that employer or an associated employer) to re-engage an employee, either in the job which he held immediately before the date of dismissal or in a different job which would be reasonably suitable in his case.

(5) In this section "date of dismissal" means –

> *(a) where the employee's contract of employment was terminated by notice, the date on which the employer's notice was given; and*
>
> *(b) in any other case, the effective date of termination.*

238A. *(1) For the purposes of this section an employee takes protected industrial action if he commits an act which, or a series of acts each of which, he is induced to commit by an act which by virtue of s.219 is not actionable in tort.*

(2) An employee who is dismissed shall be regarded for the purposes of Part X of the Employment Rights Act 1996 (unfair dismissal) as unfairly dismissed if –

(a) the reason (or, if more than one, the principal reason) for the dismissal is that the employee took protected industrial action, and

(b) subsection (3), (4) or (5) applies to the dismissal.

(3) This subsection applies to a dismissal if the date of dismissal is within the protected period.

(4) This subsection applies to a dismissal if –

(a) the date of the dismissal is after the end of that period, and

(b) the employee had stopped taking protected industrial action before the end of that period.

(5) This subsection applies to a dismissal if –

(a) the date of the dismissal is after the end of that period, and

(b) the employee had not stopped taking protected industrial action before the end of that period, and

(c) the employer had not taken such procedural steps as would have been reasonable for the purposes of resolving the dispute to which the protected industrial action relates.

(6) In determining whether an employer has taken those steps regard shall be had, in particular, to –

(a) whether the employer or a union had complied with procedures established by any applicable collective or other agreement;

(b) whether the employer or a union offered or agreed to commence or resume negotiations after the start of the protected industrial action;

(c) whether the employer or a union unreasonably refused, after the start of the protected industrial action, a request that conciliation services be used;

(d) whether the employer or a union unreasonably refused, after the start of the protected industrial action, a request that mediation services be used in relation to procedures to be adopted for the purposes of resolving the dispute;

(e) where there was agreement to use either of the services mentioned in paras. (c) and (d), the matters specified in s.238B.

(7) In determining whether an employer has taken those steps no regard shall be had to the merit of the dispute.

(7A) For the purposes of this section, "the protected period" in relation to the dismissal of an employee is the sum of the basic period and any extension period in relation to that employee.

(7B) The basic period is 12 weeks beginning with the first day of protected industrial action.

(7C) An extension period in relation to an employee is a period equal to the number of days falling on or after the first day of protected industrial action (but before the protected period ends) during the whole or any part of which the employee is locked out by his employer.

(7D) In subsections (7B) and (7C), the "first day of protected industrial action" means the day on which the employee starts to take protected industrial action (even if on that day he is locked out by his employer).

(8) For the purposes of this section no account shall be taken of the repudiation of any act by a trade union as mentioned in s.21 in relation to anything which occurs before the end of the next working day (within the meaning of s.237) after the day on which the repudiation takes place.

(9) In this section "date of dismissal" has the meaning given by s.238(5).

239. (1) Sections 237 to 238A (loss of unfair dismissal protection in connection with industrial action) shall be construed as one with Part X of the Employment Rights Act 1996 (unfair dismissal); but ss.108 and 109 of that Act (qualifying period and age limit) shall not apply in relation to s.238A of this Act.

(2) In relation to a complaint to which s.238 or 238A applies, s.111(2) of that Act (time limit for complaint) does not apply, but an employment tribunal shall not consider the complaint unless it is presented to the tribunal –

(a) before the end of the period of six months beginning with the date of the complainant's dismissal (as defined by s.238(5)); or

(b) where the tribunal is satisfied that it was not reasonably practicable for the complaint to be presented before the end of that period, within such further period as the tribunal considers reasonable.

(3) Where it is shown that the condition referred to in s.238(2)(b) is fulfilled (discriminatory re-engagement), the references in –

(a) ss.98 to 106 of the Employment Rights Act 1996; and

(b) ss.152 and 153 of this Act;

to the reason or principal reason for which the complainant was dismissed shall be read as references to the reason or principal reason he has not been offered re-engagement.

(4) In relation to a complaint under s.111 of the 1996 Act (unfair dismissal: complaint to employment tribunal) that a dismissal was unfair by virtue of s.238A of this Act –

(a) no order shall be made under s.113 of the 1996 Act (reinstatement or re-engagement) until after the conclusion of protected industrial action by any employee in relation to the relevant dispute,

(b) regulations under s.7 of the Employment Tribunals Act 1996 may make provision about the adjournment and renewal of applications (including provision requiring adjournment in specified circumstances), and

(c) regulations under s.9 of that Act may require a pre-hearing review to be carried out in specified circumstances.

TRADE UNION AND LABOUR RELATIONS (CONSOLIDATION) ACT 1992 (as amended)

Whether industrial action was official

Balfour Kilpatrick Ltd v Acheson

[2003] IRLR 683 EAT

In determining whether a strike or other industrial action has been repudiated by the trade union, so as to make the action unofficial in terms of s.237(1) thus denying those taking part the right to complain of unfair dismissal, s.21(2)(b) requires that the union must do its best to give individual written notice of the fact of repudiation to every member of the union whom it had reason to believe was taking part in the action.

Balfour Kilpatrick Ltd v Acheson

[2003] IRLR 683 EAT

In s.237(4), which provides that where an act is repudiated by the union, industrial action will not be treated as unofficial until "the end of the next working day after the day on which the repudiation takes place", "the end of the next working day" means midnight on the following working day and not the end of the period which constitutes the normal working hours for the day in question.

Whether conducting a lock-out

Express & Star Ltd v   **[1987] IRLR 422 CA**
Bunday and others
Whether there has been a lock-out or whether there has been a strike is a question to be decided on the facts and merits of each case by the employment tribunal using its industrial relations expertise. The definition of the necessary elements of a lock-out or a strike is not a question of law.

Express & Star Ltd v   **[1987] IRLR 422 CA**
Bunday and others
Although the dictionary definition of a "lock-out" as "a refusal on the part of an employer . . . to furnish work to their operatives except on conditions to be accepted by the latter collectively" is a reliable indication of what constitutes a lock-out, it would be wrong to treat the dictionary definition as if it were expressly contained in the statute and to seek to apply it word for word to any problem which may arise.

Express & Star Ltd v   **[1987] IRLR 422 CA**
Bunday and others
Whether there was a breach of contract on the part of the employer will be a material consideration in a substantial number of cases in deciding whether there was a lock-out, although a lock-out can be instituted without a breach of contract.

Whether taking part in a strike or other industrial action

Coates and Venables v   **[1982] IRLR 318 CA**
Modern Methods & Materials Ltd
Per Stephenson LJ: The meaning of "taking part in a strike" is just the sort of question which an industrial jury is best fitted to decide. An employment tribunal's decision as to whether or not an employee was taking part in a strike should not be interfered with if there was evidence upon which the employment tribunal could make its finding as to whether the employee was taking part in a strike, giving those words a meaning of which they are reasonably capable.

Manifold Industries v   **[1991] IRLR 242 EAT**
Sims
Whether an employee was taking part in industrial action at the date of dismissal must be determined as an objective fact and not by reference to what the employers knew or whether they acted properly in trying to collect information on the subject.

Bolton Roadways Ltd v   **[1987] IRLR 392 EAT**
Edwards and others
Whether an employee is or is not taking part in a strike is to be determined by evidence of what he is in fact doing or omitting to do. If his actions and omissions do not justify the conclusion that he was participating in the strike action, that settles the matter. If his actions and omissions are such as to justify the inference that he was participating in the strike, that inference cannot be invalidated by the circumstance that the employer was unaware of his actions or omissions.

Naylor and others v   **[1983] IRLR 233 EAT**
Orton & Smith Ltd and
  M D Tweddell Engineering Ltd
Following the decision of the Court of Appeal in *Coates,* there can be no error of law by the employment tribunal in making a decision under [s.238] as to whether an employee was taking part in industrial action unless upon the evidence the employment tribunal reached a conclusion which the words of the section could not reasonably bear. This might have the consequences that on the same primary facts two employment tribunals could reach diametrically opposite, but equally correct, conclusions as to whether employees took part in industrial action.

Coates and Venables v   **[1982] IRLR 318 CA**
Modern Methods & Materials Ltd
Whether an employee is taking part in a strike within the meaning of [s.238] must be judged by what the employee does and not by what he thinks or why he does it. An employee who did not cross a picket line because of fear of abuse could reasonably be regarded as taking part in the strike.
Per Stephenson LJ: If an employee stops work when his workmates come out on strike and does not say or do anything to make plain his disagreement, or which could amount to a refusal to join them, he takes part in their strike.
Per Kerr LJ: When the employee's absence from work is due to the existence of the strike in some respect, because he or she chooses not to go to work during the strike, the employee should be regarded as taking part in the strike. The employee's reasons or motives for staying out are not relevant; nor is it relevant to consider whether their utterances or actions, or silence or inaction, showed support, opposition or indifference in relation to the strike.

Sehmi v   **[2009] IRLR 807 EAT**
Gate Gourmet London Ltd
Sandhu and ors v
Gate Gourmet London Ltd
Unauthorised and unexplained absence from work at a time when industrial action is in progress will constitute participation in that industrial action.

Faust and others v   **[1983] IRLR 117 CA**
Power Packing Casemakers Ltd

The meaning of "other industrial action" in [s.238] is not restricted to action by the employee in breach of his contract of employment. The words cover a refusal to do something, such as a refusal to work overtime, whether or not it is a breach of contract, if the refusal is being used as a bargaining weapon.

Lewis and Britton v   **[1994] IRLR 4 EAT**
E Mason & Sons

One person may be able to be involved in industrial action on his own.

Norris v   **[2013] IRLR 428 EAT**
London Fire and Emergency Planning Authority

"Industrial action" connotes action taken by more than one worker acting together. To refer to a single person "taking part in" action undertaken by no one else is "unnatural": "it is like one hand clapping."

Lewis and Britton v   **[1994] IRLR 4 EAT**
E Mason & Sons

It was open to an employment tribunal to take the approach that an employee who refused to carry out an instruction which the employer was entitled to give, and which he would have been prepared to do for an extra payment, was taking part in industrial action in that his conduct was designed to coerce the employer to improve the terms and conditions of his employment.

Bolton Roadways Ltd v   **[1987] IRLR 392 EAT**
Edwards and others

Whether an employee's activity represents a breach of his obligation to attend work may be relevant to the question of whether he is taking part in a strike, but it is not an essential ingredient. Although an employee who is on holiday or away sick would not be in breach of his contractual obligation to work, he would be capable of being held to be taking part in a strike if he associated himself with the strike, attended the picket line or took part in the other activities of the strikers with a view to furthering their aims.

Lewis and Britton v   **[1994] IRLR 4 EAT**
E Mason & Sons

It was open to an employment tribunal to conclude that an employee was taking part in industrial action by making a definite threat that he and his work colleagues would not come into work the following day unless two of their colleagues were reinstated, where the threat was made at a time when further negotiations could not have been expected to take place and where the work for the following day had been allocated by the employers.

Midland Plastics v   **[1983] IRLR 9 EAT**
Till and others

The threat of taking industrial action does not itself amount to taking industrial action. The case of threatened industrial action can be distinguished from a case where some employees have started strike action and others have expressed their intention of joining in such action, such as in *Winnett v Seamarks Brothers Ltd.*

Winnett v   **[1978] IRLR 387 EAT**
Seamarks Brothers Ltd

An employee does not need to withhold his labour when he is contractually due to work in order to be taking part "in strike or other industrial action". If all the employees of a company engaged in shift work decide to stop work from the time of a meeting, those employees who are due to work on the following shifts are taking part in industrial action when they intimate that their labour will be withdrawn at a time when the current shift actually stops work. They do not only begin to take part in industrial action when the time of their shift comes and they do not actually work.

Williams v   **[1980] IRLR 222 EAT**
Western Mail & Echo Ltd

Once employees have stated that they will take strike or other industrial action and do so, they should be regarded as having done so until the action is discontinued or they indicate or state an intention of stopping it. If an employee is on strike and one day has a cold which would have prevented him from going to work, he is not to be regarded as on that day no longer taking part in a strike since he would have been on strike in any event. Similarly, if an employee who would have continued to take part in industrial action at work is prevented because he is sick from applying those sanctions he had already begun to operate, he is still taking part in industrial action.

Faust and others v   **[1983] IRLR 117 CA**
Power Packing Casemakers Ltd

Once an employment tribunal decides that an employee was, at the date of his dismissal, taking part in industrial action, the tribunal must not go into the employer's motive or reasons for dismissing.

Thompson and others v   **[1976] IRLR 308 EAT**
Eaton Ltd

The statutory provisions operate so as to exclude the jurisdiction of the tribunal even where the employer is wholly or substantially to blame for the industrial action.

Marsden and others v   **[1979] IRLR 103 EAT**
Fairey Stainless Ltd

The statutory provisions operate so as to exclude the jurisdiction of the tribunal even where a strike is "engineered" or provoked by the employers.

Date of dismissal

P & O European Ferries (Dover) Ltd v **[1989] IRLR 254 CA**
Byrne

The time at which it has to be shown that one or more employees who took part in a strike were not dismissed, for the purpose of deciding whether an employment tribunal has jurisdiction under [s.238(2)] to entertain the unfair dismissal complaint of an employee dismissed while taking part in the strike, is the conclusion of the relevant hearing at which the tribunal determines whether it has jurisdiction.

Express & Star Ltd v   **[1986] IRLR 477 EAT**
Bunday and others
For the purpose of determining whether there was a "relevant employee" who was taking part in industrial action and subsequently re-engaged, the criterion is whether that employee was taking part in industrial action at the date of the complainant's dismissal and not whether that employee was taking part in indulstrial action at the time of his own dismissal.

Manifold Industries v   **[1991] IRLR 242 EAT**
Sims
For the purpose of determining whether relevant "employees" have not been dismissed, the word "employees" must be interpreted as limited to persons who at the relevant date are still employees. Those who are dead, have retired or have voluntarily resigned fall to be disregarded.

Heath and Hammersley v   **[1973] IRLR 214 NIRC**
J F Longman
  (Meat Salesman) Ltd
Once an employer is informed that a strike is over, he no longer requires the statutory protection. Therefore, the word "date", referring to where the employee is on strike "on the date of dismissal" should be interpreted as "at the time" of dismissal. If on any given date, therefore, the employer has been told the strike is over, he is not free during the rest of that calendar day to dismiss with impunity.

Offer of re-engagement

Crosville Wales Ltd v   **[1996] IRLR 91 CA**
Tracey and others (No.2)
In a case where A, B, C and D have all been dismissed while participating in the same strike, or other industrial action, and where A and B alone have been offered re-engagement, the employment tribunal has a threefold duty: (1) to determine its own jurisdiction by determining whether the relevant collective action amounts to a strike or other industrial action and inquiring whether there had been any offers of re-engagement to the complainants; (2) where jurisdiction is established, to decide whether C and D have been unfairly dismissed because there was no qualifying reason or no sufficient qualifying reason for the discriminatory failure to re-engage; (3) where that also is established, to determine whether C and D should be regarded as having contributed to their dismissal and, if so, what reduction, if any, it would be just and equitable to make in the amount of their compensation.

Bolton Roadways Ltd v   **[1987] IRLR 392 EAT**
Edwards and others
An "offer of re-engagement" means no more and no less than that it is held open for the employee. There is no requirement

that there be a positive offer by the employer, as opposed to a tacit or implied acceptance of continuance of employment.

Crosville Wales Ltd v   **[1993] IRLR 60 EAT**
Tracey and others
A general advertising campaign offering employment to those who apply does not in itself amount to an offer of employment to any particular individual, even where the dismissed employees knew that the employers were recruiting and that offers of employment were being made.

Marsden and others v   **[1979] IRLR 103 EAT**
Fairey Stainless Ltd
A dismissed striker had been "offered re-engagement" even though he had never received a letter of offer because it had been misaddressed where he knew of the letter, knew its contents and the offer of re-engagement, and knew that it had referred to him. There is no statutory requirement that the offer of re-engagement must be in writing.

Bigham and Keogh v   **[1992] IRLR 4 EAT**
GKN Kwikform Ltd
For there to be an offer of "re-engagement" of a dismissed striker within the meaning of [s.238], the employer must have had actual knowledge of the first job from which the employee was dismissed and the reason why he was dismissed, or constructive knowledge in the sense of the means of obtaining knowledge of the fact that what is being offered is re-engagement within the meaning of [s.238].

Williams and others v   **[1982] IRLR 377 CA**
National Theatre Board Ltd
[S.238] does not require that the re-engagement offered dismissed strikers must be on the same terms and conditions in all respects as the previous employment. It is sufficient if the nature of the work and the capacity and place where the employee is to be employed are the same.

Highlands Fabricators Ltd v   **[1984] IRLR 482 EAT**
McLaughlin
An employee dismissed while on strike cannot complain of unfair dismissal where he has been offered re-engagement within three months of the date of dismissal of another employee dismissed and offered re-engagement, notwithstanding that the other employee was offered re-engagement at an earlier date than the complainant.

P & O European Ferries (Dover) Ltd v **[1989] IRLR 254 CA**
Byrne
An employer is entitled to require an employee dismissed while on strike to provide particulars which would enable the employer to know the identity of employees alleged to have been taking part in the strike who have not been dismissed and therefore are "relevant employees" for the purpose of [s.238], even though this would enable the employer to dismiss the employees identified forthwith, thereby prejudicing the claims of the complainant and other

employees dismissed while on strike as well as the continued employment of the unknown employees.

Laffin and Callaghan v   **[1978] IRLR 448 EAT**
Fashion Industries (Hartlepool) Ltd
A different standard does not apply to the fairness of non-re-engagement than that which ought to be applied when considering dismissal. Therefore, where an employee would not have been dismissed for his conduct prior to the strike, for the employers to treat his prior conduct as the reason for not re-engaging him, in circumstances where there were sufficient jobs for all the dismissed employees to do, meant that in effect he was not being re-engaged because he had gone on strike.

Edwards and others v   **[1979] IRLR 303 EAT**
Cardiff City Council
An employer does not have to show that he acted reasonably in treating his reason for not re-engaging an employee dismissed whilst on strike when another dismissed striker was re-engaged as a sufficient reason for dismissal. The statute requires the employment tribunal to determine whether an employer acted reasonably in treating the reason given as a sufficient reason for not offering re-engagement, ie whether there has been shown to be a justification for the distinction between those offered re-engagement and those who were not.

Fairness

Crosville Wales Ltd v   **[1997] IRLR 691 HL**
Tracey (No.2)
Observed (per Lord Nolan): At the stage in a case of selective re-engagement when the tribunal is considering whether the particular employee has been unfairly dismissed, it may well be essential to compare the treatment accorded to that employee with the treatment accorded to others, and to have regard to the employer's conduct and the general merits of the case. However, consideration of the matter by the tribunal does not necessarily have to extend to the collective merits or demerits of the industrial action. The preponderance of judicial opinion over the last 20 years has been to the effect that the whole policy of the relevant legislation is to withdraw the law from the field of industrial disputes, and that cannot simply be brushed aside.

4. REASONABLENESS

General test of fairness

98. *(4) Where the employer has fulfilled the requirements of sub-section (1), the determination of the question whether the dismissal was fair or unfair (having regard to the reason shown by the employer) –*

    (a) depends on whether in the circumstances (including the size and administrative resources of the employer's undertaking) the employer acted reasonably or unreasonably in treating it as a sufficient reason for dismissing the employee, and

    (b) shall be determined in accordance with equity and the substantial merits of the case.

EMPLOYMENT RIGHTS ACT 1996†

Meaning of reasonable

Iceland Frozen Foods Ltd v Jones   **[1982] IRLR 439 EAT**

The authorities establish that in law the correct approach for an employment tribunal to adopt in answering the question posed by [s.98(4)] is as follows:

(1) the starting point should always be the words of [s.98(4)] themselves;

(2) in applying the section an employment tribunal must consider the reasonableness of the employer's conduct, not simply whether they (the members of the employment tribunal) consider the dismissal to be fair;

(3) in judging the reasonableness of the employer's conduct an employment tribunal must not substitute its decision as to what was the right course to adopt for that of the employer;

(4) in many (though not all) cases there is a band of reasonable responses to the employee's conduct within which one employer might reasonably take one view, another quite reasonably take another;

(5) the function of the employment tribunal, as an industrial jury, is to determine whether in the particular circumstances of each case the decision to dismiss the employee fell within the band of reasonable responses which a reasonable employer might have adopted. If the dismissal falls within the band the dismissal is fair: if the dismissal falls outside the band it is unfair.

Post Office v Foley   **[2000] IRLR 827 CA**

HSBC Bank plc (formerly Midland Bank plc) v Madden

The "band or range of reasonable responses" approach to the issue of the reasonableness or unreasonableness of a dismissal, as expounded by Browne-Wilkinson J in *Iceland Frozen Foods Ltd v Jones* and approved and applied by the Court of Appeal, remains binding. The disapproval of that approach in *Haddon v Van Den Burgh Foods Ltd* on the basis that the expression was a "mantra" which led employment tribunals into applying what amounts to a perversity test of reasonableness, instead of the statutory test of reasonableness as it stands, and that it prevented members of employment tribunals from approaching the issue of reasonableness by reference to their own judgment of what they would have done had they been the employers, was an unwarranted departure from binding authority.

It was made clear in *Iceland Frozen Foods* that the statutory provisions did not require such a high degree of reasonableness to be shown that nothing short of a perverse decision to dismiss can be held to be unfair within the section. *Iceland Frozen Foods* also made clear that the members of a tribunal must not simply consider whether they personally think that the dismissal was fair and must not substitute their decision as to what was the right course to adopt for that of the employer. Their proper function is to determine whether the decision to dismiss the employee fell within the band of reasonable responses "which a reasonable employer might have adopted". Although it is true that if application of that approach leads the members of the tribunal to conclude that the dismissal was unfair, they are in effect substituting their judgment for that of the employer, that process must always be conducted by reference to the objective standards of the hypothetical reasonable employer which are imported by the statutory references to "reasonably or unreasonably", and not by reference to their own subjective views of what they in fact would have done as an employer in the same circumstances.

British Leyland UK Ltd v Swift   **[1981] IRLR 91 CA**

There is a band of reasonableness within which one employer might reasonably dismiss the employee whilst another would quite reasonably keep him on. It depends entirely on the circumstances of the case whether dismissal is one of the penalties which a reasonable employer would impose. If no reasonable employer would have dismissed, then the dismissal is unfair. But if a reasonable employer might reasonably have dismissed, then the dismissal is fair.

Northgate HR Ltd v Mercy   **[2008] IRLR 222 CA**

A decision can be outside the band of reasonableness without there being bad faith. The tribunal's decision that a dismissal (as a result of a glaring inconsistency in redundancy scoring) was not outside the band of reasonableness because no bad faith had been shown was an error of law.

Sainsbury's Supermarkets Ltd v Hitt   **[2003] IRLR 23 CA**

The objective standards of the reasonable employer must be applied to all aspects of the question whether an employee was fairly and reasonably dismissed.

Conlin v   **[1994] IRLR 169 CS**
United Distillers

Although failure to make express reference to the terms of [s.98(4)] or to the range of reasonable responses test may not always amount to a fatal flaw in the decision of an employment tribunal, it is essential that it should be apparent from the decision of the tribunal that the correct test has been identified and applied.

Whitbread & Co plc v   **[1988] IRLR 501 EAT**
Mills

Whether the employer acted reasonably or unreasonably in treating the reason for dismissal as sufficient must be considered as a single question, but tribunals are bound in their deliberations to pose a number of subsidiary questions, including:

A. Has the evidence shown us that the employer has complied with the pre-dismissal procedures which a reasonable employer could and should have applied in the circumstances of this case?

B. Where there is a contractual appeal process, has the employer carried it out in its essentials?

C. Where conduct is the main reason, has the evidence shown us that at the time of dismissal the employer had a reasonable suspicion amounting to belief in the guilt of the employee and if necessary has complied with the principles in *Burchell*?

D. During the disciplinary hearings and the appeal process, has the employer dealt fairly with the employee?

Lock v   **[1998] IRLR 358 EAT**
Cardiff Railway Company Ltd

In determining the fairness of dismissal on grounds of misconduct, it is an error of law for an employment tribunal to fail to have regard to the provisions of the ACAS Code of Practice on disciplinary practice and procedure.

W Devis & Sons Ltd v   **[1977] IRLR 314 HL**
Atkins

The test of fairness directs the tribunal to focus its attention on the conduct of the employer and not on whether the employee in fact suffered any injustice.

Orr v   **[2011] IRLR 317 CA**
Milton Keynes Council

For the purposes of determining whether an employer acted reasonably, the knowledge imputed to the employer is not just what the decision-maker knew but also what he or she ought reasonably to have known following a reasonable investigation. However, the employer is not to be taken to know exculpatory facts which were known to the employee's manager but were withheld from the decision-maker.

Polkey v   **[1987] IRLR 503 HL**
A E Dayton Services Ltd

Injustice to the employee is not a necessary ingredient of an unfair dismissal, although its absence will be important in relation to a compensatory award.

Effect of Human Rights Act

X v   **[2004] IRLR 625 CA**
Y

In accordance with s.3 of the Human Rights Act, an employment tribunal, so far as it is possible to do so, must read and give effect to s.98 in a way which is compatible with Convention rights. Section 3 applies to all legislation and draws no distinction between legislation governing public authorities and that governing private individuals. There would normally be no sensible grounds for treating public and private employees differently in respect of unfair dismissal.

Observed (per Mummery LJ): Whenever Human Rights Act points are raised in unfair dismissal cases, an employment tribunal should properly consider their relevance, dealing with them in a structured way, even if it is ultimately decided that they do not affect the outcome of the unfair dismissal claim. The following framework was suggested:

(1) Do the circumstances of the dismissal fall within the ambit of one or more of the articles of the Convention? If they do not, the Convention right is not engaged and need not be considered.

(2) If they do, does the state have a positive obligation to secure enjoyment of the relevant Convention right between private persons? If it does not, the Convention right is unlikely to affect the outcome of an unfair dismissal claim against a private employer.

(3) If it does, is the interference with the employee's Convention right by dismissal justified? If it is, proceed to (5) below.

(4) If it is not, was there a permissible reason for the dismissal under the ERA, which does not involve unjustified interference with a Convention right? If there was not, the dismissal will be unfair for the absence of a permissible reason to justify it.

(5) If there was, is the dismissal fair, tested by the provisions of s.98 of the ERA, reading and giving effect to them under s.3 of the HRA so as to be compatible with the Convention right?

Turner v   **[2013] IRLR 107 CA**
East Midlands Trains Ltd

The "band of reasonable responses" test provides a sufficiently robust, flexible and objective analysis of all aspects of an employer's decision to dismiss to ensure compliance with Article 8 of the European Convention on Human Rights.

X v   **[2004] IRLR 625 CA**
Y

It would not normally be fair for an employer to dismiss an employee for a reason which was an unjustified interference with the employee's private life contrary to Article 8 of the European Convention. If, however, there was a possible justification under s.98, the tribunal ought to consider Article 8 in the context of the application of s.3 of the Human Rights Act to s.98. If it would be incompatible with Article 8 to hold that the dismissal for that reason was fair, then the tribunal must, in accordance with s.3, read and give effect to s.98 so as to be compatible with Article 8.

McGowan v
Scottish Water
[2005] IRLR 167 EAT

Covert surveillance of an employee's home in order to establish whether the employers' suspicions that he was acting dishonestly were justified is not necessarily a breach of the employee's right to respect for his private life under Article 8 such as to render his dismissal unfair. Whether a surveillance operation breaches a person's right to have his private life respected is a question of proportionality.

Hill v
Governing Body of Great Tey Primary School
[2013] IRLR 274 EAT

Where an employee has been dismissed for exercising the right to freedom of speech under Article 10 of the European Convention on Human Rights, the fact that the employer is a public authority and has a duty to ensure that the employee has that freedom are relevant factors in assessing the fairness of what occurred. The tribunal's approach should have been (i) to ask whether what had occurred fell within the ambit of the right to freedom of expression and; (ii) if so, then to have held that the employer as a public body was bound to respect the exercise of that right, unless it could have been qualified by Article 10(2). That involved considering whether the restriction on the right to freedom of expression that was complained of could have been justified in accordance with Article 10(2). Accordingly, the tribunal needed to; (iii) identify the aim which the restriction on free speech sought to serve – one or more of the aims expressly set out at Article 10(2) ("interests of national security" etc); (iv) satisfy itself that the restriction or penalty imposed in the light of that aim was one prescribed by law. That did not mean, in the UK context, that it had to have been provided for by statute – a common law right would have sufficed. A contractual term requiring respect for confidential communications would, for instance, have been sufficient. So, too, would a common law right to confidentiality; (v) if so, to have considered if the restriction or penalty was "necessary in a democratic society".

Tribunal discretion

County Council of Hereford and Worcester v
Neale
[1986] IRLR 168 CA

If the employment tribunal did not err in law, its decision should not be disturbed by an appellate court unless it can be said in effect: "My goodness, that was certainly wrong."

British Telecommunications plc v
Sheridan
[1990] IRLR 27 CA

The EAT can interfere with the decision of an employment tribunal if they are satisfied that the tribunal have misdirect-
ed themselves as to applicable law, or if there is no evidence to support a particular finding of fact, or if the decision is perverse in the sense explained by May LJ in *County Council for Hereford and Worcester v Neale*. However, misunderstanding or misapplication of the facts by an employment tribunal is not a separate basis for allowing an appeal.

Piggott Brothers & Co Ltd v
Jackson and others
[1991] IRLR 309 CA

A decision of an employment tribunal can be characterised as "perverse" only if it was not a permissible option. In order to hold that a decision was not a permissible option, the EAT will almost always have to identify a finding of fact which was unsupported by any evidence, or a clear self-misdirection in law by the employment tribunal. If it cannot do that, the EAT should re-examine with the greatest care its preliminary conclusion that the decision under appeal was not a permissible option and was therefore perverse.

Piggott Brothers & Co Ltd v
Jackson and others
[1991] IRLR 309 CA

The danger in the approach to perversity as explained by May LJ is that an appellate court can very easily persuade itself that, as it certainly would not have reached the same conclusion, the tribunal that did so was "certainly wrong".

East Berkshire Health Authority v
Matadeen
[1992] IRLR 336 EAT

Perversity is a free-standing basis in law on which the EAT can interfere with the decision of an employment tribunal. Even on factual findings of an employment tribunal, the EAT can interfere if the members are satisfied in the light of their own experience and of sound industrial practice that the decision is "not a permissible option"; or that it is "a conclusion which offends reason or is one to which no reasonable employment tribunal could come"; or "so very clearly wrong that it just cannot stand"; or that it was so outrageous in its defiance of logic or of accepted standards of industrial relations that no sensible person who had applied his mind to the question and with the necessary experience could have arrived at it.

Union of Construction and Allied Trades and Technicians v
Brain
[1981] IRLR 224 CA

Per Donaldson LJ: Whether someone acted reasonably is always a pure question of fact, so long as the tribunal deciding the issue correctly directs itself on matters which should and should not be taken into account. But where Parliament has directed a tribunal to have regard to equity, which means common fairness, the tribunal's duty is very plain. It has to look at the question in the round and without regard to a lawyer's technicalities. It has to look at it in an employment and industrial relations context. It should, therefore, be very rare for any decision of an employment tribunal under this section to give rise to any question of law, and where Parliament has given to the tribunals so wide a discretion, appellate courts should be very slow to find that the tribunal has erred in law.

Retarded Children's Aid   [1978] IRLR 128 CA
  Society Ltd v
Day

Per Lord Russell: The function of the appeal tribunal is to correct errors of law where they are established and identified. Care must be taken to avoid concluding that an experienced employment tribunal by not expressly mentioning some point or breach has overlooked it, and care must also be taken to avoid, in a case where the appeal tribunal members would on the basis of the merits and the oral evidence have taken a view different from that of the employment tribunal, searching around with a fine-tooth comb for some point of law.

Williams and others v   [1982] IRLR 83 EAT
Compair Maxam Ltd

In considering whether the decision of an employment tribunal is perverse in a legal sense, the correct approach is to consider whether an employment tribunal properly directed in law and properly appreciating what is currently regarded as fair industrial practice, could have reached the decision reached.

Eclipse Blinds Ltd v   [1992] IRLR 133 CS
Wright

The weight to be attached to any evidence is a matter for the tribunal determining the facts. It is not for an appellate tribunal to decide what weight should be attached to particular facts. Furthermore, what inference is to be drawn from facts is a matter to be determined by the tribunal deciding the facts, unless there are no facts from which any particular inference could properly be drawn.

Morgan v   [1991] IRLR 89 CA
Electrolux Ltd

Where the EAT finds that an employment tribunal has erred in law in finding that an employee was unfairly dismissed, the EAT must remit the case to the tribunal unless no employment tribunal, properly directing themselves, could have come to the conclusion that the employee was not unfairly dismissed.

Wilson v   [2000] IRLR 834 CA
Post Office

Only in an extreme case, one that is very clear, will it be possible for an appellate body properly to say that an employment tribunal would inevitably have reached a particular conclusion, when in the original case, albeit proceeding upon an incorrect basis, the employment tribunal had come to the contrary conclusion. An employment tribunal is not merely a fact-finding body, it is an industrial jury. That is not merely a phrase, but a concept which is to be taken seriously.

Hennessy v   [1986] IRLR 300 CA
Craigmyle and ACAS

The Court of Appeal is a second-tier appellate court and is concerned with whether the decision of the employment tribunal was right and not with whether the Employment Appeal Tribunal was right.

Bailey v   [1980] IRLR 287 CA
BP Oil Kent Refinery Ltd

In determining whether a dismissal is fair or unfair, each case must depend on its own facts. It is unwise for the Appeal Court or the EAT to set out guidelines, and wrong to make rules and establish presumptions for employment tribunals to follow or take into account when applying [s.98(4)].

Anandarajah v   [1984] IRLR 131 EAT
Lord Chancellor's Department

Reference to cases can never be a substitute for taking the explicit directions of the statute as the guiding principle. It should seldom be necessary (and may sometimes be unwise) for an employment tribunal to frame its decision by reference to any direction other than the express terms of the statute. Although the judgment in a particular case may sometimes be found to express in concise and helpful language some concept which is regularly found in this field of inquiry, so that it becomes of great illustrative value, employment tribunals are not required, and should not be invited, to subject the authorities to the same analysis as a court of law searching in a plethora of precedent for binding or persuasive authority. The objective of Parliament when it first framed the right not to be unfairly dismissed and set up a system of employment tribunals (with a majority of lay members) to administer it, was to banish legalism and in particular to ensure that, wherever possible, parties conducting their own case would be able to face the tribunal with the same ease and confidence as those professionally represented. A preoccupation with guideline authority puts that objective in jeopardy.

Meek v   [1987] IRLR 250 CA
City of Birmingham District Council

Although the decision of an employment tribunal is not required to be an elaborate formalistic product of refined legal draftsmanship, it must contain an outline of the story which has given rise to the complaint and a summary of the factual conclusions and a statement of the reasons which have led the tribunal to reach the conclusions which it does on those basic facts. The parties are entitled to be told why they have won or lost. There should be sufficient account of the facts and of the reasoning to enable an appellate court to see whether any question of law arises.

Kent County Council v   [1985] IRLR 18 CA
Gilham and others

Where the facts are bitterly contested, it is necessary for the employment tribunal to make specific findings on contested issues to show the basis of their decision. But where the facts are not in dispute, it does not assist the parties to overburden the written decision with a lengthy recital of agreed facts.

Earl v   [1972] IRLR 115 NIRC
Slater & Wheeler (Airlyne) Ltd

In determining a question in accordance with "equity", the employment tribunal should adopt a broad approach of common sense and common fairness, eschewing all legal or other technicality. In other words, they should constitute themselves an industrial "special jury".

The relevant circumstances

W Devis & Sons Ltd v   **[1977] IRLR 314 HL**
Atkins
In determining whether a dismissal is fair an employment tribunal cannot have regard to matters of which the employer was unaware at the time of dismissal and which, therefore, could not have formed part of his reason for dismissing the employee.

Vokes Ltd v   **[1973] IRLR 363 NIRC**
Bear
The "circumstances" which an employment tribunal should take into account in determining whether a dismissal is fair or unfair embrace all relevant matters that should weigh with a good employer when deciding at a given moment in time whether or not to dismiss. The "circumstances" are not limited to those directly relating to or surrounding the employer's grounds for dismissal.

W Devis & Sons Ltd v   **[1977] IRLR 314 HL**
Atkins
If the reasons for dismissal shown by the employer appear to have been sufficient, it cannot be said that the employer acted reasonably in treating it as such if he only did so in consequence of ignoring matters which he ought reasonably to have known and which would have shown that the reason was insufficient.

West Midlands Co-operative   **[1986] IRLR 112 HL**
    Society Ltd v
Tipton
There is nothing in the language of the statute to exclude from determination of the question of reasonableness evidence which was available for consideration by the employer in the course of an appeal held pursuant to a disciplinary procedure.

Docherty v   **[2013] IRLR 874 CS**
SW Global Resourcing Ltd
If an employer takes action against an employee which amounts to a dismissal, and does so without having considered the legal consequences, or does so on a mistaken view of what those consequences would be, the dismissal may nonetheless be held to be fair; but the fact that the employer took the action in such circumstances will not *ipso facto* make the dismissal fair.

Whitbread & Co plc v   **[1988] IRLR 501 EAT**
Mills
Whether a dismissal is fair must be decided on the basis of the position after the internal appeal procedure has been completed. Matters which come to light during the appeal process may be taken into account in considering the overall "equity and substantial merits of the case".

Inner London Education Authority v   **[1981] IRLR 394 CA**
Lloyd
An employment tribunal is entitled to have regard to the conduct of an employer after the decision to dismiss has been taken but before the employee has actually been dismissed.

Alboni v   **[1998] IRLR 131 CA**
Ind Coope Retail Ltd
An employment tribunal is not only entitled but is bound to have regard to events between notice of dismissal and the date that dismissal took effect in determining whether the employers acted reasonably.

Morgan v   **[1991] IRLR 89 CA**
Electrolux Ltd
An employment tribunal may not substitute their own evaluation of a witness for that of the employer. The decision of an employment tribunal that an employer could not reasonably have accepted a witness as truthful must be based on logical and substantial grounds.

Linfood Cash & Carry Ltd v   **[1989] IRLR 235 EAT**
Thomson and another
Where the credibility of a witness before a tribunal is at issue, the relevant question is whether the employers, acting reasonably and fairly in the circumstances, could properly accept the facts and opinions which they did. The evidence is that given during the disciplinary procedures and not that given before the employment tribunal.

Burden of proof

Smith v   **[1987] IRLR 326 HL**
City of Glasgow District Council
A reason cannot reasonably be treated as a sufficient reason for dismissal where it has not been established as true or that there were reasonable grounds upon which the employer could have concluded that it was true. It is therefore an error of law for an employment tribunal to accept as a reasonably sufficient reason for dismissal a reason which, at least in respect of an important part, was neither established in fact nor believed to be true on reasonable grounds.

Post Office Counters Ltd v   **[1989] IRLR 513 EAT**
Heavey
Since 1 October 1980 when [s.98(4)] was amended, the correct direction for employment tribunals to give themselves is to use the actual wording of the statute and to remind themselves that there is now no burden of proof. It is no longer for the employer to "show" or for the tribunal to

be "satisfied" that the employer acted reasonably in dismissing the employee. When considering those reported cases containing guidelines on the application of [s.98(4)], such as *Weddel & Co Ltd v Tepper* and *British Home Stores Ltd v Burchell*, tribunals should bear in mind that it is the old law which is being examined and not the new "neutral" [s.98(4)].

Savoia v   **[1982] IRLR 166 CA**
Chiltern Herb Farms Ltd
A dismissal which is a constructive dismissal can nevertheless be fair. The words of [s.98] put the onus upon the employer to show what was the reason for dismissal. This goes beyond the simple circumstances of the employer's conduct which amounted to dismissal and involves looking into the conduct of the employee and all the surrounding circumstances. Although it will be more difficult for an employer to say that a constructive dismissal was fair, there may well be circumstances where it is possible to do so.

Cawley v   **[1985] IRLR 89 EAT**
South Wales Electricity Board
Considerations of fairness on the one hand and the considerations affecting constructive dismissal on the other are two sides of the same coin. There are not two different sets of rules for reasonableness – for the purposes of constructive dismissal and for the purposes of fairness of the dismissal. Thus the same conduct by the employer cannot be unreasonable from the standpoint of whether or not it amounts to a repudiation of the contract of employment and at the same time be reasonable conduct when looked at from the standpoint of fairness, or vice versa.

R F Hill Ltd v   **[1981] IRLR 258 EAT**
Mooney
Where a case has been conducted throughout on the basis that the only relevant question was whether there had been constructive dismissal and the employers do not submit to the employment tribunal that it had to go on to consider whether the reasonableness requirements of [s.98] had been met, the employment tribunal is under no duty to consider the matter.

Hooper v   **[1988] IRLR 517 CA**
British Railways Board
That a dismissal is in breach of contract is a factor relevant to the consideration of fairness, to be considered by the employment tribunal, but it is not decisive. An employer may well act fairly in dismissing an employee in breach of the terms of the contract of employment.

London Borough of Redbridge v   **[1978] IRLR 69 EAT**
Fishman
Many dismissals are unfair although the employer is contractually entitled to dismiss the employee. Contrariwise, some dismissals are not unfair although the employer was not contractually entitled to dismiss the employee. Although

the contractual rights and duties are not irrelevant to the statutory test of fairness, they are not of the first importance.

Treganowan v   **[1975] IRLR 247 HC**
Robert Knee & Co Ltd
Whether an employee's dismissal was without notice or whether the notice was long enough is not relevant for the purpose of determining whether the dismissal was fair or unfair. Unfair dismissal must be distinguished from the common law concept of wrongful dismissal. Therefore, that a dismissal was without notice, or without due notice, cannot of itself render a dismissal unfair.

BSC Sports & Social Club v   **[1987] IRLR 391 EAT**
Morgan
It is an error of law to hold that it was reasonable to terminate employment but that the fact of summary dismissal made the dismissal unfair. That the dismissal was summary can only be considered in the context of whether or not it was reasonable to dismiss at all. Once a decision to dismiss has been reached on reasonable grounds, it is for the employer to decide whether or not to dismiss with notice or summarily.

McCall v   **[1979] IRLR 218 EAT**
Castleton Crafts
Summary dismissal is not justified only where serious loss to the employer's business can be shown to result from the misconduct in question. It would place an unreasonable burden upon employers if they were expected to establish prejudice or loss to their enterprise before they could dismiss an employee who was behaving in an unacceptable fashion.

Size and administrative resources of undertaking

Henderson v   **[1982] IRLR 494 EAT**
Granville Tours Ltd
Though there is now a statutory requirement that an employment tribunal have regard to the size and administrative resources of the undertaking, the smallness of the undertaking does not afford any excuse or indeed explanation for a failure by the employer to carry out a proper investigation.

Bevan Harris Ltd t/a the Clyde   **[1981] IRLR 520 EAT**
   Leather Co v
Gair
Any obligation that there may be on an employer in a particular case to attempt to find alternative employment for an employee who has become incapable of performing the job that he was employed to do must be influenced to a very great extent by the size and administrative resources of the undertaking.

Meikle v [1983] IRLR 351 EAT
McPhail (Charleston Arms)
The guidelines on redundancy dismissals set out in *Williams v Compair Maxam* should be applied with caution to circumstances where the size and administrative resources of the employer are minimal.

Fair procedure

Warnings

Polkey v [1987] IRLR 503 HL
A E Dayton Services Ltd
Dismissal without a warning may not be unfair if the employer could reasonably have concluded that a warning would be utterly useless.

A J Dunning & Sons [1973] IRLR 206 NIRC
(Shop Fitters) v
Jacomb
The question of whether or not an employee should have been given a warning is not a matter of procedure; it is a matter of substance.

Grant v [1980] IRLR 461 EAT
Ampex Great Britain Ltd
A decision as to whether a warning has to be given is largely a question of fact for the employment tribunal on the circumstances of the particular case. Sometimes the degree of inadequacy is such that a warning is really not necessary although in the majority of cases, if the complaint of capability which is made is one that could or might lead to an improvement, then it is right that a warning should be given.

Wincanton Group plc v [2013] IRLR 178 EAT
Stone
Where a tribunal is considering the relevance of an earlier warning, it should take into account whether the validity of the warning is being challenged by an internal appeal and also the factual circumstances giving rise to the warning and its similarity to the conduct giving rise to the dismissal.

Wincanton Group plc v [2013] IRLR 178 EAT
Stone
A final written warning always implies, subject only to the individual terms of a contract, that any misconduct of whatever nature will often and usually be met with dismissal, and it is likely to be by way of exception that that will not occur.

Davies v [2013] IRLR 374 CA
Sandwell Metropolitan Borough Council
Where an employee has been dismissed following a final written warning, it is not the function of the employment tribunal to re-open the final warning and rule on an issue raised by the claimant as to whether the final warning should, or should not, have been issued and whether it was a legally valid warning or a "nullity". The function of the tribunal is

to apply the objective statutory test of reasonableness to determine whether the final warning was a circumstance that a reasonable employer could reasonably take into account in the decision to dismiss the claimant for subsequent misconduct. However, it is relevant for the tribunal to consider whether the final warning was issued in good faith, whether there were prima facie grounds for following the final warning procedure and whether it was manifestly inappropriate to issue the warning.

McCall v   [1979] IRLR 218 EAT
Castleton Crafts

There is no special magic about a written warning. To an intelligent man a verbal warning should be just as effective. The only advantage in a written warning might be for evidential purposes later on.

Bevan Ashford v   [1995] IRLR 360 EAT
Malin

A written warning which is ambiguous as regards the commencement date should be construed strictly against the employers who drafted it and in favour of the employee who received it. Problems may be avoided by specifying in clear terms the time, day and date on which the warning is to commence and the time, day and date on which it is to expire.

Auguste Noel Ltd v   [1990] IRLR 326 EAT
Curtis

The existence of warnings, how many there have been, the substance of the complaint on each occasion, the dates and the periods between them are all matters which an employer is entitled to take into account when deciding to dismiss for a particular offence. The mere fact that the conduct was of a different kind on those occasions when the warnings were given does not render them irrelevant.

Diosynth Ltd v   [2006] IRLR 284 CS
Thomson

It would be unreasonable for an employer to rely on an expired warning, even as part of the factual circumstances underlying a decision whether or not to dismiss. An expired warning should be removed from the personnel file.

Airbus UK Ltd v   [2008] IRLR 309 CA
Webb

It may be reasonable to rely on misconduct that is the subject of an expired warning to justify dismissal if the subsequent misconduct itself justifies dismissal but not, by means of "totting up", if the subsequent misconduct does not itself justify dismissal. *Diosynth* can be distinguished on the basis that it dealt with an expired warning used to justify a dismissal *when the conduct on its own did not justify that dismissal*, whereas this case dealt with conduct *which itself justified dismissal* and the presence or otherwise of an expired warning was used in deciding whether or not to show leniency and not dismiss.

Inquiry and investigation

British Home Stores Ltd v   [1978] IRLR 379 EAT
Burchell

In a case where an employee is dismissed because the employer suspects or believes that he or she has committed an act of misconduct, in determining whether that dismissal is unfair an employment tribunal has to decide whether the employer who discharged the employee on the ground of the misconduct in question entertained a reasonable suspicion amounting to a belief in the guilt of the employee of that misconduct at that time. This involves three elements. First, there must be established by the employer the fact of that belief; that the employer did believe it. Second, it must be shown that the employer had in his mind reasonable grounds upon which to sustain that belief. And third, the employer at the stage at which he formed that belief on those grounds, must have carried out as much investigation into the matter as was reasonable in all the circumstances of the case.

W Weddel & Co Ltd v   [1980] IRLR 96 CA
Tepper

Observed: In a case of dismissal on grounds of alleged dishonesty, the preferred legal test is that stated in *British Homes Stores Ltd v Burchell.*

Per Stephenson LJ: Employers suspecting an employee of misconduct justifying dismissal cannot justify their dismissal simply by stating an honest belief in his guilt. There must be reasonable grounds, and they must act reasonably in all the circumstances, having regard to equity and the substantial merits of the case. They do not have regard to equity in particular if they do not give him a fair opportunity of explaining before dismissing him. And they do not have regard to equity or the substantial merits of the case if they jump to conclusions which it would have been reasonable to postpone in all the circumstances until they had, per *Burchell,* "carried out as much investigation into the matter as was reasonable in all the circumstances of the case". That means that they must act reasonably in all the circumstances, and must make reasonable inquiries appropriate to the circumstances. If they form their belief hastily and act hastily upon it, without making the appropriate inquiries or giving the employee a fair opportunity to explain himself, their belief is not based on reasonable grounds and they are not acting reasonably.

Post Office v   [2000] IRLR 827 CA
Foley
HSBC Bank plc (formerly Midland Bank plc) v
Madden

Where dismissal is for a reason relating to the conduct of the employee, the tripartite approach to (a) the reason for, and (b) the reasonableness or unreasonableness of, the dismissal as expounded by Arnold J in *British Home Stores Ltd v*

Burchell, and as approved and applied by the Court of Appeal in *W Weddel & Co Ltd v Tepper*, remains binding authority. Any departure from that approach indicated in *Midland Bank Ltd v Madden* (for example, by suggesting that reasonable grounds for belief in the employee's misconduct and the carrying out of a reasonable investigation into the matter relate to establishing the reason for dismissal rather than to the reasonableness of the dismissal) was inconsistent with binding authority.

Perkin v   [2005] IRLR 934 CA
St George's Healthcare NHS Trust
There is no reason why the *Burchell* principles should be limited to conduct cases.

Sainsbury's Supermarkets Ltd v   [2003] IRLR 23 CA
Hitt
The range of reasonable responses test applies as much to the question of whether an investigation into suspected misconduct was reasonable in all the circumstances as it does to other procedural and substantive aspects of the decision to dismiss a person from his employment for a conduct reason.

Scottish Daily Record & Sunday   [1996] IRLR 665 CS
   Mail (1986) Ltd v
Laird
Where there is no real dispute on the facts, it is unlikely to be necessary for a tribunal to apply the *Burchell* test. The matter may be so obvious, and the misconduct may be of a kind which so clearly goes to the root of the relationship between the employer and employee, that application of the threefold test would be unduly elaborate.

Boys and Girls Welfare Society v   [1996] IRLR 129 EAT
McDonald
Burchell is not to be understood as saying that an employer who fails one or more of the three tests is, without more, guilty of unfair dismissal. The employment tribunal must ask itself whether dismissal fell within the range of reasonable responses.

Scottish Midland Co-operative   [1991] IRLR 261 CS
   Society Ltd v
Cullion
In applying the test laid down in *British Home Stores Ltd v Burchell*, the question to be determined is not whether, by an objective standard, the employers' belief that the employee was guilty of the misconduct in question was well-founded, but whether the employers believed that the employee was guilty and were entitled so to believe, having regard to the investigation carried out. It does not matter that the tribunal members themselves are not convinced of the employee's guilt.

British Gas plc v   [1991] IRLR 305 CA
McCarrick
Where an employee is charged with an offence, it is for the employers to reach the decision of fact whether or not they are satisfied that the employee was guilty. The decision for the employment tribunal is whether on the facts which were known or ought to have been known to the employers, they genuinely believed on reasonable grounds that the employee was guilty. It is an error of law for the tribunal to seek to reopen the factual issues on the basis of which the employers reached their conclusion.

Dick and another v   [1993] IRLR 581 CS
Glasgow University
An employment tribunal is not entitled to conclude that an employer had not carried out a reasonable investigation because, during the disciplinary procedure, the employer failed to have regard to material, when that material was never placed before him and emerged for the first time as evidence during the tribunal hearing. In determining whether the employer had carried out a reasonable investigation, the employment tribunal should consider the nature of the material which was before the employer when the decision to dismiss was taken.

ILEA v   [1988] IRLR 497 EAT
Gravett
In determining whether in all the circumstances the employer could reasonably believe that the employee was guilty of misconduct, the situations which arise can vary from the one extreme where the employee was virtually caught in the act to the other extreme where the issue is one of pure inference. As the scale moves towards the latter end, so the amount of inquiry and investigation which may be required, including questioning of the employee, is likely to increase. At some stage, the employer will need to face the employee with the information which he has. That may be during an investigation prior to a decision that there is sufficient evidence upon which to form a view or it may be at the initial disciplinary hearing. In some cases it may be that after hearing the employee's version further investigation ought fairly to be made.

A v   [2003] IRLR 405 EAT
B
In determining whether an employer carried out such investigation as was reasonable in all the circumstances, the relevant circumstances include the gravity of the charges and their potential effect upon the employee. Serious allegations of criminal misbehaviour, where disputed, must always be the subject of the most careful and conscientious investigation and the investigator carrying out the inquiries should focus no less on any potential evidence that may exculpate or at least point towards the innocence of the employee as on the evidence directed towards proving the charges.

Z v   [2014] IRLR 244 EAT
A
A bare accusation, even of something so serious as the sexual abuse of a child by a school caretaker outside work, cannot amount by itself to a substantial reason justifying a dismissal. Though an employer's decision to dismiss where there has

been an allegation (but no conviction) of child abuse may well, and indeed generally, be fair it is not inevitably so.

Salford Royal NHS Foundation   **[2010] IRLR 721 CA**
   Trust v
Roldan

It is particularly important that employers take seriously their responsibilities to conduct a fair investigation where the employee's reputation or ability to work in his or her chosen field of employment is potentially apposite.

A v   **[2003] IRLR 405 EAT**
B

Whether an employer has carried out such investigations as is reasonable in all the circumstances necessarily involves a consideration of any delays. In certain circumstances, a delay in the conduct of the investigation might of itself render an otherwise fair dismissal unfair. Where the consequence of the delay is that the employee is or might be prejudiced, for example because it has led to a failure to take statements which might otherwise have been taken, or because of the effect of delay on fading memories, this will provide additional and independent concerns about the investigative process which will support a challenge to the fairness of that process.

Ulsterbus Ltd v   **[1989] IRLR 251 NICA**
Henderson

It is not incumbent on a reasonable employer to carry out a quasi-judicial investigation into an allegation of misconduct, with a confrontation of witnesses and cross-examination of witnesses. While some employers might consider that necessary or desirable, an employer who fails to do so cannot be said to have acted unreasonably.

Santamera v   **[2003] IRLR 273 EAT**
Express Cargo Forwarding

Fairness does not require a forensic or quasi-judicial investigation for which the employer is unlikely in any event to be qualified, and for which it may lack the means. However, *Ulsterbus Ltd v Henderson* could not be read as laying down the proposition that cross-examination can never be required in any investigation carried out by a reasonable employer. There may be cases in which it will be impossible for an employer to act fairly and reasonably unless cross-examination of a particular witness is permitted. The issue under s.98(4) is always reasonableness and fairness. In each case, the question is whether or not the employer fulfils the test laid down in *British Home Stores Ltd v Burchell* and it will be for the tribunal to decide whether the employer acted reasonably and whether or nor the process was fair.

Asda Stores Ltd v   **[2002] IRLR 245 EAT**
Thompson

In investigating complaints where serious offences are allegedly involved, it is an entirely proper procedure for an employer to give a promise of confidentiality in respect of statements made by other employees. Nothing should be disclosed which in any way identifies the makers of any of the statements unless they specifically agree to be identified. If this approach means that some of the statements have to be excluded in their entirety because it is not possible to conceal the identity of the makers that is what will have to occur and the question of the fairness of the dismissal will have to be judged in due course by the employment tribunal on that basis. Knowledge of the identity of those making the allegations is not necessary for a fair hearing.

A v   **[2010] IRLR 844 EAT**
B

Where an employer receives information from a responsible public authority, under an official disclosure regime, that an employee poses a risk to children, it must, in principle and subject to certain safeguards, be entitled to treat that information as reliable. The employer cannot be expected to carry out its own independent investigation in order to test the reliability of the information provided. Nevertheless, an employer will not be acting reasonably if it takes an uncritical view of the information disclosed. The employer should insist on a sufficient degree of formality and specificity about the disclosure before contemplating taking any action against the employee on the basis of it.

Linfood Cash & Carry Ltd v   **[1989] IRLR 235 EAT**
Thomson and another

Observed: Where allegations concerning an employee's conduct are made by an informant, a careful balance must be maintained between the desirability to protect informants who are genuinely in fear and providing a fair hearing of issues for employees who are accused of misconduct. Employers may find the following guidance to be of assistance:

1. The information given by the informant should be reduced into writing. Initially these statements should be taken without regard to the fact that it may subsequently be necessary to omit certain parts of the statements before submission to others in order to preserve anonymity.

2. The following are important in taking statements: (a) Date, time and place of each or any observation or incident. (b) The opportunity and ability to observe clearly and with accuracy. (c) The circumstantial evidence, such as knowledge of a system or arrangement or the reason for the presence of the informer and why certain small details are memorable. (d) Whether the informant has suffered at the hands of the accused or has any other reason to fabricate.

3. Further investigation can then take place either to confirm or undermine the information given. Corroboration is clearly desirable.

4. Tactful inquiries may be suitable and advisable into the character and background of the informant or any other information which may tend to add or detract from the value of the information.

5. If the informant is not prepared to attend a disciplinary hearing and the employer is satisfied that the fear is genuine,

a decision will need to be made whether to continue with the disciplinary process.

6. If it is to continue, it is desirable that at each stage the member of management responsible for the hearing should himself interview the informant and satisfy himself that weight is to be given to the information.

7. The written statement of the informant, if necessary with omissions to avoid identification, should be made available to the employee and his representatives

8. If the employee or his representative raises any particular and relevant issue which should be put to the informant, it may be desirable to adjourn for the chairman to make further inquiries of the informant.

9. It is particularly important that full and careful notes should be taken.

10. If evidence from an investigating officer is to be taken at a hearing, where possible it should be prepared in a written form.

Ramsay v [2004] IRLR 754 EAT
Walkers Snack Foods Ltd

Failure to follow the guidelines set out in *Linfood Cash & Carry Ltd v Thomson* does not of itself render a dismissal unfair. In the circumstances of the present case, the employers had not acted unfairly in dismissing on the basis of witness statements from fellow employees who, for fear of reprisals, insisted that they should not be identified, even though the witness statements did not contain the detail suggested in *Linfood* and the managers involved in the disciplinary process did not personally interview the informants so as to be able to satisfy themselves as to the weight to be given to the information. This case raised two problems which were not apparent in *Linfood*: (1) the unwillingness of informants to sign a statement unless it had been sufficiently edited so as to remove any risk of identification; and (2) their unwillingness to be exposed to further questioning by other managers within the investigatory and/or disciplinary process for risk of their identities being revealed with the resulting reprisals that they feared. Within the confines of a factory in a close knit community, where retribution and reprisal were a real risk that the employers had to deal with, these were real problems which had to be balanced against issues of fairness as far as the claimants were concerned. In assessing the fairness of the employers' approach, it was therefore necessary to look at the reasons they gave for granting anonymity in the first place, the terms of that anonymity and whether it should extend to being interviewed by other managers, and the subsequent preparation of statements.

Tesco Group of Companies [1977] IRLR 63 EAT
(Holdings) Ltd v
Hill

Where employers are faced with the situation of an employee under a suspicion of dishonesty, they have a duty, as a matter of normal practice, to give the employee an opportunity for an explanation at a time when it cannot be suggested that he or she is not completely himself or herself.

Read v [1985] IRLR 93 EAT
Phoenix Preservation Ltd

The presence of police at a disciplinary inquiry without the employee's foreknowledge and consent is wholly improper.

Morley's of Brixton Ltd v [1982] IRLR 270 EAT
Minott

Judges' Rules excluding involuntary confessions have no application to an unfair dismissal case, which is concerned not with establishing the guilt of the person who made the confession but the state of mind of the person who heard the confession. Where the only relevant question is did the employer on reasonable grounds believe in the employee's guilt, it is wholly artificial to exclude from consideration the prime factor which led the employer to his view. Common sense suggests that although the employer must act fairly, his dealings with disciplinary matters are not bound by the strict technicalities of the criminal law.

Monie v [1980] IRLR 464 CA
Coral Racing Ltd

If an employer believes that a theft is the work of one of two employees or possibly both, but cannot distinguish between them, he can act reasonably if he dismisses both employees. Where there is a reasonable suspicion that one of two or possibly both employees must have acted dishonestly, it is not necessary for the employer to believe that either of them acted dishonestly.

Parr v [1990] IRLR 39 EAT
Whitbread plc

Where a group of employees could have committed a particular offence, provided that the employer's beliefs are based on solid and sensible grounds at the date of dismissal, the employer is entitled to dismiss each member of the group if: (1) an act was committed which would justify dismissal if committed by an individual; (2) there was a sufficiently thorough investigation by the employer, with appropriate procedures; (3) as a result of that investigation the employer reasonably believed that more than one person could have committed the act; (4) the employer acted reasonably in identifying the group of employees who could have committed the act and each member of the group was individually capable of doing so; (5) as between the members of the group, the employer could not reasonably identify the individual perpetrator.

Frames Snooker Centre v [1992] IRLR 472 EAT
Boyce

Where any one of a group of employees could have committed a particular offence, the fact that one or more of them was not dismissed does not render dismissal of the remainder unfair, provided that the employer is able to show solid and sensible grounds (which do not have to be related to the relevant offence) for differentiating between members of the group. There is no "all or none" principle in the dismissal of a group in this situation.

Whitbread & Co plc v   **[1988] IRLR 43 EAT**
Thomas and others

The principle in *Monie v Coral Racing Ltd* relating to "blanket dismissals" is capable of being applied to a case of capability or conduct not involving dishonesty, although such a case will be exceptional.

Henderson v   **[1982] IRLR 494 EAT**
Granville Tours Ltd

It is an error of law for an employment tribunal to hold that had an employer carried out further investigation into allegations against an employee that investigation would have supported the complaint and the result would have been the same. Such an approach is appropriate only in cases involving defects in procedure. In considering whether there has been an adequate investigation, the employment tribunal is concerned with the employer's state of mind at the moment of dismissal and the sufficiency of information to justify that state of mind. That is not simply a procedural question; it goes to the heart of the fairness of the dismissal and to whether or not the test of fairness has been fulfilled. If a man is dismissed for dishonesty on suspicion, it is no answer for an employer to say that he was convicted of the offence months later on properly prepared evidence.

Criminal proceedings

Harris and Shepherd v   **[1982] IRLR 509 CA**
Courage (Eastern) Ltd

Although it is essential that an employee should be afforded an opportunity to give an explanation and should be made to realise that the employer is contemplating dismissal, there is no hard and fast rule that once an employee has been charged with a criminal offence connected with work, an employer cannot dismiss if the employee is advised to say nothing until the trial in the criminal proceedings. If the employee chooses not to give a statement, the reasonable employer is entitled to consider whether the material he has is sufficiently indicative of guilt to justify dismissal without waiting.

Harris (Ipswich) Ltd v   **[1978] IRLR 382 EAT**
Harrison

Where an employee has been arrested and charged with a criminal offence alleged to have been committed in the course of his employment, there is nothing in the law of England and Wales to prevent an employer, before dismissing, from discussing the matter with the employee or his representative. On the contrary, it is proper to do so. What needs to be discussed is not so much the alleged offence as the action which the employer is proposing to take.

Lovie Ltd v   **[1999] IRLR 164 EAT**
Anderson

Whether an employer should carry out its own investigation after being informed that criminal charges arising in connection with his employment are being brought against an employee is a question of circumstances. It is going too far to say that the employer is precluded from carrying out any further investigation into the matter if it has already carried out some form of investigation. Equally, the employer must be careful not to trap the employee into making any sort of admission against his interests. In an extreme case when the first notice that the employer gets of the problem is the intimation that the police are bringing charges against the employee, it is incumbent upon the employer to embark upon some form of investigation involving, amongst other things, an interview with the employee to give him an opportunity to state his position. At the other end of the spectrum, the circumstances may be so blatant and sufficiently brought to the attention of the employer to warrant a reasonable belief as to guilt, that further investigation may not be necessary. Within that spectrum there are many situations which will usually require further consideration of the position by the employer, including interview after charges are brought, before dismissal can reasonably be effected.

Scottish Special Housing   **[1979] IRLR 264 EAT**
  Association v
Cooke and others

The mere fact that an employee has been charged with theft by the police does not amount to reasonable grounds for an employer, without any further information available and without undertaking any investigation, to dismiss. An employer must have sufficient information to entitle him reasonably to assume that there was guilt on the part of the employee. There are many cases where persons are initially charged with an offence and the matter proceeds no further. There are cases were persons are eventually acquitted and where more than one person is involved, there is always the possibility that not all will be found guilty. Notwithstanding that investigation into the matter may be limited by the prospect of future criminal proceedings, some inquiry at least may disclose the nature of the information upon which the police were proceeding.

Carr v   **[1976] IRLR 220 CS**
Alexander Russell Ltd

Where an employee was caught red-handed by the police with the employer's property, was charged with theft and made no protestations of innocence to the employer, the employer did not act unreasonably in dismissing the employee rather than awaiting the outcome of the criminal proceedings.

Scottish Special Housing   **[1979] IRLR 265 EAT**
  Association v
Linnen

Where an employee reasonably appears to have been caught red-handed, dismissal without further investigation may be appropriate.

P v   **[1992] IRLR 362 CA**
Nottinghamshire County Council

When an employee has pleaded guilty to a criminal offence or has been found guilty by the decision of a court or the verdict of a jury, it is reasonable for an employer to believe that the offence has been committed by the employee.

Securicor Guarding Ltd v   [1994] IRLR 633 EAT
P
The mere fact that an employee in a sensitive position has been charged with a criminal offence unconnected with work will not justify the employer in dismissing him, rather than suspending him or moving him away from the sensitive position until the truth of the matter is determined.

Rhondda Cynon Taf County   [2008] IRLR 868 EAT
  Borough Council v
Close
It may be reasonable for employers to rely on witness statements obtained by the police, particularly if those statements were made closer to the relevant time, the employers get confirmation from the witnesses that they stand by those statements and they allow cross-examination of those witnesses.

Natural justice and fair hearings

Slater v   [1989] IRLR 16 CA
Leicestershire Health Authority
The rules of natural justice do not form an independent ground upon which a decision to dismiss may be attacked, although a breach will clearly be an important matter when an employment tribunal considers the question raised in [s.98(4)].

McLaren v   [1988] IRLR 215 CA
National Coal Board
Standards of fairness are immutable. Acceptable reasons for dismissing may change in a varying industrial situation, but the standards of fairness never change. Thus, no amount of heat in industrial conflict can justify failing to give an employee an opportunity of offering an explanation, though it may create a situation in which conduct which would not normally justify dismissal becomes conduct which does justify dismissal.

Khanum v   [1978] IRLR 215 EAT
Mid-Glamorgan Area
  Health Authority
There are only three basic requirements of natural justice which have to be complied with during the proceedings of a domestic disciplinary inquiry; firstly, that the person should know the nature of the accusation against him; secondly, that he should be given an opportunity to state his case; and thirdly, that the tribunal should act in good faith.

R v   [2001] IRLR 442 CA
Chief Constable of Merseyside Police
The requirements of judicial impartiality which would be understood to apply to any judge should not be assumed inexorably to apply to a Chief Constable conducting disciplinary proceedings in accordance with his operational responsibilities. A Chief Constable who is simultaneously involved in two sets of proceedings, where in one he is named as a defendant and in the other he is adjudicating on the conduct of the officer who made the allegation, is not in the same position as a judge conducting a trial involving an individual with whom he is personally involved in separate litigation. Where there is no disqualifying personal interest, a Chief Constable is vested with a statutory responsibility to hear disciplinary proceedings against an officer. It could not be accepted, therefore, that in every case where a police officer is proceeding against the Chief Constable in the employment tribunal, the Chief Constable must disqualify himself, on grounds that he would be sitting as a judge in his own cause, from adjudicating in any disciplinary proceedings where the outcome would have any bearing on the proceedings before the tribunal.

Hussain v   [1999] IRLR 420 CA
Elonex plc
There is no universal requirement of natural justice or general principle of law that in all cases an employee must be shown copies of witness statements obtained by an employer about the employee's conduct. It is a matter of what is fair and reasonable in each case. What emerges from the authorities is not that there is a failure of natural justice where witness statements are obtained but not disclosed, but that there is a failure of natural justice if the essence of the case on the employee's conduct is contained in statements which have not been disclosed to him, and where he has not otherwise been informed of the nature of the case against him.

Panama v   [2003] IRLR 278 CA
London Borough of Hackney
Fairness demands that serious allegations of dishonesty must be put with sufficient formality and at an early enough stage to provide a full opportunity for answer.

Slater v   [1989] IRLR 16 CA
Leicestershire Health
  Authority
Although it is a general principle that a person who holds an inquiry must be seen to be impartial, merely because the person conducting a disciplinary hearing had carried out a preliminary investigation did not mean that he was unable to conduct a fair inquiry.

Slater v   [1989] IRLR 16 CA
Leicestershire Health
  Authority
As a general rule, if a person has been a witness, he should not hold the inquiry. However, there are exceptions to that general rule.

Gray Dunn & Co Ltd v   [1980] IRLR 23 EAT
Edwards
The concept of natural justice does not include the automatic right to be present throughout a disciplinary hearing, provided the interests of the employee are safeguarded by his duly accredited representatives.

R (Puri) v　　　　　　　　　**[2011] IRLR 582 QBD**
Bradford Teaching Hospital NHS Trust
In ordinary disciplinary proceedings, where all that could be at stake is the loss of a specific job, Article 6 ECHR is not engaged, but it is engaged if the effect of the proceedings could be to deprive an employee of the right to practise his or her profession, and that issue should be decided by asking whether the outcome will have a substantial influence or effect on the determination of that right.

Opportunity to appeal

West Midlands Co-operative　　　**[1986] IRLR 112 HL**
　Society Ltd v
Tipton
A dismissal is unfair if the employer unreasonably treats his reason as a sufficient reason to dismiss the employee, either when he makes his original decision to dismiss or when he maintains that decision at the conclusion of an internal appeal. A dismissal may also be held to be unfair when the employer has refused to entertain an appeal to which the employee was contractually entitled and thereby denied to him the opportunity of showing that, in all the circumstances, the employer's reason for dismissing him could not reasonably be treated as sufficient.

Rowe v　　　　　　　　　　**[1982] IRLR 177 EAT**
Radio Rentals Ltd
It is very important that internal appeals procedures run by commercial companies (which usually involve a consideration of the decision to dismiss by one person in line management by his superior) should not be cramped by legal requirements imposing impossible burdens on companies in the conduct of their personnel affairs. In general, it is inevitable that those involved in the original decision to dismiss must be in daily contact with their superiors who will be responsible for deciding the appeal. Therefore, the appearance of total disconnection between the two cannot be achieved. Moreover, at the appeal hearing, the initial dismisser is very often required to give information as to the facts to the person hearing the appeal. Rules about total separation of functions and lack of contact between those hearing the appeal and those involved in the original decision, therefore, cannot be applied in the majority of cases. The correct approach was indicated by Lord Denning in *Ward v Bradford Corporation* (1971) LGR 27 where he said, "We must not force these disciplinary bodies to become entrammelled in the nets of legal procedure. So long as they act fairly and justly, their decision should be supported."

Byrne v　　　　　　　　　　**[1992] IRLR 505 EAT**
BOC Ltd
A person may be disqualified from hearing an appeal not only where he was personally involved in the events that led

to the dismissal or in the decision to dismiss, but also through involvement in the investigation. A person who investigates an alleged disciplinary breach may become so involved in that matter that it realistically becomes his cause so as to disentitle him from being a person who can conduct a fair appeal from a decision at the disciplinary hearing in which he played no part.

Tower Hamlets Health Authority v　　**[1989] IRLR 394 CA**
Anthony
Where a warning is a prerequisite to dismissal under the disciplinary procedure, in considering whether or not to dismiss, a reasonable employer should take into account the fact that there has been a formal warning but should bear in mind that the warning is subject to an appeal which has yet to be determined. Similarly, the fact of the warning and that it is still subject to an undetermined appeal are circumstances which an employment tribunal, as an industrial jury, should take into account in deciding whether or not the employer acted reasonably in dismissing the employee. Where, for example, the appeal against the warning was due to be determined the day after the dismissal, the tribunal may well take the view that the employer acted unreasonably in not awaiting the outcome of the appeal. Where the timescale is in weeks or months, the fact of the warning, provided it was given on adequate evidence and not for any oblique or improper motive, and the fact that it is still subject to appeal remain throughout circumstances which should be taken into account in determining the fairness of the dismissal.

Chrystie v　　　　　　　　　**[1976] IRLR 336 EAT**
Rolls-Royce (1971) Ltd
An employee who fails to appeal against dismissal under the employer's disciplinary procedure cannot be regarded as having acquiesced in his dismissal.

Failure to follow a fair procedure

Polkey v　　　　　　　　　　**[1987] IRLR 503 HL**
A E Dayton Services Ltd
An employer having prima facie grounds to dismiss will in the great majority of cases not act reasonably in treating the reason as a sufficient reason for dismissal unless and until he has taken the procedural steps which are necessary in the circumstances of the case to justify that course of action.

Whitbread & Co plc v　　　　　**[2001] IRLR 275 CA**
Hall
Where misconduct is admitted by the employee, the requirement of reasonableness in s.98(4) of the Employment Rights Act 1996 relates not only to the outcome in terms of the penalty imposed by the employer but also to the process at which the employer arrived at that decision. Accordingly, the

employment tribunal should not simply ask whether dismissal fell within the "band of reasonable responses" but should also apply that test to the procedure used in reaching the decision to dismiss.

Stoker v   **[1992] IRLR 75 CA**
Lancashire County Council
A reasonable employer can be expected to comply with the full requirements of the procedure in its own disciplinary code.

West London Mental Health   **[2014] IRLR 227 SC**
   NHS Trust v
Chhabra
There is an implied contractual right to a fair disciplinary process.

Taylor v   **[2006] IRLR 613 CA**
OCS Group Ltd
If an early stage of a disciplinary process is defective and unfair in some way then it does not matter whether or not an internal appeal is technically a rehearing or a review, only whether the disciplinary process as a whole is fair. After identifying a defect a tribunal will want to examine any subsequent proceeding with particular care. Their purpose in so doing will be to determine whether, due to the fairness or unfairness of the procedures adopted, the thoroughness or lack of it of the process and the open-mindedness (or not) of the decision-maker, the overall process was fair, notwithstanding any deficiencies at an early stage.

Crawford v   **[2012] IRLR 402 CA**
Suffolk Mental Health Partnership NHS Trust
It is for the employer to ensure that a fair procedure is adopted. It cannot be enough for an employer to say that although a fair procedure was not adopted, the responsibility for failing to remedy it lies at the door of the employee for failing to alert him to the error.

Disciplinary rules

Ladbroke Racing Ltd v   **[1983] IRLR 154 CS**
Arnott and others
The statutory test of fairness is superimposed on the employer's disciplinary rules, so that a rule which specifically states that a breach will result in dismissal does not in itself necessarily meet the requirements of [s.98(4)]. The standard of acting reasonably set by [s.98(4)] requires an employer to consider all the facts relevant to the nature and cause of the breach, including the degree of its gravity. Where there is a rule prohibiting a specific act for which the stated penalty is instant dismissal, an employer does not satisfy [s.98(4)] if he imposes that penalty without regard to any facts or circumstances other than the breach itself.

John Lewis plc v   **[2001] IRLR 139 EAT**
Coyne
A reference in disciplinary rules to dishonesty normally being regarded as serious misconduct which would normally lead to dismissal indicates that dismissal is not an inevitable consequence of such conduct. The duty on the employers to act fairly and reasonably requires that they should investigate the seriousness of the offence in the particular case.

Elliott Brothers (London) Ltd v   **[1979] IRLR 92 EAT**
Colverd
There is no rule of law that a disciplinary rule must indicate that an employee will inevitably be dismissed if he commits the offence in question in order to entitle the employer to dismiss.

Procter v   **[1992] IRLR 7 EAT**
British Gypsum Ltd
The use of the word "liable" or "may" in disciplinary rules is not something upon which reliance can be placed to indicate that there is a general practice that dismissal would not be the likely result of the misconduct in question.

Ulsterbus Ltd v   **[1989] IRLR 251 NICA**
Henderson
There may be circumstances in which it would be unreasonable for an employer to dismiss an employee for a minor misdemeanour without warning that dismissal might result from such an act. However, where it would be obvious to any employee that a particular offence was a most serious one which was likely to lead to dismissal, dismissal for such an offence is not unreasonable even though it was not made clear in the disciplinary procedure that the offence would merit dismissal.

The Distillers Company   **[1982] IRLR 47 EAT**
   (Bottling Services) Ltd v
Gardner
Disciplinary rules are not meant to be exhaustive. A catalogue of offences which carry the potential sanction of dismissal contained in company rules may occasionally be useful in assessing the quality of an offence but it does not follow that an offence which does not fall within it can never merit dismissal.

W Brooks & Son v   **[1984] IRLR 379 EAT**
Skinner
Whether or not an employer is justified in treating a particular matter of conduct as sufficient to justify dismissal must include the question whether, in a particular case, the employee knew that his conduct would merit summary dismissal. Though there is much conduct which any employee will know will result in instant dismissal, there are also instances of conduct, particularly those which have been dealt with in other ways at other times by the employer, which the employee may well consider will not merit summary dismissal.

C A Parsons & Co Ltd v   **[1978] IRLR 65 EAT**
McLoughlin

It ought not to be necessary for anybody to have in black-and-white in the form of a rule that a fight is something which is going to be regarded very gravely by management.

West London Mental Health   **[2009] IRLR 512 EAT**
  NHS Trust v
Sarkar

Employers who attempt to negotiate a settlement of a dispute through a conflict resolution procedure which could only lead to a formal written warning are not precluded, if those negotiations break down, from raising that matter afresh through a formal disciplinary procedure which could result in dismissal.

Christou v   **[2013] IRLR 379 CA**
London Borough of Haringey

The doctrine of *res judicata* does not apply to the exercise of disciplinary power by an employer even though a disciplinary body set up by an employer can be described as a "domestic tribunal". It is wrong to describe the exercise of disciplinary power by the employer as a form of adjudication. The purpose of disciplinary procedures is not to allow a body independent of the parties to determine a dispute between them. Even where the procedures provide a panoply of safeguards of a kind typically found in adjudicative bodies, as is sometimes the case in the public sector in particular, that does not alter their basic function. It is far removed from the process of litigation or adjudication, which is in essence where this doctrine bites.

Gray Dunn & Co Ltd v   **[1980] IRLR 23 EAT**
Edwards

Where employers negotiate a detailed disciplinary agreement with a recognised union, they are entitled to assume that all employees who are members of the union know of and are bound by its provisions.

W Brooks & Son v   **[1984] IRLR 379 EAT**
Skinner

It does not always follow that an employer who has reached agreement with a trade union is justified in taking the view that all employees will be fixed with knowledge of what has been agreed.

Consistency

The Post Office v   **[1981] IRLR 221 CA**
Fennell

The word "equity" in the phrase "having regard to equity and the substantial merits of the case" in [s.98(4)] comprehends the concept that employees who behave in much the same way should have meted out to them much the same punishment. An employment tribunal is entitled to say that where that is not done and one man is penalised much more heavily than others who have committed similar offences in the past, the employer has

not acted reasonably in treating whatever the offence is as a sufficient reason for dismissal.

Hadjioannou v   **[1981] IRLR 352 EAT**
Coral Casinos Ltd

The emphasis in [s.98(4)] is on the particular circumstances of the individual employee's case. An argument by a dismissed employee that the treatment he received was not on a par with that meted out in other cases is relevant in determining the fairness of the dismissal in only three sets of circumstances. First, it may be relevant if there is evidence that employees have been led by an employer to believe that certain categories of conduct will be either overlooked, or at least will not be dealt with by the sanction of dismissal. Second, there may be cases where evidence in relation to other cases supports an inference that the purported reason stated by the employer is not the real or genuine reason for dismissal. Third, evidence as to decisions made by an employer in truly parallel circumstances may be sufficient to support an argument, in a particular case, that it was not reasonable on the part of the employer to visit the particular employee's conduct with the penalty of dismissal and that some lesser penalty would have been appropriate in the circumstances. employment tribunals should scrutinise arguments based upon disparity with particular care and there will not be many cases in which the evidence supports the proposition that there are other cases which are truly similar, or sufficiently similar to afford an adequate basis for argument. It is of the highest importance that flexibility should be retained and employers and tribunals should not be encouraged to think that a tariff approach to industrial misconduct is appropriate.

Paul v   **[1995] IRLR 305 CA**
East Surrey District Health Authority

Where arguments based upon disparity are raised, employment tribunals should heed the warning in *Hadjioannou v Coral Casinos* and scrutinise them with particular care. Ultimately the question for the employer is whether in the particular case dismissal is a reasonable response to the misconduct proved. If the employer has an established policy applied for similar misconduct, it would not be fair to change the policy without warning. If the employer has no established policy but has on other occasions dealt differently with misconduct properly regarded as similar, fairness demands that he should consider whether in all the circumstances, including the degree of misconduct proved, more serious disciplinary action is justified. However, an employer is entitled to take into account not only the nature of the conduct and the surrounding facts but also any mitigating personal circumstances affecting the employee concerned.

Securicor Ltd v   **[1989] IRLR 356 CA**
Smith

Where two employees are dismissed for the same incident and one is successful on appeal but the other is not, in determining the fairness of the latter's dismissal the question is whether the appeal panel's decision was so irrational that no employer could reasonably have accepted it.

London Borough of Harrow v [1996] IRLR 256 EAT
Cunningham

Where two employees who have committed the same joint offence are treated differently by the employer, the employment tribunal should direct itself in accordance with the Court of Appeal's judgment in *Securicor v Smith* and ask whether the distinction made by the employer rendered the dismissal within the band of reasonable responses open to the employer or was so irrational that no employer could reasonably have made it. The employer is entitled to take into account aggravating factors, such as one employee's poor disciplinary record when compared with the other, as well as any mitigating circumstances affecting one employee compared with the other.

Procter v [1992] IRLR 7 EAT
British Gypsum Ltd

The requirement that employers must act consistently between all employees means that, before reaching a decision to dismiss, an employer should consider truly comparable cases of which he knew or ought reasonably to have known. The overriding principle must be, however, that each case must be considered on its own facts and with freedom to consider mitigating aspects.

Cain v [1990] IRLR 168 EAT
Leeds Western Health Authority

Consistency must be consistency as between all employees of the employer. It is no answer to a complaint of inconsistency to say that different cases were considered by different members of management.

Conlin v [1994] IRLR 169 CS
United Distillers

In determining whether the employers have acted consistently, the question is not whether they were consistent in issuing final warnings as between employees who committed similar offences, but whether there was any inconsistency in the action which they took after those warnings had been issued.

Specific tests of fairness

Conduct

Strouthos v [2004] IRLR 636 CA
London Underground Ltd

An employee should only be found guilty of the offence with which he has been charged. It is a basic proposition, whether in criminal or disciplinary proceedings, that the charge against the defendant or the employee facing dismissal should be precisely framed, and that evidence should be confined to the particulars given in the charge. Care must be taken with the framing of a disciplinary charge and the circumstances in which it is permissible to go beyond that charge in a decision to take disciplinary action are very limited. Where care has clearly been taken to frame a charge formally and put it formally to an employee, the normal result must be that it is only matters charged which can form the basis for a dismissal.

Salford Royal NHS [2010] IRLR 721 CA
 Foundation Trust v
Roldan

Where there is an allegation of misconduct and the evidence consists of diametrically conflicting accounts of an alleged incident with no, or very little, evidence to provide corroboration one way or the other, employers are not obliged to believe one employee and to disbelieve another. The requirement is to form a genuine belief on reasonable grounds that the misconduct has occurred. The evidence of the accuser should be tested. There will be cases where it is perfectly proper for the employers to say that they are not satisfied that they can resolve the conflict of evidence and accordingly do not find the case proved. It would be perfectly proper in such a case for the employer to give the alleged wrongdoer the benefit of the doubt without feeling compelled to have to come down in favour of one side or the other.

Trusthouse Forte Hotels Ltd v [1977] IRLR 186 EAT
Murphy

It would place an unreasonable burden upon employers whose employee had been proved to be guilty of theft of the employers' property entrusted to his care that the employer should not be entitled to dismiss fairly.

British Railways Board v [1994] IRLR 235 CA
Jackson

It was fair to dismiss an employee for intending to sell goods for his own gain, where he had been discovered before he had actually infringed the rule. The employment tribunal's finding that the employers had "jumped the gun" because the rule had not yet been infringed was the kind of legalism which tribunals should try to avoid.

P v   [1992] IRLR 362 CA
Nottinghamshire County Council
The employers had no option but to take the view that a
school groundsman could not continue in employment which
brought him into even casual contact with young girls, after
he pleaded guilty to a charge of indecent conduct with his
daughter.

United Distillers v   [1992] IRLR 503 EAT
Conlin
A second offence of deliberate fraud on the employer so
obviously strikes at the fundamental relationship of trust and
confidence that there would have to be some clear reason
to justify a decision that dismissal falls outside the range of
reasonable responses open to an employer.

John Lewis plc v   [2001] IRLR 139 EAT
Coyne
There are two aspects to dishonesty, the objective and the
subjective, and judging whether there has been dishonesty
involves going through a two-stage process. First, it must be
decided whether according to the ordinary standards of
reasonable and honest people, what was done was dishonest. If so, then secondly, consideration must be given to
whether the person concerned must have realised that what
he or she was doing was by those standards dishonest.

Denco Ltd v   [1991] IRLR 63 EAT
Joinson
Unauthorised use of, or tampering with, computers can be
compared with dishonesty. For an employee deliberately to
use an unauthorised password in order to enter or to attempt to
enter a computer known to contain information to which he
is not entitled is gross misconduct which prima facie will
attract summary dismissal.

John Lewis plc v   [2001] IRLR 139 EAT
Coyne
Using an employer's telephone for personal calls is not necessarily dishonest. The test of dishonesty is not simply an
objective one. What one person believes to be dishonest may
in some circumstances not be dishonest to others.

Harris (Ipswich) Ltd v   [1978] IRLR 382 EAT
Harrison
In determining whether dismissal of an employee charged
with a criminal offence connected with his employment is fair,
the function of an employment tribunal is not to determine the
employee's guilt or innocence of the alleged crime but to consider the behaviour of the employers in terms of the statutory
test of fairness.

Thus, where an employee is charged with a criminal
offence alleged to have been committed in the course of
employment, and consequently dismissed, it does not follow that because he is later acquitted, the dismissal was
unfair. It will not always be wrong to dismiss the employee
before his guilt has been established. For, quite apart from

guilt, involvement in the alleged criminal offence often
involves a serious breach of duty or discipline. For example, the cashier charged with a till offence, guilty or not, is
often in breach of company rules in the way in which the
till has been operated. The employee who removes goods
from the premises without express permission, guilty or not,
is often in breach of the company's rules in taking his
employer's goods from the premises without express permission; and it is irrelevant to that matter that a jury may
be in doubt whether he intended to steal them. What it is
right to do, therefore, in a case of this kind, will depend on
the exact circumstances, including the employer's disciplinary code; sometimes it may be right to dismiss the
employee, sometimes to retain him, sometimes to suspend
him on full pay and sometimes to suspend him without pay.
The size of the employer, the nature of the business and the
number of employees are also relevant factors.

London Ambulance Service   [2009] IRLR 563 CA
 NHS Trust v
Small
An employment tribunal hearing an unfair dismissal case has
a different role when it is determining whether the dismissal
was unfair than, if it so finds, determining whether compensation should be reduced on grounds of contributory fault.
Whereas a tribunal must make findings of fact relating to the
employee's conduct in order to assess contributory fault, in
determining liability the tribunal should focus its fact-finding
on the employer's conduct of the dismissal. It is not the role of
the tribunal to conduct a re-hearing of the facts which formed
the basis of the employer's decision to dismiss. The tribunal's
proper role is objectively to review the fairness of the employee's dismissal by the employer.

Sehmi v   [2009] IRLR 807 EAT
Gate Gourmet London Ltd
Sandhu and ors v
Gate Gourmet London Ltd
Where an employee withdraws his labour in the course of
industrial action which was not protected and, after he has
ceased to participate in that action, he is dismissed on
grounds of having taken it, his withdrawal of labour may
amount to gross misconduct justifying dismissal, as it is a
fundamental breach of the contract. However, the essential
issue is not one of contract but whether it was within the
range of reasonable responses for the company to dismiss the
employee for taking part in the industrial action. Such a dismissal may not be unfair under the ERA 1996 even if it takes
place without any form of hearing or any examination of the
circumstances.

Trusthouse Forte (Catering) Ltd v   [1984] IRLR 382 EAT
Adonis
That the employee was aware that his conduct was wrong
and would probably result in his dismissal does not amount
to a justification for the action taken by the employer for
the purposes of [s.98(4)]. The employment tribunal must

look to what the employer did and whether that conduct was reasonable.

Brito-Babapulle v   [2013] IRLR 854 EAT
Ealing Hospital NHS Trust
Even if an employee has been dismissed for gross misconduct, that does not necessarily mean that dismissal must be within the range of reasonable responses. Mitigating factors must always be taken into account, such as long service, the consequences of dismissal and having a previously unblemished record.

British Leyland UK Ltd v   [1981] IRLR 91 CA
Swift
The conduct of an employee after an offence is discovered is a relevant consideration for an employer to take into account in deciding whether it is reasonable to dismiss. If an employee persistently lies about the matter, that is a breach of trust which would influence any reasonable employer to dismiss.

Farrant v   [1998] IRLR 176 EAT
The Woodroffe School
The lawfulness of the employer's instruction is not determinative of the fairness of the dismissal of an employee for refusing to obey that instruction.

Union of Construction and Allied   [1981] IRLR 224 CA
  Trades and Technicians v
Brain
Per Donaldson LJ: Where the conduct complained of is a refusal to obey an instruction given to the employee by the employer, the primary factor which falls to be considered by the reasonable employer in deciding whether or not to dismiss is whether the employee is acting reasonably in refusing to obey the instructions.

Turner v   [1981] IRLR 23 EAT
Vestric Ltd
Where there is a breakdown in the working relationship of two employees, before deciding whether to dismiss one or the other, the employers must take reasonable steps to try and improve the relationship so that it can be said that not only is there a breakdown but that their relationship is irremediable.

Boychuk v   [1977] IRLR 395 EAT
H J Symons Holdings Ltd
Although there are limits upon an employer's discretion to dismiss an employee because he or she will not accept the employer's standards in relation to attire, hair and behaviour, it is necessary to strike a balance according to the circumstances of the particular case between the need of the employer to control the business for which he is responsible in the interests of the business and the reasonable freedom of the employee. Whilst an employer cannot impose an unreasonable restriction on the basis of a foolish or unreasonable

judgment of what could be expected to be offensive, a reasonable employer should be allowed to decide what, upon reflection and mature consideration, could be expected to be offensive to customers and fellow employees. There is no necessity for the employer to wait and see whether the business is damaged or what disruption is caused, before he takes steps.

P v   [1992] IRLR 362 CA
Nottinghamshire County Council
In an appropriate case and where the size and administrative resources of the employer's undertaking permit, it may be unfair to dismiss without the employer first considering whether the employee can be offered some other job, notwithstanding that it may be clear that he cannot be allowed to continue in his original job. However, the question of alternative employment does not have to be investigated before giving notice to dismiss, as opposed to before the dismissal is effected by the notice.

Strouthos v   [2004] IRLR 636 CA
London Underground Ltd
Length of service is a factor which can properly be considered in deciding whether the reaction of an employer to an employee's conduct is an appropriate one.

Working in competition

Davidson and Maillou v   [1980] IRLR 360 EAT
Comparisons
An employer is entitled to defend himself against unfair competition from his employee and take whatever reasonable steps are necessary in order to achieve that end.

Harris & Russell Ltd v   [1973] IRLR 221 NIRC
Slingsby
That an employee is seeking employment with a competitor is a wholly insufficient reason to dismiss, unless it can be shown that there are reasonably solid grounds for supposing that he is doing so in order to abuse his confidential position and information with his present employer. In the nature of things, when an employee changes employment it is more than likely that he will be seeking fresh employment with someone in the same line of business and therefore a competitor of his present employer.

Laughton and Hawley v   [1986] IRLR 245 EAT
Bapp Industrial Supplies Ltd
The proposition stated in *Harris & Russell Ltd v Slingsby* applies where the employee seeks to set up in competition on his own account. An employee who is intending to leave to set up in competition on his own account commits no breach of contract justifying dismissal in doing so unless either there is a specific term in his contract to that effect which does not fall foul of the doctrine against restraint of trade, or he is intending to use the confidential information of his employer other than for the benefit of the employer.

Marshall v   **[1992] IRLR 294 EAT**
Industrial Systems &Control Ltd

The employers were entitled to dismiss their managing director after discovering that he had formed a plan with another manager to set up in competition and take away the business of their best client, and that he tried to induce another key employee to join in that venture. Such circumstances were entirely different from merely forming an intention to set up in competition with the employer, as in *Laughton*.

Capability

Taylor v   **[1978] IRLR 82 CA**
Alidair Ltd

The correct test of fairness is whether the employer honestly and reasonably held the belief that the employee was not competent and whether there was a reasonable ground for that belief.

Polkey v   **[1987] IRLR 503 HL**
A E Dayton Services Ltd

Per Lord Bridge: In a case of incapacity, an employer will normally not act reasonably unless he gives the employee fair warning and an opportunity to mend his ways and show that he can do the job.

Cook v   **[1977] IRLR 132 EAT**
Thomas Linnell & Sons Ltd

Although employers must act reasonably when removing from a particular post an employee whom they consider to be unsatisfactory, it is important that the operation of unfair dismissal legislation should not impede employers unreasonably in the efficient management of their business.

Alidair Ltd v   **[1976] IRLR 420 EAT**
Taylor

There are activities in which the degree of professional skill which must be required is so high, and the potential consequences of the smallest departure from that high standard so serious, that one failure to perform in accordance with those standards is enough to justify dismissal. The passenger-carrying airline pilot, the scientist operating the nuclear reactor, the chemist in charge of research into the possible effect of thalidomide, the driver of the Manchester to London express, the driver of an articulated lorry full of sulphuric acid, are all in the situation in which one failure to maintain the proper standard of professional skill can bring about a major disaster.

Gair v   **[1983] IRLR 368 CS**
Bevan Harris Ltd

Whether an employer acts fairly in dismissing an employee on grounds of lack of capability rather than offering to demote the employee depends upon whether the decision to dismiss is outside the band of reasonableness.

Ill health and absence

Spencer v   **[1976] IRLR 373 EAT**
Paragon Wallpapers Ltd

In cases where an employee is dismissed on grounds of ill health, the basic question that has to be determined when looking at the fairness of the dismissal is whether, in all the circumstances, the employer can be expected to wait any longer and, if so, how much longer? Matters to be taken into account are the nature of the illness, the likely length of the continuing absence, the need of the employer to have done the work which the employee was engaged to do and the circumstances of the case.

Smiths Industries Aerospace &   **[1986] IRLR 434 EAT**
   Defence Systems Ltd v
Brookes

A contractual term providing that employment would be terminated by statutory minimum notice if the employee was incapacitated for a specified period did not mean that the employers could not lawfully dismiss an employee on grounds of ill health until his incapacity had lasted for that specified period.

Discussion and consultation

Spencer v   **[1976] IRLR 373 EAT**
Paragon Wallpapers Ltd

In cases of ill health, though an employee ought not to be dismissed without some prior communication between him and the employer, a "warning" is not appropriate. By its association with cases of misconduct, "warning" carries with it the suggestion that the employee is being required to change or improve his conduct. That is not the case where the absence is due to ill health and in some such cases, some damage could be done by a written warning unaccompanied by a more personal touch. Usually what is required is a discussion of the position between the employer and the employee so that the situation can be weighed up, bearing in mind the employer's need for work to be done and the employee's need for time to recover his health.

East Lindsey District Council v   **[1977] IRLR 181 EAT**
Daubney

Unless there are wholly exceptional circumstances, before an employee is dismissed on grounds of ill health, it is necessary that he should be consulted and the matter discussed with him, and that in one way or another, steps should be taken by the employer to discover the true medical position. Discussions and consultation will often bring to light facts and circumstances of which the employers were unaware and which will throw new light on the problem. Or the employee may wish to seek medical advice on his own account which, brought to the notice of the employers' medical advisers, will cause them to change their opinion. If the employee is not consulted and given an opportunity to state his case, an injustice may be done. Though the steps that employers should take may vary, if in every case employers take such steps as are sensible according to the circumstances, to consult the employee and to discuss the matter with him, and to inform themselves upon the true medical position, it will be found in practice that all that is necessary has been done. Only in the rarest possible circumstances can a failure to consult be justified on the grounds that discussion and consultation would have been fruitless.

BS v [2014] IRLR 131 CSIH
Dundee City Council
There is a distinction when taking into account long service for the purpose of an ill health dismissal as compared with a dismissal for misconduct. While long service will often be relevant in a misconduct case as indicating that what the employee has done can be treated as a temporary aberration, the critical question in an ill health case is whether the length of the employee's service, and the manner in which he worked during that period, yields inferences that indicate that the employee is likely to return to work as soon as he can.

A Links & Co Ltd v [1991] IRLR 353 CS
Rose
In deciding whether an employer acted fairly in dismissing an employee on grounds of ill health, an employment tribunal must determine, as a matter of fact and judgment, what consultation, if any, was necessary or desirable in the known circumstances of the particular case; what consultation, if any, in fact took place; and whether or not that consultation process was adequate in all the circumstances.

Patterson v [1977] IRLR 137 EAT
Messrs Bracketts
What is required in a particular case as far as the employer informing himself about the true situation of the employee's health is concerned will depend on the circumstances of each case. But the principle is twofold: first, that there should be consultation or discussion with the employee; and second, that such other steps as are necessary should be taken to enable the employer to form a balanced view about the employee's health. In some cases that will require consultation with the doctors; in other cases it will not.

Williamson v [1977] IRLR 303 EAT
Alcan (UK) Ltd
The purpose of discussion and consultation is partly to enable the true medical position to be discerned. But it is also necessary because it is reasonably fair and good practice that a man who is going to be dismissed should have a say in the matter. Further, quite apart from the medical condition, his whole employment situation requires to be assessed and considerations of alternative employment taken into account.

Looking for alternative work

Merseyside & North Wales [1975] IRLR 60 HC
Electricity Board v
Taylor
Whether, before dismissing on grounds of incapacity, an employer should offer the employee alternative work, depends upon the circumstances of each case. There is no rule of law that an employer is obliged to create a special job for such an employee. Nor is there a rule of law which obliges the employer in an ill-health case to find other work for the employee.

Shook v [1986] IRLR 46 EAT
London Borough of Ealing
An employer's right to enforce mobility under a contract of employment does not carry with it a reciprocal duty in law to provide work elsewhere in the organisation if the employee is incapacitated from performing any role in which he is currently engaged.

Carricks (Caterers) Ltd v [1980] IRLR 259 EAT
Nolan
Though employers cannot be expected to go to unreasonable lengths in seeking to accommodate someone who is not able to carry out his job to the full extent, what is reasonable is very largely a question of fact and degree for the employment tribunal.

Safety

Liverpool Area Health Authority [1977] IRLR 471 EAT
(Teaching) Central & Southern District v
Edwards
That an employer may be held to have breached his common law duty to take reasonable care of his employees if, disregarding medical opinion, an employee is continued in employment and is subsequently injured, must be a factor that a reasonable employer can take into account without unfairness.

Pension provision

First West Yorkshire Ltd [2008] IRLR 182 EAT
t/a First Leeds v
Haigh
In addition to the usual steps of obtaining medical evidence, undergoing consultation and considering alternative employment, if an employer provides an enhanced pension on ill-health retirement they will also be expected to take reasonable steps to ascertain whether an employee is entitled to benefit from that before choosing to dismiss.

Disabled employees

HJ Heinz Co Ltd v [2000] IRLR 144 EAT
Kenrick
A disability-related dismissal which is not justified under the Disability Discrimination Act is not automatically unfair in

terms of s.98(4) of the Employment Rights Act. Separate consideration must be given to the matters falling for consideration under s.98(4).

Royal Liverpool Children's   [2006] IRLR 351 EAT
NHS Trust v
Dunsby
An employer may take into account disability-related absences in operating a sickness absence procedure. The DDA does not impose an absolute obligation on an employer to refrain from dismissing an employee who is absent on grounds of ill health due to disability. The question is whether or not the employer is justified in taking the disability-related absences into account. Note, however, that this case does not deal with whether not taking into account some, or all, disability-related absences might be regarded as a reasonable adjustment.

Intermittent absence

International Sports Co Ltd v   [1980] IRLR 340 EAT
Thomson
Where an employee has an unacceptable level of intermittent absences due to minor ailments, what is required is first, that there should be a fair review by the employer of the attendance record and the reasons for it; and second, appropriate warnings after the employee has been given an opportunity to make representations. If there is then no adequate improvement in the attendance record, in most cases the employer will be justified in treating the persistent absences as a sufficient reason for dismissing the employee. In such a case, the principles set out in *Spencer v Paragon Wallpapers* and *East Lindsey District Council v Daubney* are not applicable. It would be placing too heavy a burden on the employer to require him to carry out a formal medical investigation. Even if he did, such an investigation would rarely be fruitful because of the transient nature of the employee's symptoms and complaints.

Lynock v   [1988] IRLR 510 EAT
Cereal Packaging Ltd
In determining whether to dismiss an employee with a poor record of sickness absence, an employer's approach should be based on sympathy, understanding and compassion. Factors which may prove important include the nature of the illness; the likelihood of it recurring or of some other illness arising; the length of the various absences and the periods of good health between them; the need of the employer to have done the work of the employee; the impact of the absences on those who work with the employee; the adoption and exercise of a policy in connection with absence due to sickness; the importance of a personal assessment in the ultimate decision; and the extent to which the difficulty of the situation and the position of the employer have been explained to the employee.

Lynock v   [1988] IRLR 510 EAT
Cereal Packaging Ltd
A disciplinary approach involving warnings is not appropriate in a case of intermittent sickness absence, but the employ-

ee should be cautioned that the stage has been reached when it has become impossible to continue with the employment.

The Post Office v   [1977] IRLR 422 EAT
Jones
In a case involving frequent absences from work, whether or not the employer is entitled to make his decision whether or not to dismiss the employee on his own upon the evidence, or whether in every case where illness is involved there should be a final medical opinion, is something that the employment tribunal must decide for itself. Whilst *Spencer v Paragon Wallpapers* emphasised the need for employers to establish what the true medical position of the employee is before deciding whether or not to dismiss, that case dealt with one illness, one absence, which was the first absence.

Lynock v   [1988] IRLR 510 EAT
Cereal Packaging Ltd
In a case of unconnected intermittent periods of absence, there is no obligation on an employer to make medical inquiries or to provide medical evidence to an employment tribunal since it is impossible to give a reasonable prognosis or projection of what will happen in the future.

International Sports Co Ltd v   [1980] IRLR 340 EAT
Thomson
Where an employee was absent for about 25% of the time in the last 18 months of her employment and the employers had investigated her attendance record and issued warnings, a reasonable employer was entitled to say "enough is enough".

Maternity

Hilton International Hotels (UK) Ltd v   [1994] IRLR 270 EAT
Kaissi
An employee who is off work for pregnancy or maternity, but who has no statutory or contractual right to return to work, does not lose or forfeit her right not to be unfairly dismissed. As the contract of employment continues until dismissal, there continues with it a statutory right not to be unfairly dismissed. Therefore, an employment tribunal did not err in finding that the dismissal of the respondent while she was off work after the birth of her baby was unfair because the employers had been informed that she was sick, yet made no further investigation of her situation before terminating the contract.

Redundancy dismissals

Standard of proof

Williams and others v   [1982] IRLR 83 EAT
Compair Maxam Ltd
Where dismissal is for redundancy, the employment tribunal must be satisfied that it was reasonable to dismiss each of the

claimants on the grounds of redundancy. It is not enough to show that it was reasonable to dismiss an employee; it must be shown that the employer acted reasonably in treating redundancy "as a sufficient reason for dismissing the employee". Therefore, if the circumstances of the employer make it inevitable that some employee must be dismissed, it is still necessary to consider the means whereby the claimant was selected to be the employee to be dismissed and the reasonableness of the steps taken by the employer to choose the claimant, rather than some other employee, for dismissal.

Redland Roof Tiles Ltd v   **[1979] IRLR 10 EAT**
Eveleigh
In determining whether a redundancy dismissal meets the general test of fairness, what has to be considered is not whether or not there was a genuine redundancy situation but how the employer acted in the face of the redundancy in dismissing the employee.

Moon and others v   **[1976] IRLR 298 EAT**
Homeworthy Engineering (Northern) Ltd
In hearing a complaint of unfair dismissal, the employment tribunal can investigate the operating of a redundancy situation, including questions such as unfair selection or lack of notice. There cannot be any investigation into the reasons for creating redundancies or into the rights and wrongs of the declared redundancy.

Cox v   **[1978] IRLR 157 EAT**
Wildt Mellor Bromley Ltd
In a case of alleged unfair redundancy, in addition to showing that the employee was dismissed for redundancy, upon what basis the selection was made and how it was applied in practice, an employer must be prepared to deal in outline at least with any general points which a reasonable employer would consider to be important, such as efforts to find the employee other employment or to assist him.

Tocher v   **[1981] IRLR 55 EAT**
General Motors Scotland Ltd
An employee who volunteers for redundancy cannot be held to have been unfairly dismissed.

General guidelines

Polkey v   **[1987] IRLR 503 HL**
A E Dayton Services Ltd
Per Lord Bridge: In a case of redundancy, the employer will not normally act reasonably unless he warns and consults any employees affected or their representative, adopts a fair basis on which to select for redundancy and takes such steps as may be reasonable to avoid or minimise redundancy by redeployment within his own organisation.

Langston v   **[1998] IRLR 172 EAT**
Cranfield University
It is implicit in a claim of unfair dismissal by reason of

redundancy that the unfairness incorporates unfair selection, lack of consultation and failure to seek alternative employment. Since there is now no onus on either party to establish the reasonableness or unreasonableness of the dismissal, it is incumbent upon the employment tribunal to consider each of these three questions. Normally, therefore, an employer can be expected to lead some evidence as to the steps which were taken to select the employee for redundancy, to consult him and/or his trade union and to seek to find him alternative employment, and the tribunal would be expected to refer to these three issues on the facts of the particular case in explaining its reasons for concluding that the employer acted reasonably or unreasonably in dismissing the employee by reason of redundancy.

Williams and others v   **[1982] IRLR 83 EAT**
Compair Maxam Ltd
Although it would be impossible to lay down detailed procedures which all reasonable employers would follow in all circumstances, there is a generally accepted view in industrial relations that, in cases where employees are represented by an independent union recognised by the employer, reasonable employers will seek to act in accordance with the following principles:

1. The employer will seek to give as much warning as possible of impending redundancies so as to enable the union and employees who may be affected to take early steps to inform themselves of the relevant facts, consider possible alternative solutions and, if necessary, find alternative employment in the undertaking or elsewhere.

2. The employer will consult the union as to the best means by which the desired management result can be achieved fairly and with as little hardship to the employees as possible. In particular, the employer will seek to agree with the union the criteria to be applied in selecting the employees to be made redundant. When a selection has been made, the employer will consider with the union whether the selection has been made in accordance with these criteria.

3. Whether or not an agreement as to the criteria to be adopted has been agreed with the union, the employer will seek to establish criteria for selection which so far as possible do not depend solely upon the opinion of the person making the selection but can be objectively checked against such things as attendance record, efficiency at the job, experience or length of service.

4. The employer will seek to ensure that the selection is made fairly in accordance with these criteria and will consider any representations the union may make as to such selection.

5. The employer will seek to see whether instead of dismissing an employee he could offer him alternative employment.

These principles should be departed from only where some good reason is shown to justify such departure.

Rolls-Royce Motors Ltd v   **[1985] IRLR 184 EAT**
Dewhurst and others
A breach of the guidelines set out in *Compair Maxam* is not grounds in itself for a finding of unfair dismissal.

Grundy (Teddington) Ltd v   **[1983] IRLR 98 EAT**
Plummer and Salt

The judgment in *Compair Maxam* was not intended to suggest that failure to act in accordance with one or more of the five principles in that decision would necessarily involve the conclusion that the dismissal was unfair. It should be emphasised that: (a) the five points in *Compair Maxam* are dealing with what a reasonable employer will seek to do if circumstances permit. The extent to which any one or more of them applies in a given case depends on the circumstances of that case; (b) an employer's failure to adopt any one or more of those practices does not necessarily lead to a finding of unfair dismissal. The employment tribunal must look at the circumstances of the case in the round having those considerations in mind. Whether in the circumstances of a particular case the employer acted reasonably in not taking any step, and whether any unjustified failure to adopt such procedure renders the dismissal unfair, is a matter for the employment tribunal to decide in the light of all the circumstances of the case in reaching the conclusion whether the dismissal was reasonable within the meaning of [s.98(4)].

A Simpson & Son (Motors) v   **[1983] IRLR 401 EAT**
Reid and Findlater

The observations contained in *Compair Maxam* do not embody principles of law but standards of behaviour applicable only in situations where substantial redundancies arise in enterprises where there is an independent recognised union. The five so-called principles were never intended to be considered in each and every redundancy case, being ticked off as in a shopping list as to whether or not they had been complied with and, in the event of any one or more not having been complied with, automatic unfairness arising.

Unfair selection

Capita Hartshead Ltd v   **[2012] IRLR 814 EAT**
Byard

Provided that the employer has genuinely applied its mind to who should be in the pool for consideration for redundancy, "then it will be difficult, but not impossible, for an employee to challenge it".

British Aerospace plc v   **[1995] IRLR 433 CA**
Green and others

Observed (per Waite LJ): In general, an employer who sets up a system of selection which can reasonably be described as fair and applies it without any overt sign of conduct which mars its fairness, will have done all that the law requires of him.

Buchanan v   **[1983] IRLR 417 CS**
Tilcon Ltd

Where an employee's only complaint is that he was unfairly selected for redundancy and no other complaints are made, all the employers have to prove is that their method of selection was fair in general terms and that it was applied reasonably in the case of that employee. In doing so, it is sufficient to call witnesses of reasonable seniority to explain the circumstances in which dismissal of the employee came about. It is imposing too high a burden on the employers to demand that they prove the accuracy of the information upon which they had acted in selecting the employee for redundancy.

British Aerospace plc v   **[1995] IRLR 433 CA**
Green and others

In cases of alleged unfair selection for redundancy, documents relating to assessments of retained employees are not likely to be relevant in any but the most exceptional circumstances. The question for the employment tribunal, which must be determined separately for each claimant, is whether that claimant was unfairly dismissed, not whether some other employee could have been fairly dismissed. The tribunal is not entitled to embark upon a re-assessment exercise. Therefore, a claimant who alleges that the selection process was unfairly applied in practice and who seeks an order for disclosure must specify the respect in which he claims that the process was unfairly applied with sufficient particularity to demonstrate the relevance of the material the disclosure of which is sought.

John Brown Engineering Ltd v   **[1997] IRLR 90 EAT**
Brown and others

A fair redundancy selection process requires that individual employees have the opportunity to contest selection, either by themselves or through their trade unions. In order to do so, the employees need to know how they themselves have been assessed and, therefore, a policy decision to withhold all markings in a particular selection process may result in individual unfairness. It may be invidious to publish the whole identified "league tables", but in choosing not to do so, the employer must run the risk that he is not acting fairly in respect of individual employees.

FDR Ltd v   **[1995] IRLR 400 EAT**
Holloway

Where there is an issue as to whether redundancy selection criteria were applied fairly and reasonably in the case of a particular employee, an employment tribunal, of necessity, has to know the employee's markings and how they compare with the other employees in the pool in order to determine whether the system had been applied fairly and reasonably to the employee. The tribunal is not bound to accept the employer's assertion that the criteria were applied fairly. It was over-literal to read the Court of Appeal's decision in *British Aerospace v Green* as indicating that documents relating to retained employees are not relevant.

King and others v   **[1996] IRLR 199 CS**
Eaton Ltd

Observed: employment tribunals should not be reviewing the markings of employees for redundancy selection purposes. The decision of the EAT in *FDR v Holloway* was irreconcilable with that of the Court of Appeal in *British Aerospace v Green*, which was correct.

King v
[1998] IRLR 686 CS
Eaton Ltd (No.2)
Observed: In an appropriate case, an employment tribunal can enquire into the marking and assessments of those selected for redundancy, whether at the stage of enquiry into the merits or at the stage of remedy and *Polkey* reduction.

Eaton Ltd v
[1995] IRLR 75 EAT
King and others
In selecting employees to be made redundant, a senior manager is entitled to rely on assessments of employees made by those having direct knowledge of their work. There is no material difference between the position of a senior manager who relies on such assessments and that of one who relies on information in company records. In both cases, the senior manager is relying on the proper performance of the work done by those appointed to do it and in the absence of some reason to think that the work has not been properly done, there is no reason why he should not so rely. It is not necessary for those who actually carried out the assessment to give evidence before the employment tribunal to explain why the employee was marked in a particular way.

N C Watling & Co Ltd v
[1978] IRLR 255 EAT
Richardson
The fairness of the dismissal is to be judged by the objective standard of the way in which a reasonable employer in those circumstances, in that line of business, would have behaved. It has to be recognised that there are circumstances where more than one course of action may be reasonable. In the case of redundancy, for example, and where selection of one or two employees from a larger number is in issue, there often are cases where equally reasonable, fair, sensible and prudent employers would take different courses, one choosing "A", another "B" and another "C". In those circumstances for an employment tribunal to say that it was unfair to select "A" for dismissal, rather "B" or "C", merely because had they been the employers that is what they would have done, is to apply the test of what the particular employment tribunal itself would have done and not the test of what a reasonable employer would have done. It is in this sense that it is said that the test is whether what has been done is something which "no reasonable management would have done".

BL Cars Ltd v
[1983] IRLR 58 EAT
Lewis
The question that falls to be asked in determining whether an employee was unfairly selected for redundancy is "Was the selection one which a reasonable employer could have made?" This involves considering the criteria which were adopted and whether the employers have demonstrated that they fairly applied those criteria to this redundancy. In the normal case of a large employer, that would usually involve the employers showing that in selecting the particular employee, they had compared

him in relation to his length of service, his job and his skills with those others who might be made redundant. In the ordinary case, though not invariably, that would involve evidence from the person who made the selection indicating that the rating of each person who might be made redundant had been made and that as a result it emerged fairly and genuinely that the employee was one of those who rated worst under those heads.

Williams and others v
[1982] IRLR 83 EAT
Compair Maxam Ltd
The purpose of having, so far as possible, objective criteria for redundancy selection is to ensure that redundancy is not used as a pretext for getting rid of employees whom some manager wishes to get rid of for other reasons. Except in cases where the criteria can be applied automatically (eg last in first out), in any selection for redundancy elements of personal judgment are bound to be required thereby involving the risk of judgment being clouded by personal animosity. Unless some objective criteria are included, it is extremely difficult to demonstrate that the choice was not determined by personal likes and dislikes alone.

Watkins v
[2011] IRLR 382 EAT
Crouch t/a Temple Bird Solicitors
Using the criterion "the overall requirements of the business" separately but in addition to scoring employees on other criteria, requires care to be taken because: (1) it may be too subjective to satisfy the requirement of objectivity which tries to eliminate decisions being made on a basis which cannot withstand close scrutiny; (2) it may be a statement of the obvious as all redundancy exercises aim to retain employees best equipped to help the business trade profitably in the future; and (3) if that was to be a factor it should probably have been reflected in the selection criteria themselves so that all members of the workforce would have been scored on it.

Smiths Industries Aerospace
[1996] IRLR 656 EAT
and Defence Systems v
Rawlings
The protection against dismissal in a redundancy exercise afforded to union-elected health and safety representatives is neutral. They must not be disadvantaged by reason of the performance of their health and safety duties but, equally, they are not entitled to any advantage over their fellow employees in the selection pool. The duties of health and safety representatives do not form part of the employee's contractual duties, and it would be wrong to assess their performance of such duties for the purposes of redundancy selection.

Boulton & Paul Ltd v
[1994] IRLR 532 EAT
Arnold
An offer to retain an employee under notice of dismissal on grounds of redundancy at the expense of another employee cannot prevent a finding of unfair dismissal on the basis that the employee had the opportunity of staying employed. It is unfair to put the onus on the employee to decide who is to be selected for dismissal.

Morgan v   **[2011] IRLR 376 EAT**
Welsh Rugby Union

When examining the fairness of the process of selection for a new role created by a reorganisation following a redundancy exercise, (1) the principal test for the tribunal to apply is that set out in section 98(4) of the ERA 1996, (2) the criteria set out in *Williams v Compair Maxam* for selecting employees to be made redundant do not apply in the context of selecting between candidates for a new role, and (3) the case of *Ralph Martindale v Harris* (UKEAT/0166/07), which involved the selection process for a new position, does not contain any principles of law which must be followed in such situations.

Warnings and consultation

King and others v   **[1996] IRLR 199 CS**
Eaton Ltd

Although the consultation required of an employer before dismissing on grounds of redundancy may be directly with the employees concerned or with their representatives, such consultation must be fair and proper. The definition set out by Glidwell LJ in *R v British Coal Corporation ex parte Price* – that "fair consultation means (a) consultation when the proposals are still at a formative stage; (b) adequate information on which to respond; (c) adequate time in which to respond; and (d) conscientious consideration by an authority of a response to consultation" – would be adopted.

Rowell v   **[1995] IRLR 195 EAT**
Hubbard Group Services Ltd

The obligation to consult about dismissal on grounds of redundancy is separate from the obligation to warn of impending redundancies.

Elkouil v   **[2002] IRLR 174 EAT**
Coney Island Ltd

There is no separate duty on an employer to warn an employee of impending redundancy. Warning and consultation are part of the same single process of consultation which should begin with a warning that the employee is at risk.

De Grasse v   **[1992] IRLR 269 EAT**
Stockwell Tools Ltd

While the size of the undertaking may affect the nature or formality of the consultation process, it cannot excuse the lack of any consultation at all. However informal the consultation may be, it should normally take place.

Grundy (Teddington) Ltd v   **[1983] IRLR 98 EAT**
Plummer and Salt

Although in one sense proper consultation is a "procedural" matter, it has a direct bearing on the substantive decision to select the particular employee since a different employee might have been selected if, as a result of proper consultation, different criteria had been adopted or had been applied differently.

Graham v   **[1986] IRLR 90 EAT**
ABF Ltd

The more vague and subjective the criteria adopted for redundancy selection, the more powerful the need for the employee to be given an opportunity of personal consultation before he is judged by it.

Rolls-Royce Motor Cars Ltd v   **[1993] IRLR 203 EAT**
Price and others

Full consultation with a union on the choice of criteria to be applied in a redundancy situation does not mean that there is no obligation on the employer to consult with the union or the employees concerned about the application of the criteria to individuals. Nor is there any rigid rule that the obligation on the employer is only to consult either the union or the employees about the application of the redundancy selection criteria.

Looking for alternative work

Thomas & Betts Manufacturing Ltd v   **[1980] IRLR 255 CA**
Harding

The obligation on an employer to look for alternative work for a redundant employee is not limited to looking for another job in the same section of the business that the dismissed employee worked. Moreover, it is not an error of law for an employment tribunal to hold that it is unfair to dismiss an employee on grounds of redundancy rather than offering them alternative work, even if to offer that alternative work would mean dismissing another employee.

Stacey v   **[1986] IRLR 3 EAT**
Babcock Power Ltd (Construction Division)

Fair industrial practice requires an employer to offer a long-standing employee given notice of dismissal for redundancy the opportunity of new employment which arises during his notice period before filling the vacancies with newly recruited employees.

Avonmouth Construction Co Ltd v   **[1979] IRLR 14 EAT**
Shipway

Implicit in the duty to look for alternative employment in a redundancy situation is a responsibility on the employer not simply to look, but to give careful consideration to the possibility of offering the employee another job. That a vacant position would involve demotion is something primarily for the employee to worry about.

Barratt Construction Ltd v   **[1984] IRLR 385 EAT**
Dalrymple

Since there is no longer an onus on an employer to show that he acted reasonably, the employment tribunal must decide the question of reasonableness on the evidence before them in accordance with equity and the substantial merits of the case. Although the principle that a reasonable employer will not make an employee redundant if he can employ him elsewhere still holds good, in the absence of evidence as to the availability of alternative employment, it is not for the employment tribunal to speculate as to what further steps might have been taken and to draw an inference adverse to the employer because he did not take them.

Modern Injection Moulds Ltd v Price   [1976] IRLR 172 EAT

When making an offer of alternative employment to a redundant employee, the employer should give the employee sufficient information upon which he can make a realistic decision whether to take the job or not. Whilst it will depend upon the circumstances of every case as to how much information and information upon what subjects should be given, it is necessary for the employer to inform the employee of the financial prospects of the new job.

Elliot v Richard Stump Ltd   [1987] IRLR 215 EAT

If an offer of alternative employment made to a redundant employee was made on terms which were not reasonable, prima facie that would justify the conclusion that a dismissal consequent upon refusal of that offer was unfair.

Gwent County Council v Lane   [1977] IRLR 337 EAT

Where an employee is on a temporary short-term contract which is not renewed for reasons of redundancy, the obligation on the employer to attempt to find alternative employment for the employee is not as stringent as in the case of a permanent employee. In particular, there is no general rule that the employee has a right to priority of appointment to an available suitable position over any other suitable candidate.

Bowater Containers Ltd v McCormack   [1980] IRLR 50 EAT

An employer cannot be expected to offer an alternative job in circumstances where that would contravene an agreement with the union.

Octavius Atkinson & Sons Ltd v Morris   [1989] IRLR 158 CA

There is no right to complain of an unfair failure to re-engage. Therefore, an employer's failure to offer an employee re-sengagement on alternative work could not render the earlier termination of his employment on grounds of redundancy retrospectively unfair.

Other substantial reason

Catamaran Cruisers Ltd v Williams and others   [1994] IRLR 386 EAT

Where an employee is dismissed for refusing to accept new terms of a contract of employment which are much less favourable than the terms of the old contract, the correct test is to balance the disadvantage of the new contract from the employee's point of view and the benefit to the employers in imposing the changes. There is no principle of law that if the new terms are much less favourable to an employee than the old terms, dismissal of the employee for refusing to accept them will be unfair unless the business reasons are so pressing that it is vital for the survival of the employer's business that the new terms be accepted.

Richmond Precision Engineering Ltd v Pearce   [1985] IRLR 179 EAT

In determining whether an employer has acted reasonably in dismissing an employee who refused to agree to changes in his terms and conditions of employment consequent upon a reorganisation, employment tribunals should confine themselves to the question posed under [s.98(4)] and approach the question on the basis of considering the range of response open to an employer in the circumstances. The task of weighing the advantages to the employer of implementing the proposed changes against the disadvantages to the employee is merely one factor which the tribunal has to take into account in determining the question in accordance with equity and the substantial merits of the case. It does not follow that because there are disadvantages to the employee, the employer acted unreasonably in treating his refusal to accept the changes as a reason for dismissing him.

St John of God (Care Services) Ltd v Brooks and others   [1992] IRLR 546 EAT

Whether the new terms and conditions offered by the employer were those which a reasonable employer could offer is only one element in the test for whether the dismissal of an employee for refusing to accept substantial changes in terms and conditions is reasonable. It is wrong to look at the employer's offer alone because that necessarily excludes from consideration everything that happened between the time the offer was made and the dismissal, including the potentially significant factor of whether other employees accepted the offer.

Martin v Automobile Proprietary Ltd   [1979] IRLR 64 EAT

In determining whether it is fair to dismiss individual employees who refuse to go along with a reorganisation, the vital question is whether the employer acted fairly and reasonably with reference to the individual, not whether or not they consulted with some representative body.

Garside and Laycock Ltd v Booth   [2011] IRLR 735 EAT

In determining whether an employer has acted reasonably in dismissing an employee who had refused to accept a pay cut, it was not relevant to ask (a) whether the employer was in a situation so desperate that the only way of saving the business was to propose stringent reductions in pay and conditions, or (b) whether the employee's refusal was reasonable, and it was important to consider the question in accordance with equity, and thus to take into account factors such as (i) upon whom of the workforce the pay cuts would fall, (ii) the extent to which the workforce were or were not persuaded by reasons which were not good and proper reasons for adopting a common approach in favour of cuts, and (iii) whether there were other cost saving measures which the employer might have taken.

Banerjee v   **[1979] IRLR 147 EAT**
City & East London Area Health
  Authority
In the case of dismissal following a policy of reorganisation, in order to show that the dismissal was reasonable in all the circumstances, the employer must be able to adduce evidence as to how the decision to rationalise was made, of the consideration which was given to the matter, of the pros and cons which were considered and of the importance which was attached to the different features which went into the decision. Alternatively, a witness should be called who can give that information.

Oakley v   **[1988] IRLR 34 CA**
The Labour Party
Where a reorganisation is simply a pretext for getting rid of an employee, it must inevitably follow that the dismissal was unfair.

Pillinger v   **[1979] IRLR 430 EAT**
Manchester Area Health Authority
If an employer relies on the decision of some other body as another substantial reason to justify a dismissal, he must show what the reason for that dismissal was and that, in the circumstances, he acted reasonably. That funds needed to pay salaries have been withdrawn is a factor to be taken into account. But it is not conclusive and consideration must be given to what steps the employer took before the dismissal. Where an employer is dismissing because funds have been withdrawn by a third party, it is essential, to be fair, that the employer should seek to ascertain the reason for the withdrawal and explain this to the employee concerned. Otherwise there is a serious danger that some misunderstanding might occur.

Dobie v   **[1983] IRLR 278 EAT**
Burns International Security
  Services (UK) Ltd
Whether a dismissal at the behest of a third party was a fair dismissal for some other substantial reason involves a two-stage analysis. The first stage is to see whether the employer justified the reason for dismissal and at this stage the employment tribunal has to have regard only to the conduct of the employer and not to whether the employee suffered any injustice. If the employer passes the first test, then what has to be determined is whether the dismissal was fair having regard to equity and the substantial merits of the case, including possible injustice to the employee. If an employee was told at the time of the making of the contract that his employment could be terminated at the behest of a third party, then

if he is dismissed in those circumstances, he cannot complain that the employer is acting contrary to equity or that his dismissal is unreasonable according to the substantial merits of the case. But if he is not so told, the position is different.

Kelman v   **[1983] IRLR 432 EAT**
G J Oram
Once it has been established that the reason for dismissal was that it was impracticable for employment to continue and that this was a substantial reason for dismissal within the meaning of [s.98(1)(b)], it is extremely difficult to conclude that it was unreasonable in terms of [s.98(4)] for the employer to dismiss on this account.

Transfer of undertakings

McGrath v   **[1985] IRLR 323 EAT**
Rank Leisure Ltd
A dismissal connected with a business transfer for an economic, technical or organisational reason entailing changes in the workforce is automatically to be treated as "some other substantial reason" within the meaning of [s.98(1)(b)], but it is then thrown back into the mainstream of [s.98] and must pass the test of reasonableness under [s.98(4)].

Meikle v   **[1983] IRLR 351 EAT**
McPhail (Charleston Arms)
Dismissal for an economic reason entailing changes to the workforce within the meaning of reg. 8(2) of the Transfer of Undertakings (Protection of Employment) Regulations 1981 is analogous to redundancy, so that it is reasonable to have regard to what has been said to be the duty of an employer faced with a redundancy situation in the context of [s.98(4)] of the Employment Rights Act.

Nationwide Building Society v   **[2010] IRLR 922 EAT**
Benn
Where a dismissal occurs as a result of changes in terms and conditions of employment on a transfer of an undertaking, whether an employer has complied with its consultation obligations under TUPE is not a factor which is directly applicable to assessment of the fairness of the dismissal under the ERA 1996 where no breach of the TUPE consultation requirements has been established by a successful claim under those regulations, but it is open to the tribunal to have regard to the extent and nature of any consultation, both collective and individual, engaged in by the respondent on the changes in terms and conditions in deciding whether the dismissal was fair.

5. REMEDIES

112. *(1) This section applies where on a complaint under s.111 an employment tribunal finds that the grounds of the complaint are well founded.*

(2) The tribunal shall –

    (a) explain to the complainant what orders may be made under s.113 and in what circumstances they may be made, and

    (b) ask him whether he wishes the tribunal to make such an order.

(3) If the complainant expresses such a wish, the tribunal may make an order under s.113.

(4) If no order is made under s.113, the tribunal shall make an award of compensation for unfair dismissal (calculated in accordance with ss.118–126) to be paid by the employer to the employee.

Re-employment

113. *An order under this section may be –*

    (a) an order for reinstatement (in accordance with s.114), or

    (b) an order for re-engagement (in accordance with s.115),

as the tribunal may decide.

114. *(1) An order for reinstatement is an order that the employer shall treat the complainant in all respects as if he had not been dismissed.*

(2) On making an order for reinstatement the tribunal shall specify –

    (a) any amount payable by the employer in respect of any benefit which the complainant might reasonably be expected to have had but for the dismissal (including arrears of pay) for the period between the date of termination of employment and the date of reinstatement,

    (b) any rights and privileges (including seniority and pension rights) which must be restored to the employee, and

    (c) the date by which the order must be complied with.

(3) If the complainant would have benefited from an improvement in his terms and conditions of employment had he not been dismissed, an order for reinstatement shall require him to be treated as if he had benefited from that improvement from the date on which he would have done so but for being dismissed.

(4) In calculating for the purposes of subsection (2)(a) any amount payable by the employer, the tribunal shall take into account, so as to reduce the employer's liability, any sums received by the complainant in respect of the period between the date of termination of employment and the date of reinstatement by way of –

    (a) wages in lieu of notice or ex gratia payments paid by the employer, or

    (b) remuneration paid in respect of employment with another employer,

and such other benefits as the tribunal thinks appropriate in the circumstances.

115. *(1) An order for re-engagement is an order, on such terms as the tribunal may decide, that the complainant be engaged by the employer, or by a successor of the employer or by an associated employer, in employment comparable to that from which he was dismissed or other suitable employment.*

(2) On making an order for re-engagement the tribunal shall specify the terms on which re-engagement is to take place, including –

    (a) the identity of the employer,

    (b) the nature of the employment,

    (c) the remuneration for the employment,

    (d) any amount payable by the employer in respect of any benefit which the complainant might reasonably be expected to have had but for the dismissal (including arrears of pay) for the period between the date of termination of employment and the date of re-engagement,

    (e) any rights and privileges (including seniority and pension rights) which must be restored to the employee, and

    (f) the date by which the order must be complied with.

(3) In calculating for the purposes of subsection (2)(d) any amount payable by the employer, the tribunal shall take into account, so as to reduce the employer's liability, any sums received by the complainant in respect of the period between the date of termination of employment and the date of re-engagement by way of –

    (a) wages in lieu of notice or ex gratia payments paid by the employer, or

    (b) remuneration paid in respect of employment with another employer,

and such other benefits as the tribunal thinks appropriate in the circumstances.

116. *(1) In exercising its discretion under s.113 the tribunal shall first consider whether to make an order for reinstatement and in so doing shall take into account –*

    (a) whether the complainant wishes to be reinstated,

    (b) whether it is practicable for the employer to comply with an order for reinstatement, and

    (c) where the complainant caused or contributed to some extent to the dismissal, whether it would be just to order his reinstatement.

(2) If the tribunal decides not to make an order for reinstatement it shall then consider whether to make an order for re-engagement and, if so, on what terms.

(3) In so doing the tribunal shall take into account –

    (a) any wish expressed by the complainant as to the nature of the order to be made,

    (b) whether it is practicable for the employer (or a successor or an associated employer) to comply with an order for re-engagement, and

    (c) where the complainant caused or contributed to some extent to the dismissal, whether it would be just to order his re-engagement and (if so) on what terms.

(4) Except in a case where the tribunal takes into account contributory fault under subsection (3)(c) it shall, if it orders re-engagement, do so on terms which are, so far as is reasonably practicable, as favourable as an order for reinstatement.

(5) Where in any case an employer has engaged a permanent replacement for a dismissed employee, the tribunal shall not take that fact into account in determining, for the purposes of subsection (1)(b) or (3)(b), whether it is practicable to comply with an order for reinstatement or re-engagement.

(6) Subsection (5) does not apply where the employer shows –

    (a) that it was not practicable for him to arrange for the dismissed employee's work to be done without engaging a permanent replacement, or

    (b) that –

       (i) he engaged the replacement after the lapse of a reasonable period, without having heard from the dismissed employee that he wished to be reinstated or re-engaged, and

       (ii) when the employer engaged the replacement it was no longer reasonable for him to arrange for the dismissed employee's work to be done except by a permanent replacement.

117. *(1) An employment tribunal shall make an award of compensation, to be paid by the employer to the employee, if –*

(a) *an order under s.113 is made and the complainant is reinstated or re-engaged, but*

(b) *the terms of the order are not fully complied with.*

(2) Subject to s.124, the amount of the compensation shall be such as the tribunal thinks fit having regard to the loss sustained by the complainant in consequence of the failure to comply fully with the terms of the order.

(2A) There shall be deducted from any award under subsection (1) the amount of any award made under s.112(5) at the time of the order under s.113.

(3) Subject to subsections (1) and (2), if an order under s.113 is made but the complainant is not reinstated or re-engaged in accordance with the order, the tribunal shall make –

(a) *an award of compensation for unfair dismissal (calculated in accordance with ss.118–126), and*

(b) *except where this paragraph does not apply, an additional award of compensation of an amount not less than 26 nor more than 52 weeks' pay,*

to be paid by the employer to the employee.

(4) Subsection (3)(b) does not apply where –

(a) *the employer satisfies the tribunal that it was not practicable to comply with the order.*

(7) Where in any case an employer has engaged a permanent replacement for a dismissed employee, the tribunal shall not take that fact into account in determining for the purposes of subsection (4)(a) whether it was practicable to comply with the order for reinstatement or re-engagement unless the employer shows that it was not practicable for him to arrange for the dismissed employee's work to be done without engaging a permanent replacement.

(8) Where in any case an employment tribunal finds that the complainant has unreasonably prevented an order under s.113 from being complied with, in making an award of compensation for unfair dismissal it shall take that conduct into account as a failure on the part of the complainant to mitigate his loss.

EMPLOYMENT RIGHTS ACT 1996 (as amended)

General principles

Pirelli General Cable Works Ltd v   **[1979] IRLR 190 EAT**
Murray
The requirements of [s.112(2)] of the Act are mandatory and require that in every case where a dismissal is found to be unfair, the employment tribunal must explain reinstatement and re-engagement and ask if the complainant wants such an order made. If he says he does, then it must go on to consider whether or not to make either order in the light of the provisions of [s.116] and give both complainant and employer the opportunity to be heard, before exercising its discretion to make such an order or not. This procedure must be followed even in a case where the complainant is professionally represented.

Cowley v   **[1995] IRLR 153 CA**
Manson Timber Ltd
Failure by an employment tribunal to comply with the procedure laid down in [s.112(2)] does not make any decision on compensation a nullity and of no effect in law. An order

made without proper compliance with [s.112] can be set aside by the EAT if it appears that failure to comply with the statutory duty led to the possibility of injustice or unfairness.

Qualcast (Wolverhampton) Ltd v   **[1979] IRLR 98 EAT**
Ross
"Expediency" – which means a state of things which is favourable to the fulfilment of some objective which is in mind, such as the general furtherance of the industrial objectives of the employer – is not a matter which is a proper ground on which a tribunal should decide whether or not to exercise its discretion as to reinstatement. The employment tribunal is required by the statutory provisions to consider three things: the wishes of the employee; whether it is practicable for the employer to comply with the order; and, where the employee caused or contributed to some extent to the dismissal, whether it would be just to order his reinstatement.

King v   **[2012] IRLR 280 EAT**
Royal Bank of Canada Europe Ltd
The issue of whether it is practicable for the employer to reinstate or re-engage the employee must be determined by reference to the circumstances which obtain as at the date such an order would take effect (not as at the date of dismissal).

Whether practicable to make order

Port of London Authority v   **[1994] IRLR 9 CA**
Payne and others
Before ordering re-engagement, an employment tribunal must make a determination or assessment on the evidence before it as to whether it is practicable for the employer to comply with such an order. However, the determination at this stage is of necessity provisional.

Meridian Ltd v   **[1977] IRLR 425 EAT**
Gomersall and another
In deciding whether it is practicable to order reinstatement, an employment tribunal should look at the circumstances of the case taking a broad commonsense view and not try to analyse in too much detail the application of the word "practicable". An employment tribunal may fall into error if it approaches the question of reinstatement on the basis of general objective rules, guidelines and principles.

Clancy v   **[2001] IRLR 331 EAT**
Cannock Chase Technical College
Where an employment tribunal directs itself correctly on the law and hears and accepts evidence as to impracticability and then sets out its reasoning clearly and fully, a plea that the tribunal's refusal to order re-employment was perverse is virtually impossible. Of all the subjects properly to be left to the exclusive province of an employment tribunal

as an "industrial jury", few can be more obviously their territory than the issue of "practicability" within s.116(1)(b) and s.116(3)(b).

Coleman and Stephenson v　　　**[1974] IRLR 343 CA**
Magnet Joinery Ltd
"Practicable" means not merely "possible" but "capable of being carried into effect with success". If re-engagement would inevitably lead to serious industrial strife, it would not be practicable or in accordance with equity that the employees should be re-engaged.

Nothman v　　　**[1980] IRLR 65 CA**
London Borough of Barnet (No.2)
The unfair dismissal legislation is not designed to enable complainants to re-establish or vindicate their reputation or anything of that kind. It is concerned with whether they are fairly or unfairly dismissed and once a conclusion is reached that they were unfairly dismissed, the question is how reasonably and most sensibly to compensate the unfairly dismissed employee. Where, as in the present case, the employee believes himself to be a victim of a conspiracy by his employers, he is not likely to be a satisfactory employee in any circumstances if reinstated or re-engaged.

Wood Group Heavy Industrial　　　**[1998] IRLR 680 EAT**
**　Turbines Ltd v**
Crossan
Where there is a breakdown in trust and confidence, the remedy of re-engagement has very limited scope and will be practicable only in the rarest of cases.

Enessy Co SA t/a The Tulchan　　　**[1978] IRLR 489 EAT**
**　Estate v**
Minoprio and Minoprio
Observed: It is one thing to make an order for reinstatement where the employee concerned works in a factory or other substantial organisation. It is another to do so in the case of a small employer with few staff. Where there must exist a close personal relationship, reinstatement can only be appropriate in exceptional circumstances and to enforce it upon a reluctant employer is not a course which an employment tribunal should pursue unless persuaded by powerful evidence that it would succeed.

Contributory fault

Boots Co plc v　　　**[1986] IRLR 485 EAT**
Lees-Collier
Where a tribunal finds or would be justified in finding that, for the purposes of the compensatory award, the employee had not caused or contributed to his dismissal, they need not address their minds separately to [s.116(1)(c)] and whether it would be just and equitable to order reinstatement where the employee caused or contributed to some extent to the dismissal.

Nairne v　　　**[1989] IRLR 366 CS**
Highlands & Islands Fire Brigade
An order for re-engagement should not have been made where the degree of contribution by the employee to which the employment tribunal had regard was a rate of contribution which no reasonable tribunal could have considered was appropriate.

Terms of order

Artisan Press v　　　**[1986] IRLR 126 EAT**
Srawley and Parker
"Reinstatement" in [s.114] means treating the employee as if he had not been dismissed. It cannot be on less favourable terms than he previously enjoyed. If an employer reinstates an employee on less favourable terms, therefore, it is a failure to comply at all with an order for reinstatement within the meaning of [s.117(3)], rather than a failure fully to comply with the order within the meaning of [s.117(1)]. [Section 117(1)] refers to failure by the employer to comply with ancillary matters which may be specified in the reinstatement order and not to the terms of the order for reinstatement as such.

McBride v　　　**[2013] IRLR 297 CS**
Strathclyde Police Joint Board
Reinstatement is unconditional and involves being returned in all respects to the contractual position existing at the time of dismissal.

O'Laoire v　　　**[1991] IRLR 170 CA**
Jackel International Ltd
Only benefits arising from contractual improvements are covered by the express requirement of [s.114(3)] that a person who is reinstated must be treated as having benefited from any improvement in terms and conditions of employment since the dismissal.

O'Laoire v　　　**[1990] IRLR 70 CA**
Jackel International Ltd
Observed: Arrears of pay between the date of termination and the date by which an employee is to be reinstated should be specified in a reinstatement order by reference to rates of pay or other formulae rather than an actual lump sum since, in theory, reinstatement might take place earlier than the stipulated date. Provision should not be made in a reinstatement order for what is to happen if reinstatement takes place after the stipulated date. Once that date has passed there can be no reinstatement pursuant to the order.

Electronic Data Processing Ltd v　　　**[1986] IRLR 8 EAT**
Wright
If the terms of a tribunal's order for re-engagement are ambiguous or silent as to an important point, it is open to them thereafter to give effect to their intentions by filling out the terms of the order.

Lilley Construction Ltd v   **[1984] IRLR 483 EAT**
Dunn

Employment tribunals should not adopt the practice of making directions that an offer of re-engagement should be made on specified terms within a stated period in lieu of making a re-engagement order in the full form required by [s.115(2)].

Rank Xerox (UK) Ltd v   **[1995] IRLR 568 EAT**
Stryczek

As a matter of law, an employment tribunal cannot order re-engagement on significantly more favourable terms than the employee would have enjoyed if he had been reinstated in his former job.

Electronic Data Processing Ltd v   **[1986] IRLR 8 EAT**
Wright

Where re-engagement is ordered in a lower-paid capacity, the amount payable by the employer in respect of the employee's interim loss in accordance with [s.115(2)(d)] is based on the higher-paid original job.

City & Hackney Health Authority v   **[1990] IRLR 47 EAT**
Crisp

There is no jurisdiction for an employment tribunal to reduce the amount payable under a re-engagement order in respect of loss of earnings between termination and re-engagement on the ground that the employee failed to mitigate that loss.

British Airways v   **[2014] IRLR 683 EAT**
Valencia

Re-engagement is engagement in a different role (albeit comparable or otherwise suitable) and may involve a change in the identity of the employer, the nature of the employment or the terms as to remuneration. To order that the claimant be re-employed in the role he held before dismissal on precisely the same terms and conditions on which he had previously been employed is wrong in principle and not permitted by the statutory scheme as a re-engagement.

Whether practicable to comply with order

Port of London Authority v   **[1994] IRLR 9 CA**
Payne and others

The final conclusion as to practicability is made when an order for re-engagement has been made but not complied with, and the size of the additional award is being considered. The burden of proof rests on the employer. However, the test is "practicability" not "possibility". The employer does not have to show that re-engagement was impossible. It is a matter of what is practicable in the circumstances of the employer's business at the relevant time. Although an employment

tribunal should carefully scrutinise the reasons advanced by the employer, due weight should be given to the commercial judgment of the management. The standard should not be set too high. The employer cannot be expected to explore every possible avenue which ingenuity might suggest.

Port of London Authority v   **[1994] IRLR 9 CA**
Payne and others

It is not practicable to comply with a re-engagement order if there is no suitable available vacancy. The employer is not required to invite applications for voluntary severance from the existing workforce.

Freemans plc v   **[1984] IRLR 486 EAT**
Flynn

A re-engagement order does not place a duty on the employers to search for and find a place for the dismissed employee, irrespective of vacancies that may arise.

Cold Drawn Tubes Ltd v   **[1992] IRLR 160 EAT**
Middleton

Reinstatement cannot be a practicable option where it would result either in redundancies or significant overmanning.

Compensation

O'Laoire v   **[1990] IRLR 70 CA**
Jackel International Ltd

A reinstatement order is wholly unenforceable. If such an order is not complied with, whether wholly or in part, the complainant's only remedy is to apply to the employment tribunal under [s.117] for an award of compensation. The monetary provisions of a reinstatement order do not create a cause of action enforceable through the County Courts.

Parry v   **[2005] IRLR 193 CA**
National Westminster Bank plc

Where an employer refuses to comply with an order for reinstatement, the employee is not entitled to receive the sum specified in the reinstatement order under s.114(2)(a) in respect of arrears of pay and benefits between the date of dismissal and the date of reinstatement as a separate head of compensation, as well as a maximum compensatory award under s.124(1) and an additional award under s.117(3)(b). The amount specified in s.114(2)(a) forms part of the compensatory award to which the statutory cap applies, subject to the provisions of s.124(4) which permit the limit to be exceeded only "to the extent necessary to enable the aggregate of the compensatory and additional awards fully to reflect the amount specified as payable under s.114(2)(a)". Thus, where the amount specified under s.114(2)(a) itself exceeds the statutory cap, that limit will be exceeded so as to permit "full reflection" but any other elements of the compensatory award will not be recoverable because of the statutory cap.

Artisan Press v   **[1986] IRLR 126 EAT**
Srawley and Parker

If an employer reinstates an employee on less favourable terms, or where the purported reinstatement is a sham, the effect is that there is no reinstatement in law and the employee is entitled, therefore, to an additional award.

Mabirizi v   **[1990] IRLR 133 EAT**
National Hospital for
   Nervous Diseases

The additional award is not intended to be a precisely calculated substitute for financial loss but rather a general solatium to be arrived at by fixing the appropriate point on the scale.

Morganite Electrical Carbon Ltd v   **[1987] IRLR 363 EAT**
Donne

While there is a wide discretion as to the matters which can properly be taken into account by an employment tribunal in deciding where in the range the additional award should fall, some sort of proper assessment and balancing must take place. One factor would ordinarily be the view that the tribunal takes of the conduct of the employer in refusing to comply with the re-employment order. It would also be material for the tribunal to take into account the extent to which the compensatory award has met the actual loss suffered by the claimant and to reflect that the statutory limit meant that the tribunal's view as to the true nature of the loss had to be cut down so as to accord with that limit.

Mabirizi v   **[1990] IRLR 133 EAT**
National Hospital for
   Nervous Diseases

In fixing the level of the additional award, an employment tribunal can reflect their finding that the employers had a genuinely felt objection to reinstating the employee, notwithstanding an earlier finding that it would not be impracticable for the employers to comply with a reinstatement order.

Mabirizi v   **[1990] IRLR 133 EAT**
National Hospital for
   Nervous Diseases

It is wrong in principle to use as a factor for fixing the additional award something which is properly and adequately covered by the compensatory award. However, an employee's failure to mitigate loss can be treated as a relevant factor in setting the level of the additional award where that failure is treated only as a general factor going to the merits of the case, as distinct from something producing a quantifiable reduction in a sum to which the employee was otherwise entitled.

Compensation

118. *(1) Where a tribunal makes an award of compensation for unfair dismissal under s.112(4) or 117(3)(a), the award shall consist of –*
- *(a) a basic award (calculated in accordance with ss.119–122 and 126), and*
- *(b) a compensatory award (calculated in accordance with ss.123, 124, 124A and 126).*

119. *(1) Subject to the provisions of this section, ss.120–122 and s.126, the amount of the basic award shall be calculated by –*
- *(a) determining the period, ending with the effective date of termination, during which the employee has been continuously employed,*
- *(b) reckoning backwards from the end of that period the number of years of employment falling within that period, and*
- *(c) allowing the appropriate amount for each of those years of employment.*

(2) In subsection (1)(c) "the appropriate amount" means –
- *(a) one and a half week's pay for a year of employment in which the employee was not below the age of 41,*
- *(b) one week's pay for a year of employment (not within para. (a)) in which he was not below the age of 22, and*
- *(c) half a week's pay for a year of employment not within para. (a) or (b).*

(3) Where 20 years of employment have been reckoned under subsection (1), no account shall be taken under that subsection of any year of employment earlier than those 20 years.

120. *(1) The amount of the basic award (before any reduction under s.122) shall not be less than £5,676* where the reason (or, if more than one, the principal reason) –*
- *(a) in a redundancy case, for selecting the employee for dismissal, or*
- *(b) otherwise, for the dismissal,*

is one of those specified in s.100(1)(a) and (b), 101A(d), 102(1) or 103.

  (1A) ...

  (1B) ...

  (1C) Where an employee is regarded as unfairly dismissed by virtue of s.104F (blacklists) (whether or not the dismissal is unfair or regarded as unfair for any other reason), the amount of the basic award of compensation (before any reduction is made under s.122) shall not be less than £5,000.

121. *The amount of the basic award shall be two weeks' pay where the tribunal finds that the reason (or, where there is more than one, the principal reason) for the dismissal of the employee is that he was redundant and the employee –*
- *(a) by virtue of s.138 is not regarded as dismissed for the purposes of Part XI, or*
- *(b) by virtue of s.141 is not, or (if he were otherwise entitled) would not be, entitled to a redundancy payment.*

122. *(1) Where the tribunal finds that the complainant has unreasonably refused an offer by the employer which (if accepted) would*

---

* It is anticipated that this sum will be increased by statutory instrument where the appropriate date falls on or after 6 April 2015.

have the effect of reinstating the complainant in his employment in all respects as if he had not been dismissed, the tribunal shall reduce or further reduce the amount of the basic award to such extent as it considers just and equitable having regard to that finding.

(2) Where the tribunal considers that any conduct of the complainant before the dismissal (or, where the dismissal was with notice, before the notice was given) was such that it would be just and equitable to reduce or further reduce the amount of the basic award to any extent, the tribunal shall reduce or further reduce that amount accordingly.

(3) Subsection (2) does not apply in a redundancy case unless the reason for selecting the employee for dismissal was one of those specified in s.100(1)(a) and (b), 101A(d), 102(1) or 103; and in such a case subsection (2) applies only to so much of the basic award as is payable because of s.120.

(3A) Where the complainant has been awarded any amount in respect of the dismissal under a designated dismissal procedures agreement, the tribunal shall reduce or further reduce the amount of the basic award to such extent as it considers just and equitable having regard to that award.

(4) The amount of the basic award shall be reduced or further reduced by the amount of –
(a) any redundancy payment awarded by the tribunal under Part XI in respect of the same dismissal, or
(b) any payment made by the employer to the employee on the ground that the dismissal was by reason of redundancy (whether in pursuance of Part XI or otherwise).

(5) Where a dismissal is regarded as unfair by virtue of s.104F (blacklists), the amount of the basic award shall be reduced or further reduced by the amount of any basic award in respect of the same dismissal under s.156 of the Trade Union and Labour Relations (Consolidation) Act 1992 (minimum basic award in case of dismissal on grounds related to trade union membership or activities).

123. (1) Subject to the provisions of this section and ss.124, 124A and 126, the amount of the compensatory award shall be such amount as the tribunal considers just and equitable in all the circumstances having regard to the loss sustained by the complainant in consequence of the dismissal in so far as that loss is attributable to action taken by the employer.

(2) The loss referred to in subsection (1) shall be taken to include –
(a) any expenses reasonably incurred by the complainant in consequence of the dismissal, and
(b) subject to subsection (3), loss of any benefit which he might reasonably be expected to have had but for the dismissal.

(3) The loss referred to in subsection (1) shall be taken to include in respect of any loss of –
(a) any entitlement or potential entitlement to a payment on account of dismissal by reason of redundancy (whether in pursuance of Part XI or otherwise), or
(b) any expectation of such a payment,
only the loss referable to the amount (if any) by which the amount of that payment would have exceeded the amount of a basic award (apart from any reduction under s.122) in respect of the same dismissal.

(4) In ascertaining the loss referred to in subsection (1) the tribunal shall apply the same rule concerning the duty of a person to mitigate his loss as applies to damages recoverable under the common law of England and Wales or (as the case may be) Scotland.

(5) In determining, for the purposes of subsection (1), how far any loss sustained by the complainant was attributable to action taken by the employer, no account shall be taken of any pressure which by –
(a) calling, organising, procuring or financing a strike or other industrial action, or
(b) threatening to do so,
was exercised on the employer to dismiss the employee; and that question shall be determined as if no such pressure had been exercised.

(6) Where the tribunal finds that the dismissal was to any extent caused or contributed to by any action of the complainant, it shall reduce the amount of the compensatory award by such proportion as it considers just and equitable having regard to that finding.

(6A) Where –
(a) the reason (or principal reason) for the dismissal is that the complainant made a protected disclosure, and
(b) it appears to the tribunal that the disclosure was not made in good faith,
the tribunal may, if it considers it just and equitable in all the circumstances to do so, reduce any award it makes to the complainant by no more than 25%.

(7) If the amount of any payment made by the employer to the employee on the ground that the dismissal was by reason of redundancy (whether in pursuance of Part XI or otherwise) exceeds the amount of the basic award which would be payable but for s.122(4), that excess goes to reduce the amount of the compensatory award.

(8) Where the amount of the compensatory award falls to be calculated for the purposes of an award under s.117(3)(a), there shall be deducted from the compensatory award any award made under s.112(5) at the time of the order under s.113.

124. (1) The amount of –
(a) any compensation awarded to a person under s.117(1) and (2), or
(b) a compensatory award to a person calculated in accordance with s.123,
shall not exceed the amount specified in subsection (1ZA).

(1ZA) The amount specified in this subsection is the lower of –
(a) £76,574*, and
(b) 52 multiplied by a week's pay of the person concerned.

(1A) Subsection(1) shall not apply to compensation awarded, or a compensatory award made, to a person in a case where he is regarded as unfairly dismissed by virtue of s.100, 103A, 105(3) or 105(6A).

(3) In the case of compensation awarded to a person under s.117(1) and (2), the limit imposed by this section may be exceeded to the extent necessary to enable the award fully to reflect the amount specified as payable under s.114(2)(a) or s.115(2)(d).

(4) Where –
(a) a compensatory award is an award under para. (a) of subsection (3) of s.117, and
(b) an additional award falls to be made under para. (b) of that subsection,
the limit imposed by this section on the compensatory award may be exceeded to the extent necessary to enable the aggregate of the compensatory and additional awards fully to reflect the amount specified as payable under s.114(2)(a) or s.115(2)(d).

---

* It is anticipated that this sum will be increased by statutory instrument where the appropriate date falls on or after 6 April 2015.

(5) The limit imposed by this section applies to the amount which the employment tribunal would, apart from this section, award in respect of the subject matter of the complaint after taking into account –

> *(a) any payment made by the respondent to the complainant in respect of the matter, and*
>
> *(b) any reduction in the amount of the award required by any enactment or rule of law.*

124A. *Where an award of compensation for unfair dismissal falls to be –*

> *(a) reduced or increased under [s.207A of the Trade Union and Labour Relations (Consolidation) Act 1992 (effect of failure to comply with Code: adjustment of awards)], or*
>
> *(b) increased under s.38 of that Act (failure to give statement of employment particulars),*

the adjustment shall be in the amount awarded under s.118(1)(b) and shall be applied immediately before any reduction under s.123(6) or (7).

126. *(1) This section applies where compensation falls to be awarded in respect of any act both under –*

> *(a) the provisions of this Act relating to unfair dismissal, and*
>
> *(b) the Equality Act 2010.*

(2) An employment tribunal shall not award compensation under either of those Acts in respect of any loss or other matter which is or has been taken into account under the other by the tribunal (or another employment tribunal) in awarding compensation on the same or another complaint in respect of that act.

EMPLOYMENT RIGHTS ACT 1996 (as amended)

207A Effect of failure to comply with Code: adjustment of awards
(1) This section applies to proceedings before an employment tribunal relating to a claim by an employee under any of the jurisdictions listed in Schedule A2.

(2) If, in the case of proceedings to which this section applies, it appears to the employment tribunal that –

> *(a) the claim to which the proceedings relate concerns a matter to which a relevant Code of Practice applies,*
>
> *(b) the employer has failed to comply with that Code in relation to that matter, and*
>
> *(c) that failure was unreasonable,*

the employment tribunal may, if it considers it just and equitable in all the circumstances to do so, increase any award it makes to the employee by no more than 25%.

(3) If, in the case of proceedings to which this section applies, it appears to the employment tribunal that –

> *(a) the claim to which the proceedings relate concerns a matter to which a relevant Code of Practice applies,*
>
> *(b) the employee has failed to comply with that Code in relation to that matter, and*
>
> *(c) that failure was unreasonable,*

the employment tribunal may, if it considers it just and equitable in all the circumstances to do so, reduce any award it makes to the employee by no more than 25%.

(4) In subsections (2) and (3), "relevant Code of Practice" means a Code of Practice issued under this Chapter which relates exclusively or primarily to procedure for the resolution of disputes.

(5) Where an award falls to be adjusted under this section and under s.38 of the Employment Act 2002, the adjustment under this section shall be made before the adjustment under that section.

(6) The Secretary of State may by order amend Schedule A2 for the purpose of –

> *(a) adding a jurisdiction to the list in that Schedule, or*
>
> *(b) removing a jurisdiction from that list.*

(7) The power of the Secretary of State to make an order under subsection (6) includes power to make such incidental, supplementary, consequential or transitional provision as the Secretary of State thinks fit.

(8) An order under subsection (6) shall be made by statutory instrument.

(9) No order shall be made under subsection (6) unless a draft of the statutory instrument containing it has been laid before Parliament and approved by a resolution of each House.

Schedule A2
TRIBUNAL JURISDICTIONS TO WHICH SECTION 207A APPLIES

...

Section 111 of that Act (unfair dismissal).

**TRADE UNION AND LABOUR RELATIONS
(CONSOLIDATION) ACT 1992 (as amended)**

General principles

Norton Tool Co v   **[1972] IRLR 86 NIRC**
Tewson
The general principles for calculating unfair dismissal compensation are twofold: first, to compensate fully but not award a bonus; second, the amount to be awarded is what is just and equitable in all the circumstances having regard to the loss sustained by the complainant. Loss in this context does not include injury to feelings. The burden of proving loss lies with the complainant. The employment tribunal has a duty to set out its reasoning in sufficient detail to show the principles upon which it proceeded.

An award of unfair dismissal compensation should include the following heads of damage:
1. Immediate loss of wages.
2. Future loss of wages.
3. Loss arising from the manner of dismissal.
4. Loss of protection in respect of unfair dismissal.

Dunnachie v   **[2004] IRLR 727 HL**
Kingston upon Hull City Council
Section 123(1) of the Employment Rights Act does not allow for the recovery of non-economic loss resulting from a dismissal. It only permits recovery of pecuniary loss. It does not cover injury to feelings, humiliation or distress.

The decision of the NIRC in *Norton Tool Co Ltd v Tewson* that only economic loss could be compensated was generally assumed to reflect the correct legal position and was consistently applied at all levels until called into question by Lord Hoffmann in *Johnson v Unisys Ltd*. The observation of Lord Hoffman that *Norton Tool* had construed "loss" too narrowly, though lending support to his reasoning, was *obiter*. The language which he used in introducing his comments was not the language of a Law Lord inviting the House to overrule a long-standing decision on a point of statutory construction which was not in issue and not explored in opposing arguments.

Stuart Peters Ltd v   **[2009] IRLR 941 CA**
Bell
The Norton Tool principle that an employee who is unfairly dismissed without notice does not have to give credit for any earnings during the notice period does not apply in a case of constructive dismissal. The Norton Tool principle was expressly based on a precept of good industrial practice: the employer should either give notice or pay the appropriate wages in lieu, and should not be in a better position if they failed to comply with that practice than if they did. Lord Justice Elias reasons that the same considerations as to what is good industrial relations practice do not apply to a case of alleged constructive dismissal. It is not "a general practice, let alone good practice, for the employer to make a payment in lieu of notice at the point when an employee resigns in response to an alleged repudiatory breach".

Polkey v   **[1987] IRLR 503 HL**
A E Dayton Services Ltd
In considering whether an employee would still have been dismissed even if a fair procedure had been followed, there is no need for an all or nothing decision. If the employment tribunal thinks there is a doubt whether or not the employee would have been dismissed, this element can be reflected by reducing the normal amount of compensation by a percentage representing the chance that the employee would still have lost his employment.

Hill v   **[2013] IRLR 274 EAT**
Governing Body of Great Tey Primary School
It is wrong to adopt a "review" approach to making a *Polkey* deduction, asking whether, if a fair procedure had been adopted resulting in dismissal, the tribunal would have found the dismissal fair, and applying the range of reasonable responses to that assessment. The correct approach is "predictive": "could the employer fairly have dismissed and, if so, what were the chances that the employer would have done so?"

Software 2000 Ltd v   **[2007] IRLR 568 EAT**
Andrews
The s.98A(2) exercise of determining whether the employer has shown that the employee would have been dismissed if a fair procedure had been followed, and the assessment of whether, instead, the dismissal is unfair but subject to a *Polkey* reduction, are exercises which run in parallel. There are five possible outcomes:
1. The evidence from the employer may be so unreliable that the exercise of seeking to reconstruct what might have been is too uncertain to make any prediction, though the mere fact that an element of speculation is involved is not a reason for refusing to have regard to the evidence.

2. The employer may show that if fair procedures had been complied with, the dismissal would have occurred when it did in any event. The dismissal will then be fair in accordance with s.98A(2).
3. The tribunal may decide there was a chance of dismissal but it was less than 50%, in which case compensation should be reduced.
4. The tribunal may decide that employment would have continued, but only for a limited period.
5. The tribunal may decide that employment would have continued indefinitely because the evidence that it might have terminated earlier is so scant that it can effectively be ignored.

Dignity Funerals Ltd v   **[2005] IRLR 189 CS**
Bruce
In deciding whether to make a compensatory award in accordance with s.123(1), a tribunal has to consider two main questions: whether the claimant's dismissal was one of the causes of his wage loss; and, if it was, what compensatory award would be just and equitable in all the circumstances. The former question is one of fact; the latter is one of discretion.

Simrad Ltd v   **[1997] IRLR 147 EAT**
Scott
The assessment of a compensatory award in accordance with s.123(1) involves a three-stage process requiring firstly, factual quantification of losses claimed. Secondly, the tribunal must consider the extent to which any or all of those losses are attributable to dismissal or action taken by the employer. The word "attributable" implies that there has to be a direct and natural link between the losses claimed and the conduct of the employer in dismissing, on the basis that the dismissal was the causa causans of the particular loss, ie the immediate cause, and not that it simply arose by reason of a causa sine qua non, ie but for the dismissal the loss would not have arisen. If that is the only connection, the loss is too remote. Thirdly, the phrase "just and equitable" requires the tribunal to look at the conclusions it draws from the first two questions and determine whether, in all the circumstances, it remains reasonable to make the relevant award.

GAB Robins (UK) Ltd v   **[2008] IRLR 317 CA**
Triggs
Losses sustained by a claimant, which are caused by a breach of contract that pre-dates the termination of the employment contract, are not recoverable under a constructive unfair dismissal claim because they are not incurred *in consequence of the dismissal*, and can only be claimed in a separate contractual action.

Leonard v   **[1998] IRLR 693 CS**
Strathclyde Buses Ltd
An employment tribunal has to apply the statutory test for assessing a compensatory award as a whole and assess what is just and equitable having regard to the loss so far as it is attributable to the employer. The extent to which the tribunal can have regard to what followed after dismissal is primarily a matter for it to assess on the particular facts. To introduce

principles of foreseeability or remoteness in the technical sense in which those concepts apply in other legal contexts is inconsistent with the discretionary approach which has governed the assessment of unfair dismissal compensation ever since *Norton Tool Co Ltd v Tewson.*

Townson v   **[1981] IRLR 382 EAT**
The Northgate Group Ltd
The only particular circumstance to which the statute directs the employment tribunal's attention in assessing compensatory awards is the complainant's loss flowing from the dismissal. In general terms that will be the lost earnings between the date of dismissal and the date of obtaining new employment, bearing in mind the employee's obligation to mitigate his loss. After looking at the actual loss, in deciding what is just and equitable, the tribunal must then look at all the circumstances. This includes asking the question, "How unfair was the unfair dismissal?"

Babcock FATA Ltd v   **[1987] IRLR 173 CA**
Addison
The object of unfair dismissal compensation is to compensate the employee fully but not to award a bonus. The statutory provisions provide no basis for an award of wages over and above the period of loss in addition to wages due for the period already paid.

Morgans v   **[2005] IRLR 234 EAT**
Alpha Plus Security Ltd
The statutory basis for recovery of compensation for unfair dismissal in s.123 is the reimbursement of loss suffered. The actual pecuniary loss is the maximum sum that a complainant can be awarded. Where a complainant has suffered a lesser loss by virtue of his receipt of benefits which would not have been paid had he remained in employment, or because of earnings from a new employer, he must give credit for them. Loss which is in fact recovered and recouped by receipt of monies from third parties is simply not a loss suffered. If credit is not given, then the tribunal would be compensating the claimant in a greater amount than the loss he or she has suffered.

Paggetti v   **[2002] IRLR 861 EAT**
Cobb
Where a claimant's actual wage is below the statutory minimum wage, the higher figure must be used for calculating a "week's pay" for the purposes of assessing the basic award, and the net weekly wage to which the applicant was entitled under his contract of employment for the purposes of calculating the loss of earnings element of the compensatory award. To do otherwise would be to disregard the legal obligation of the employer to pay the statutory minimum wage.

Lifeguard Assurance Ltd v   **[1977] IRLR 56 EAT**
Zadrozny and another
The purpose of assessing compensation is not to express disapproval of industrial relations policy but to compensate the employee for financial loss. The employment tribunal, in assessing compensation, should not fall into the benevolent error of awarding compensation not for some loss due to the unfair nature of the dismissal but more out of sympathy for the predicament in which the employee finds himself.

Bentwood Bros (Manchester) Ltd v   **[2003] IRLR 364 CA**
Shepherd
Given that an employment tribunal, as the industrial jury, can be expected to make broad-brush assessments which reflect the tribunal's local knowledge and experience, the Court of Appeal, like the EAT, will be reluctant to interfere with a tribunal's assessment of loss.

Burlo v   **[2007] IRLR 145 CA**
Langley
There is no principle of law under which precepts of good industrial or employment practice should be applied in assessing the compensatory award under s.123 of ERA 1996, if the result of such application would be an award greater than the loss caused to the employee as a consequence of the dismissal.

Gallop v   **[2013] IRLR 23 EAT**
Newport City Council
A tribunal may not reduce compensation to reflect the chance that a settlement may have been reached. They must not enquire into negotiations between the parties before them where no agreement is reached and where there has been no clear and unequivocal waiver of privilege by the parties.

Just and equitable

Dignity Funerals Ltd v   **[2005] IRLR 189 CS**
Bruce
A compensatory award depends on proof of loss. Therefore, any application of the just and equitable principle must be underpinned by findings in fact establishing that the loss was caused to a material extent by the dismissal. If the dismissal was not a cause of the claimant's loss of wages, no award is due. If it was the sole cause, the full award will normally be appropriate. Where dismissal is merely one of two or more concurrent causes of the employee's loss, or where the dismissal was a cause of his loss for only part of the period, a just and equitable award would in all likelihood be of less than the full amount of the wage loss.

Morgans v   **[2005] IRLR 234 EAT**
Alpha Plus Security Ltd
The concept of justice and equity does not enable recovery of a greater sum than the actual loss suffered. There is no room for the approach of the NIRC in *Norton Tool Co Ltd v Tewson* or of the Court of Appeal in *Babcock FATA Ltd v Addison* whereby "the employee is to be treated as having suffered a loss in so far as he recovers less than he would have received in accordance with good industrial practice".

Neither by way of penalising an employer for an unfair industrial practice nor by way of adopting some broad brush just and equitable approach is there any basis for treating a loss which has not occurred as having occurred.

O'Donoghue v   **[2001] IRLR 615 CA**
Redcar & Cleveland Borough Council
An employment tribunal must award such compensation as is "just and equitable". If the facts are such that a tribunal, while finding that a claimant has been dismissed unfairly (whether substantively or procedurally), concludes that, but for the dismissal, the claimant would have been bound soon thereafter to be dismissed fairly by reason of some course of conduct or characteristic attitude which the employer reasonably regards as unacceptable but which the employee cannot or will not moderate, then it is just and equitable that compensation for the unfair dismissal should be awarded on that basis. Accordingly, in this case, the tribunal was entitled to find that the claimant's divisive and antagonistic approach to her colleagues would inevitably have led to her fair dismissal within a further period of six months and to therefore regard the date six months after the date of her termination as a cut-off point for the purposes of assessing her unfair dismissal compensation.

W Devis & Sons Ltd v   **[1977] IRLR 314 HL**
Atkins
In assessing unfair dismissal compensation, an employment tribunal is entitled to have regard to subsequently discovered misconduct and, if they think fit, to award nominal or nil compensation. It cannot be just and equitable that a sum should be awarded in compensation when in fact the employee has suffered no injustice in being dismissed. There is no inconsistency in finding that there was an unfair dismissal and in awarding no compensation. An employee may bring about his dismissal wholly by his own misconduct and yet that dismissal, which would otherwise have been held to have been fair, may be held to be unfair through a failure to follow the correct procedure. In such a case, the just and equitable award may be one of nil compensation. Parliament cannot possibly have intended that a dishonest employee who has successfully concealed his defalcations up to the time of dismissal, whose conduct, if known, would justify his summary dismissal, should, in addition to the proceeds of his dishonesty, obtain compensation from his employers.

Soros and Soros v   **[1994] IRLR 264 EAT**
Davison and Davison
Post-dismissal conduct is not relevant in determining the amount of compensation which is "just and equitable in all the circumstances".

Edwards v   **[2001] IRLR 733 EAT**
Governors of Hanson School
The law does not require that questions of responsibility for the illness of a claimant which made dismissal inevitable must be ignored when deciding whether or not it is just and equitable to make a compensatory award for unfair dismissal. The words "just and equitable" enable an employment tribunal to take full account of the conduct of the employer and the employee, provided that the award remains compensation of the employee rather than punishment of the employer. If it is found that misconduct for which the employers were liable caused or contributed to the claimant's ill health leading to his dismissal, it is for the tribunal to assess whether it would be just and equitable that a compensatory award should follow and, if so, to what extent.

Trico-Folberth Ltd v   **[1989] IRLR 396 CA**
Devonshire
That an employee *could* have been fairly dismissed on another ground does not mean that it is not just and equitable for the employee to receive a compensatory award.
Per Nourse LJ: It cannot be just and equitable for an employee to be deprived of the compensation to which he would otherwise be entitled if the employers would not have relied on that other ground.

Courage Take Home Trade Ltd v   **[1986] IRLR 427 EAT**
Keys
Whether it would be just and equitable to award compensation to an employee who, before presenting his complaint of unfair dismissal, accepted a sum from his employer "in full and final settlement", depends upon the facts of the case.

Standard of proof

Tidman v   **[1977] IRLR 218 EAT**
Aveling Marshall Ltd
It is the duty of the employment tribunal itself to raise the five categories of compensatory award: (1) the immediate loss of wages; (2) the manner of dismissal; (3) future loss of wages; (4) loss of protection in respect of unfair dismissal; and (5) loss of pension rights. It would be contrary to the spirit of the legislation if it were held that simply because a man himself did not put forward a particular ground that, thereby, he might forever be prevented from raising it. It is the duty of the employment tribunal itself to inquire into the various heads of damage. It is the responsibility of the aggrieved person, once the categories have been investigated, to prove the loss and, therefore, it is essential that the difference between the inquiry into the categories and the proof of any loss under any one of those categories should always be borne in mind.

Copson and another v   **[1974] IRLR 247 NIRC**
Eversure Accessories Ltd
In the assessment of awards of compensation for unfair dismissal, the burden of proving the loss and its extent is on the claimant, though the information needed, particularly as far as pensions are concerned, might well be in the hands of the

employer. Tribunals therefore should be vigilant in ensuring that claimants are aware that they can ask the tribunal to use its powers to order the employer to disclose documents which are relevant to the issues to be decided.

Assessing loss

Notice period

Burlo v   **[2007] IRLR 145 CA**
Langley
The principle set out in *Norton Tool Co Ltd v Tewson*, that in calculating an unfairly dismissed employee's compensation an employee who is dismissed without notice should receive a full notice payment without having to give credit for sums earned from other employers during the notice period, should be applied unless and until the House of Lords decides otherwise.

Hilti (GB) Ltd v   **[1974] IRLR 53 NIRC**
Windridge
In calculating an employee's loss of earnings due to an unfair dismissal, "net" pay should be used in respect of all periods, including the notice period.

Loss of earnings

Scope v   **[2007] IRLR 155 CA**
Thornett
Any assessment of future loss of earnings inevitably involves a speculative element and where there is evidence that the employment would not have continued indefinitely then that must be taken into account.

Dench v   **[1998] IRLR 653 CA**
Flynn & Partners
A loss consequent upon unfair dismissal does not necessarily cease when a claimant gets employment of a permanent nature at an equivalent or higher salary than the employee previously enjoyed. To regard such an event as always putting an end to the attribution of the loss to the unfair dismissal could lead to an award which is not just and equitable. What the tribunal has to determine is whether the loss in question was caused by the unfair dismissal or by some other cause.

Tradewinds Airways Ltd v   **[1981] IRLR 272 EAT**
Fletcher
In determining how the dismissal affected the employee's future job prospects and consequent earnings, the employment tribunal is required to compare the employee's salary prospects for the future in each job and see as best they can how long it will take the employee to reach in his new job the equivalent salary to that he would have reached had he remained with his old employers. The amount of short-fall,

measured by reference to difference in net take home pay, during the period before he reaches parity is his future loss.

Kinzley v   **[1987] IRLR 490 EAT**
Minories Finance Ltd
The loss sustained by a complainant in consequence of his dismissal should be based on what he was entitled to, whether or not he was receiving it at the time he was dismissed. Any dispute as to the terms of the contract and the amount properly payable to the employee under it should be investigated by the tribunal. Until the tribunal have determined the base figure, they cannot properly exercise their discretion and decide what is fair and reasonable having regard to the loss sustained.

York Trailer Co Ltd v   **[1973] IRLR 348 NIRC**
Sparkes
An anticipated salary increase should be taken into account in assessing loss of earnings where the evidence reveals a high probability that such an increase would be paid.

Morganite Electrical Carbon Ltd v   **[1987] IRLR 363 EAT**
Donne
There is no justification either in the statute or in practice for limiting future loss to any particular period. The amount of compensation is governed by a statutory maximum but, subject to that, the range must be determined by the evidence in any particular case.

Port of Tilbury (London) Ltd v   **[2005] IRLR 92 EAT**
Birch
It is not necessarily an error of law for a tribunal to award more than a claimant claims. Especially where a claimant is not legally represented, a tribunal may feel that it is necessary to do so in order to do justice.

Bateman v   **[1974] IRLR 101 NIRC**
British Leyland UK Ltd
How long an employee is likely to suffer loss flowing from his dismissal is a matter to be estimated by the tribunal on the basis of its members' collective knowledge of industrial relations in its own area.

Fougère v   **[1976] IRLR 259 EAT**
Phoenix Motor Co Ltd
In estimating the length of time that a successful complainant is likely to remain unemployed for the purpose of assessing compensation for unfair dismissal, an employment tribunal should take into account as one of the circumstances the personal characteristics of the person dismissed, such as that he was elderly or in poor health, provided these characteristics existed at the date of dismissal.

Wardle v   **[2011] IRLR 604 CA**
Credit Agricole Corporate and
** Investment Bank**
When awarding compensation for dismissal, future loss of

earnings should normally be assessed only up to the point when there is a more than 50% chance that the employee would have obtained a job at an equivalent salary level.

Kingston upon Hull City Council v   [2003] IRLR 843 EAT
Dunnachie (No.3)
HSBC Bank plc v
Drage
In calculating unfair dismissal compensation for future loss of earnings, the Ogden tables should only be relied upon where it is established that there is a prima facie career-long loss.

James W Cook & Co (Wivenhoe) Ltd   [1990] IRLR 386 CA
   (in liquidation) v
Tipper and others
An employee unfairly dismissed on grounds of redundancy cannot be awarded compensation for loss of wages beyond the date when he would have been dismissed in any event because the business closed down.

Delanair Ltd v   [1976] IRLR 340 EAT
Mead
Where an employee is unfairly dismissed on grounds of redundancy, the assessment of his compensation depends on whether the employment tribunal finds that he would have been fairly made redundant at a later date.

Young's of Gosport Ltd v   [1977] IRLR 433 EAT
Kendell
In relating the possibility of redundancy to future loss, an employment tribunal should not speculate and should not come to a conclusion as to the likelihood of a dismissal in any event due to redundancy without there being some evidence to support that sort of conclusion.

Elkouil v   [2002] IRLR 174 EAT
Coney Island Ltd
There is no rigid rule that compensation falls to be calculated by assessing how long the consultation process would have taken and assuming that the employee would have been employed for that further period and that that was the measure of his loss. In this case, it was clear to the employers some ten weeks prior to dismissing the claimant that he was going to be made redundant, and they should have started the consultation process at that stage by warning the claimant that he was at risk. Had they done so, the claimant would have had the opportunity of looking for another job some ten weeks earlier than he in fact could. He therefore lost the chance of being re-employed substantially earlier than he was and the appropriate measure of compensation was ten weeks' pay.

Barrel Plating and Phosphating   [1976] IRLR 262 EAT
   Co Ltd v
Danks
The assessment of compensation for unfair dismissal can include a sum to take account of loss of earnings after the

employee has reached normal retiring age. That employees over normal retiring age are excluded from making a complaint of unfair dismissal does not mean that Parliament can be taken to have extended that statutory guillotine to the quantum of compensation. If it had been the intention of the draftsman to restrict compensation to the determination of benefits likely to accrue before normal retiring age (or 65 in the case of a man, 60 in the case of a woman), the draftsman would have expressly stated that limitation in the provisions dealing with the calculation of compensation. Where there is evidence therefore on which to conclude that an employee would, had he not been unfairly dismissed, have continued working after retirement age, such loss of earnings can be taken into account.

F C Shepherd & Co Ltd v   [1985] IRLR 275 EAT
Jerrom
Where an apprentice is unfairly dismissed during the course of his apprenticeship, the employment tribunal is entitled to find that his opportunities of acquiring skilled status are thereby severely reduced and to fix at a substantial figure the sum required to compensate him for such diminution.

Dignity Funerals Ltd v   [2005] IRLR 189 CS
Bruce
Where a claimant suffers loss in the period after dismissal because he is prevented from working due to ill health, the employment tribunal must decide whether the illness was caused to any material extent by the dismissal itself; whether, if so, it had continued to be so caused for all or part of the period up to the hearing; and, if it was so still caused at the date of the hearing, for how long it would continue to be so caused. It is essential that the tribunal should make clear-cut findings on these questions before any question of a compensatory award can arise.

Dunnachie v   [2003] IRLR 384 EAT
Kingston upon Hull City Council
Williams v
Southampton Institute
Dawson v
Stonham Housing Association Ltd
Psychiatric illness may result in economic loss where a claimant can show that, by virtue of an "internal reason" such as a psychiatric or other illness or condition or a mental state of mind such as stress, distress or depression, he or she was not physically or mentally fit to take up alternative employment as early or as suitably as they would otherwise have done and/or ever; or that by virtue of "external reasons" such as stigma damage, loss of professional status, loss of reputation or embarrassment vis à vis potential alternative employers, notwithstanding that the claimant was trying to find alternative employment and would ordinarily have been able to achieve it, no or no suitable employer was prepared to employ him or her, at any rate on terms that would not cause continuing loss. Recovery will only arise if

such condition or state of mind impact upon continued employment.

Eastwood v [2004] IRLR 733 HL
Magnox Electric plc
McCabe v
Cornwall County Council
Observed (per Lord Steyn): Contrary to the assumption of the majority of the House of Lords in *Johnson v Unisys Ltd*, an award under s.123(1) cannot compensate an employee for any psychiatric injury resulting from the employer's conduct. The jurisdiction of an employment tribunal does not extend to awarding compensation "in respect of personal injuries". A claim in contract or tort for damages for psychiatric injury is a claim in respect of personal injuries. There is no reason to give the words "in respect of personal injuries" in the statutory regime governing employment tribunals any different meaning. On the plain meaning of those words, claims for financial loss caused by psychiatric injury are excluded from the jurisdiction of employment tribunals.

Hough and others v [1991] IRLR 194 EAT
Leyland DAF Ltd
In assessing compensation where the employee has been unfit for work since dismissal, a tribunal should take account of the loss of any sickness benefit which attached to the former employment.

Hilton International Hotels (UK) Ltd v [1994] IRLR 267 EAT
Faraji
An employee might be entitled to compensation for loss of earnings notwithstanding that he was in receipt of state invalidity benefit during the relevant period. The employment tribunal is entitled to look behind the payment of the benefit, inquire what the nature of the disability was and decide whether it was attributable to the action of the employer in unfairly dismissing the employee.

Sheffield Forgemasters [2009] IRLR 192 EAT
International Ltd v
Fox
A claimant is not precluded from claiming compensation for loss of future earnings in respect of the periods for which he was receiving incapacity benefit merely on the grounds that he was receiving those benefits, though, of course, credit must be given for the sums received. The mere fact that an employee might be deemed "incapable of work" for the purpose of claiming incapacity benefit does not mean that he or she is unable to work. Accordingly, tribunals must consider all the evidence before deciding if the claimant would have earned any money in a period for which compensation is being claimed.

Justfern Ltd v [1994] IRLR 164 EAT
D'Ingerthorpe and others
In calculating the employee's economic loss, the employment tribunal was entitled to make no allowance for an education-

al grant in respect of a course he had embarked upon following his dismissal, on the ground that it would not be just and equitable for the employers to benefit from the employee's efforts to improve himself.

Other losses

Melia v [2006] IRLR 117 CA
Magna Kansei Ltd
An employment tribunal is entitled to make an allowance for delayed payment of past earnings. This does not represent an award of interest. It recognises that money that is paid later than it should have been gives rise to a loss. Where there is also a loss of future earnings that is subject to a deduction for accelerated payment it would be just and equitable to treat the two losses in a consistent way.

Harvey v [1995] IRLR 416 EAT
Institute of the Motor Industry
There is no rule of law requiring an award for loss of statutory rights.

Puglia v [1996] IRLR 70 EAT
C James & Sons
Where an employment tribunal finds that the employee would have been fairly dismissed in any event at a later date, it is entitled not to make an award for loss of statutory rights.

Brownson v [1978] IRLR 73 EAT
Hire Service Shops Ltd
Loss of overtime earnings can be taken into account in assessing an employee's loss of earnings and other benefits for the purposes of calculating his compensatory award.

Tradewinds Airways Ltd v [1981] IRLR 272 EAT
Fletcher
Tax free allowances which were paid to the employee to reimburse him for expenses necessarily incurred in the course of his job and in respect of which there was no profit element are not properly to be included in the calculation of the compensatory award.

Daley v [1981] IRLR 385 EAT
A E Dorsett (Almar Dolls) Ltd
Loss of a service-related notice entitlement is a head of damage that can be reflected in the compensatory award. A claim for compensation for loss of entitlement to notice is not a claim in respect of loss of earnings over a period. It is a claim for compensation for the loss of an intangible benefit, namely that of being entitled, in the course of employment, to a longer notice than might otherwise be the case. That loss of service-related notice entitlement does provide a sustainable head of damage was accepted by the NIRC in 1974 in *Hilti (GB) Ltd v Windridge*. Though in that case the NIRC thought that the employment tribunal's award of net pay for half the period of notice was somewhat high, they

held that it was not sufficiently high for them to interfere. Given that economic conditions are worse now than they were in 1974, it could be that the benefit of longer notice is more valuable than it was then. In the present case, it would do no injustice to either side to award under this head a sum equivalent to half the employee's statutory notice entitlement.

Arthur Guinness Son & Co (GB) Ltd v   **[1989] IRLR 288 EAT**
Green
In compensating an employee for loss of entitlement to long notice, the practice is to award a sum calculated by multiplying net pay by a fraction of the statutory max-imum period of notice of 12 weeks but the convention is never to award a sum based on a multiplier of more than six weeks.

S H Muffett Ltd v   **[1986] IRLR 488 EAT**
Head
The significance of loss of service-related notice entitlement depends upon the double contingency that the dismissed employee will get a new job and that he will be dismissed from that job before building up his notice entitlement to what it was in his previous job. The employment tribunal must consider the remoteness or otherwise of these contingencies using their knowledge of local conditions.

Leonard v   **[1998] IRLR 693 CS**
Strathclyde Buses Ltd
A compensatory award can reflect an increase in the value of shares in the company which an employee had to sell back to the employers on termination.

Gardiner-Hill v   **[1982] IRLR 498 EAT**
Roland Berger Technics Ltd
Expenses incurred by an unfairly dismissed employee in setting up his own business following the dismissal is an expense to which he was put as a result of the dismissal and is a recoverable head of damage.

Malik v   **[1997] IRLR 462 HL**
BCCI
An employee may be compensated for loss of reputation caused by the employer's breach of the implied term of trust and confidence which prejudicially affects the employee's future prospects so as to give rise to continuing financial losses.

Fox v   **[2013] IRLR 812 CA**
British Airways plc
Unfair dismissal compensation may include loss of the chance of a death-in-service benefit despite it only being payable on the death of the employee, as it forms part of an employee's employment benefits. Ordinarily, the amount recoverable by the employee would be the cost of the employee buying such a benefit. However, in the unusual circumstances where an employee dies shortly after his dis-

missal, the employee's estate is entitled to recover, on behalf of the deceased employee, the full amount of the benefit which would have been payable had he been in employment at the time of his death. This is because an employment tribunal, when assessing loss, is entitled to take into account the situation as it is known, and does not have to assess the loss as at the date of the alleged unlawful dismissal.

Loss of pension rights

This is a recognised head of damage in accordance with the Norton Tool principles. Because of the complexities involved in assessing compensation for loss of pension rights, in 1980 a document was drawn up by the Government Actuary's Department for the guidance of employment tribunals. This has been superseded by a set of guidelines* prepared by a committee of employment tribunal judges, in consultation with the Actuary's Department. These give general guidance on several aspects of pension loss with specific recommendations on the three main heads of loss: loss of pension rights from the date of dismissal to the date of the hearing; loss of future rights; and loss of enhancement of accrued rights. An appendix sets out the revised Government Actuary's Department paper and tables on assessing loss.

Port of Tilbury (London) Ltd v   **[2005] IRLR 92 EAT**
Birch
There is no duty on an employment tribunal to follow the guidelines in the booklet "Employment Tribunals: Compensation for loss of pension rights". The tribunal's first duty is to consider any credible evidence and submissions put forward by the parties in order to ascertain whether a fair and equitable assessment of the loss of pension rights can be worked out on that basis. If it cannot, the tribunal must explain adequately why not. Where there is little forthcoming from the parties, the booklet may assist the tribunal in making its assessment.

Bingham v   **[1992] IRLR 298 EAT**
Hobourn Engineering Ltd
There is no error of law in not giving precise effect to the guidelines set out in the booklet. In each case, it is a question of evaluating the facts on either side to see what adjustment should be made or whether the guidelines are a safe guide at all.

Griffin v   **[2014] IRLR 962 CA**
Plymouth Hospital NHS Trust
The simplified approach to the calculation of pension loss in the guidelines is not appropriate where the former member of a final salary scheme has found a new job where the employer makes contributions to a money purchase scheme. In those circumstances, the substantial loss approach should be used.

---

* *Employment Tribunals: Compensation for loss of pension rights.* Available online or from the Office for Public Sector Information.

Aegon UK Corp Services Ltd v   [2009] IRLR 1042 CA
Roberts

In calculating compensation for financial loss, different principles of causation should not be applied to different aspects of the remuneration package. Lord Justice Elias states: "I do not accept that pensions have some special status in this calculation. The pension is simply part of the overall remuneration package – in essence deferred remuneration – albeit an important part, and must be assessed accordingly."

Clancy v   [2001] IRLR 331 EAT
Cannock Chase Technical College

A system of computation based on the value of the employers' contributions is not appropriate in assessing loss of pension rights under a scheme which yields not only an income benefit but also a lump sum arising as of right rather than by commutation. The 1991 guidelines on compensation for loss of pension rights provide no yardstick for the computation of loss in such a case.

Manpower Ltd v   [1983] IRLR 281 EAT
Hearne

In no circumstances should the assessment of loss of pension rights require the employee to produce, or the employment tribunal to insist upon, elaborate statistical or other evidence on the point. If employers wish to adduce elaborate evidence, they do so at their own expense and risk. The complications inherent in assessing loss of pension rights provide no exception to the general rough and ready approach to the assessment of unfair dismissal compensation.

TBA Industrial Products Ltd v   [1984] IRLR 48 EAT
Locke

In applying a withdrawal factor, the employment tribunal can take account of the probability that the employee would have been fairly dismissed on grounds of his performance and therefore would not have remained in the employer's employ until normal retiring age.

Prescribed element

Mason v   [1982] IRLR 454 EAT
Wimpey Waste Management

Paragraph 5(2) of the Employment Protection (Recoupment of Unemployment Benefit and Supplementary Benefit) Regulations 1977 provides in terms that the amount of the prescribed element must be reduced by the same proportion that a compensatory award is reduced by to bring it down to the statutory maximum.

Mason v   [1982] IRLR 454 EAT
Wimpey Waste Management

Where there is a successful appeal to the EAT followed by a further hearing before an employment tribunal, the period covered by the prescribed element terminates when the second employment tribunal reaches its conclusion.

Basic award

Fenton v   [1986] IRLR 64 EAT
Stablegold Ltd

Given a relevant transfer and given a dismissal beforehand made unfairly by the transferor, followed by a re-engagement and subsequent unfair dismissal by the transferee, the joint effect of the Employment Protection (Consolidation) Act and the Transfer of Undertakings Regulations is to establish the necessary continuity of employment and transfer liability so as to enable a basic award to be claimed in both cases from the transferee.

Brownson v   [1978] IRLR 73 EAT
Hire Service Shops Ltd

Loss of overtime earnings should not be taken into account in calculating an employee's basic award.

Boorman v   [1995] IRLR 553 CA
Allmakes Ltd

Section [122(4)] applies to reduce the basic award by the amount of a statutory redundancy payment made by the employer only where the dismissal was in fact by reason of redundancy. It is not enough that the employer made an ex gratia payment to the employee which was expressed as being on the ground that the dismissal was for redundancy, even if the employee accepted that description at the time.

Chelsea Football Club and Athletic   [1981] IRLR 73 EAT
Co Ltd v
Heath

Whether an employee is still entitled to a basic award if he has already received an ex gratia payment from his employer depends upon the nature of the payment. If an employer admits that he has unfairly dismissed an employee and pays him an amount specifically referable to the basic award for which he is liable under the Act, the employee is still entitled to go to an employment tribunal and ask for a declaration that he was unfairly dismissed and entitled to the basic award. But the employer is entitled to say that he has paid the basic award and, in those circumstances, the tribunal is not obliged by the provisions of the statute to make another order in the employee's favour.

Similarly, if the employer denies that there has been an unfair dismissal but pays the employee a sum on the basis that, if he is wrong, that will be the amount of the basic award, and if an employment tribunal then finds that the employee was unfairly dismissed, the employer is entitled to say that he has already paid the basic award and the tribunal is not required to make such an award.

However, where a general payment is made, rather than a specific payment in respect of the basic award, whether that payment is to be taken to have included any rights which the employee might have under the statute is a question of construction in each case.

Mitigation

Hardy v   **[2004] IRLR 420 EAT**
Polk (Leeds) Ltd

A compensatory award is based on compensating the victim of an unfair dismissal for his or her loss; it is not a penal award, penalising the employers for their conduct. There is the same duty to mitigate that loss, so far as the employee is concerned, as there is at common law, which means that the employee must take reasonable steps to obtain alternative employment.

Bessenden Properties Ltd v   **[1974] IRLR 338 CA**
Corness

Questions relating to the duty of dismissed employees to mitigate their loss are questions of fact for the employment tribunal to determine. Where one party seeks to allege that another party has failed to mitigate a loss, the burden of proof is on the party making that allegation.

Wilding v   **[2002] IRLR 524 CA**
British Telecommunications plc

Per Sedley LJ: It is not enough for the wrongdoer to show that it would have been reasonable to take the steps he has proposed. He must show that it was unreasonable of the innocent party not to take them. This is an important legal distinction, reflecting the fact that if there is more than one reasonable response open to the wronged party, the wrongdoer has no right to determine his choice. It is only where the wrongdoer can show affirmatively that the other party acted unreasonably in relation to his duty to mitigate that the defence will succeed.

Fyfe v   **[1989] IRLR 331 EAT**
Scientific Furnishings Ltd

The decision in *Bessenden Properties Ltd v Corness* that it is for the employers to make good their claim that the employee failed to mitigate his loss is binding. The wording of [s.123(4)] that "the tribunal shall apply the same rule concerning the duty of a person to mitigate his loss as applies to damages recoverable under common law", does not shift the onus of proof in an unfair dismissal case from the employer to the employee. The wording of [s.123(4)] is merely to direct that the common law rules on mitigation are to apply and it has long been settled under those rules that the onus is on the defendant.

Wilding v   **[2002] IRLR 524 CA**
British Telecommunications plc

In determining whether a dismissed employee has failed in his duty to mitigate his loss by refusing of an offer of re-employment, the following principles apply: (i) it is the duty of the employee to act as a reasonable person unaffected by the prospect of compensation from their former employer; (ii) the onus is on the former employer as the wrongdoer to show that the employee had failed in his duty to mitigate his loss by unreasonably refusing an offer of re-employment; (iii) the test of reasonableness is an objective one based on the totality of the evidence; (iv) in applying that test, the circumstances in which the offer was made and refused, the attitude of the former employer, the way in which the employee had been treated, and all the surrounding circumstances, including the employee's state of mind, should be taken into account; (v) the court or tribunal must not be too stringent in its expectations of the injured party.

F & G Cleaners Ltd v   **[2012] IRLR 892 EAT**
Saddington

If a TUPE transferee refuses to engage the employees of the transferor as employees but offers them work on a self-employed basis and on "substantially less attractive" terms, the employees cannot be said to have unreasonably failed to mitigate their loss if they do not accept such an offer.

Gardiner-Hill v   **[1982] IRLR 498 EAT**
Roland Berger Technics Ltd

In the case of failure to mitigate, it is not appropriate for the employment tribunal to make a percentage reduction in the total sum of compensation. In order to show a failure to mitigate, what has to be shown is that if a particular step had been taken, the dismissed employee, after a particular time, on a balance of probabilities, would have gained employment. From then onwards, the loss flowing from the unfair dismissal would have been extinguished or reduced by his income from that other source. In fixing the amount to be deducted for a failure to mitigate, therefore, it is necessary for the employment tribunal to identify what step should have been taken, the date on which that step would have produced an alternative income and, thereafter to reduce compensation by the alternative income which would have been earned.

Prestwick Circuits Ltd v   **[1990] IRLR 191 CS**
McAndrew

Conduct before dismissal is not relevant to the question of mitigation of loss.

Sweetlove v   **[1979] IRLR 195 EAT**
Redbridge & Waltham Forest Area
   Health Authority

An unreasonable refusal by a dismissed employee of an offer by the employer to reinstate him deprives the employee of the right to claim any loss. An unreasonably refused offer of reinstatement means either that the employee has failed to mitigate his loss or that the loss he suffered flowed from his own act and not that of his employer. In the same way that accepting an offer of reinstatement would restore all the employee's rights, including his existing pension rights and the opportunity of earning future wages and acquiring future pension rights, so an unreasonable refusal of an offer of reinstatement deprives the employee of the right to claim any loss.

A G Bracey v   **[1973] IRLR 210 NIRC**
Iles

The duty of mitigation does not require the dismissed employee to take the first job that comes along, irrespective of pay and job prospects. The dismissed employee has a duty to act reasonably in order to mitigate his loss. It may be more reasonable in the interests both of the employee and the employer, who has to pay compensation, for the employee to wait a little time, provided he uses the time well and seeks a better-paid job which will reduce his overall loss and the amount of compensation which his previous employer ultimately has to pay.

Daley v   **[1981] IRLR 385 EAT**
A E Dorsett (Almar Dolls) Ltd

Though in certain circumstances an employment tribunal may find that it was reasonable for a dismissed employee not to accept subsequent employment because thereunder he would be receiving less than the unemployment benefit or any other benefit he might be obtaining from the State, they should be slow to do so.

Bessenden Properties Ltd v   **[1973] IRLR 365 NIRC**
Corness

A dismissed employee cannot be said to have mitigated his loss if he refuses new work simply by measuring prospective jobs against the definition of suitable alternative employment in the redundancy payments provisions. The test is whether the person who is said to have failed to mitigate the damage acted reasonably in all the circumstances. In deciding whether he acted reasonably, a useful test is for the tribunal to ask itself whether, if the complainant had no hope of recovering compensation from anybody else, and if he had consulted merely his own interests, and acted reasonably in all the circumstances, he would have accepted the new job in mitigation of the loss he had suffered. If the answer is yes, then he should have taken the job and the fact that he is able to look to his previous employer for compensation provides him with no excuse for not doing so.

Gardiner-Hill v   **[1982] IRLR 498 EAT**
Roland Berger Technics Ltd

An employee does not necessarily fail to mitigate his loss by setting up in business on his own account after being dismissed rather than trying to get another job. The question that must be asked is whether what he did was reasonable. A claimant who has suffered by the wrongful act of another party is entitled to recover the loss that flows from that wrongful act. The duty on the claimant is to take such steps as are reasonable in all the circumstances to reduce the loss he suffers from the wrongful act.

Aon Training Ltd v   **[2005] IRLR 891 CA**
Dore

Where a dismissed employee attempts to mitigate his loss by setting up his own business, and the employment tribunal is satisfied that mitigation in that way was reasonable in the circumstances, the conventional way to assess compensation requires

the tribunal first to calculate what sum represents loss of remuneration. It should then consider the costs incurred in mitigating loss and such a sum, if reasonably incurred, should be added to the loss. From that sum should be deducted the earnings from the new business.

Seligman & Latz Ltd v   **[1979] IRLR 130 EAT**
McHugh

An employee who has been constructively dismissed does not fail in his duty to mitigate his loss by not processing a claim through the company's grievance procedure. Since once there has been a fundamental breach that has been accepted, the contract is at an end, it cannot be prayed in aid that after the breach the employee should have applied the grievance procedure.

Lock v   **[1994] IRLR 444 EAT**
Connell Estate Agents

Failure by an employee to operate the internal appeals procedure after dismissal cannot as a matter of law amount to a failure to mitigate loss under [s.123(4)]. *Hoover v Forde* was wrongly decided on this point and *William Muir (Bond 9) Ltd v Lamb* was preferred.

Sturdy Finance Ltd v   **[1979] IRLR 65 EAT**
Bardsley

An employee does not fail to mitigate his loss of pension rights by choosing to take a refund of his contributions rather than a deferred pension. There is no rule of law which requires an employee to take a deferred pension rather than a refund of contributions. Where a failure to mitigate is alleged, the onus is on the party making the allegation. It is therefore for the employer to show that it was wholly unreasonable for an employee to take his contributions and not to opt for a deferred pension.

Lock v   **[1994] IRLR 444 EAT**
Connell Estate Agents

A basic award can never be reduced on grounds of a failure to mitigate. [Section 123(4)] applies only to the compensatory award and there is no corresponding provision relating to the basic award.

Contributory fault

Nelson v   **[1979] IRLR 346 CA**
BBC (No. 2)

In determining whether to reduce an employee's unfair dismissal compensation on grounds of his contributory fault, an employment tribunal must make three findings. First, there must be a finding that there was conduct on the part of the employee in connection with his unfair dismissal which was culpable or blameworthy. Notwithstanding that there is no express reference in the statutory provisions to culpability or blameworthiness, this can be implied on the grounds that it could never be just or equitable to reduce a successful complainant's compensation unless the conduct on his part relied upon as contributory was culpable or blameworthy. In this connection, the concept of culpability or blameworthiness does not necessarily involve only conduct amounting to a breach of contract or a tort. It includes conduct of that kind but it also includes conduct which, while not amounting to a breach of contract or a tort, is nevertheless perverse or foolish or bloody-minded. It may also include action which, though not meriting any of those more pejorative epithets, is nevertheless unreasonable in the circumstances. But all unreasonable conduct is not necessarily culpable or blameworthy; it must depend upon the degree of unreasonableness involved.

Second, there must be a finding that the matters to which the complaint relates were caused or contributed to, to some extent, by action that was culpable or blameworthy. In this context, the expression "matters to which the complaint relates" means the unfair dismissal itself and the word "action" comprehends not only behaviour or conduct which consists of doing something but also behaviour or conduct which consists of doing nothing or in declining or being unwilling to do something.

Third, there must be a finding that it is just and equitable to reduce the assessment of the complainant's loss to a specified extent.

Friend v   **[2001] IRLR 819 CA**
Civil Aviation Authority
Observed (per Chadwick LJ): An employment tribunal is not required to, and should not, embark on a consideration of the question of contributory fault under s.123(6) unless it has satisfied itself, under s.123(1), that some part of the loss sustained by the complainant in consequence of the dismissal is attributable to action taken by the employer. If no part of the loss is attributable to action taken by the employer, then s.123 is not engaged. It is for this reason, if for no other, that a reduction of 100% under s.123(6) can be appropriate only in exceptional circumstances. Such a decision requires the tribunal to satisfy itself that, although some part of the loss sustained is attributable to action taken by the employer, nevertheless the complainant's contribution to the dismissal makes it just and equitable that he should receive no compensatory award.

Morrison v   **[1989] IRLR 361 NICA**
Amalgamated Transport & General
  Workers' Union
The authorities establish the following principles and guidelines for determining contributory fault: (i) the tribunal must take a broad commonsense view of the situation; (ii) that broad approach should not necessarily be confined to a particular moment, not even the moment when employment is terminated; (iii) what has to be looked for in such a broad approach over a period is conduct on the part of the employee which is culpable or blameworthy or otherwise unreasonable; and (iv) the employee's culpability or unreasonable conduct must have contributed to or played a part in the dismissal.

Hutchinson v   **[1981] IRLR 318 EAT**
Enfield Rolling Mills Ltd
In order for unfair dismissal compensation to be reduced on grounds of the employee's contributory fault, there has to be a causal link between the actions of the employee and the dismissal. The employment tribunal must find that the action of the employee caused or contributed to the dismissal, and the amount of the reduction is the amount which is just and equitable having regard to that finding. The tribunal cannot simply point to some bad behaviour of the employee and say that by reason of that matter, they are going to reduce compensation.

Polentarutti v   **[1991] IRLR 457 EAT**
Autokraft Ltd
A finding of contributory fault does not require that the action of the complainant was the sole or principal or operative cause of the dismissal.

Hollier v   **[1983] IRLR 260 CA**
Plysu Ltd
In considering whether compensation should be reduced on grounds of the employee's contribution to the dismissal, the employment tribunal's function is to take a broad commonsense view of the situation, to decide what part, if any, the employee's own conduct played in causing or contributing to the dismissal and then, in the light of that finding, to decide what, if any, reduction should be made in the assessment of the employee's loss. The apportionment of the responsibility for the dismissal is so obviously a matter of impression, opinion and discretion that the EAT is not entitled to interfere with the employment tribunal's conclusion on that matter unless there is either a plain error of law or the conclusion is one which no reasonable tribunal could have reached on the evidence.

Warrilow v   **[1984] IRLR 304 EAT**
Robert Walker Ltd
The principles of law to be applied when considering whether an apportionment of contributory fault can stand are precisely the same as the principles which apply and which bind an appellate court in relation to appeals where the question in issue arises under the Law Reform (Contributory Negligence) Act 1945: the proportion of culpability is a matter for the tribunal of fact and can be interfered with only where there has been some failure by that tribunal to appreciate some material aspect of fact or where some improper emphasis has been laid on some other aspect of fact.

Tele-Trading Ltd v   **[1990] IRLR 430 CA**
Jenkins
The provision in [s.123(6)] for a reduction in compensation on grounds of contributory fault applies where, for example, an employee was guilty of conduct of which the employer became aware and as a result dismissed him. The dismissal may be unfair, perhaps because the employer failed to give

any prior warning or failed to carry out a proper investigation but, nevertheless, when assessing compensation the employment tribunal can consider how far the misconduct caused or contributed to the dismissal.

Slaughter v   **[1990] IRLR 426 CA**
C Brewer & Sons Ltd
Cases of unfair dismissal on grounds of ill health will rarely give rise to a reduction in compensation on grounds of contributory fault. In ill-health cases, instances where an act or omission on the part of the employee was a contributory factor within the guidance given in *Nelson v BBC (No. 2)* (see above) will be infrequent. One possible example might be where the employee had blatantly and persistently refused to obtain appropriate medical reports or attend for medical examination.

Sutton & Gates (Luton) Ltd v   **[1978] IRLR 486 EAT**
Boxall
The question of contributory fault can arise in a case which, though referred to as a "capability" case is really a "conduct" case. The degree of contribution in such a case may be very high where the so-called incapability was due to the employee's own fault in the sense that he was lazy, negligent or idle or did not try to improve.

Maris v   **[1974] IRLR 147 NIRC**
Rotherham County Borough
  Council
In determining whether compensation should be reduced on grounds of contributory fault, the employment tribunal should ignore the technical reason why the dismissal was unfair and look at the realities of the situation to see to what extent, if any, the employee contributed to his own ultimate dismissal.

Jamieson v   **[1975] IRLR 348 CS**
Aberdeen County Council
A reduction in compensation on grounds of the employee's contributory fault can be based on a consideration of aspects of his conduct other than the stated reasons for dismissal.

Polentarutti v   **[1991] IRLR 457 EAT**
Autokraft Ltd
There is no legal requirement that exceptional circumstances must be shown before a finding of contributory fault can be made in a constructive dismissal case.

Polentarutti v   **[1991] IRLR 457 EAT**
Autokraft Ltd
That the employers failed to show the reason for dismissal does not preclude a finding of contribution by the employee. Constructive dismissal and contributory fault are separate and distinct processes and there can be a reduction in compensation both where the employers have discharged the onus of showing what the reason for dismissal was and where they have failed to do so.

Garner v   **[1977] IRLR 206 EAT**
Grange Furnishing Ltd
In the case of constructive dismissal resulting from a series of small incidents, when looking at the question of contribution, the employment tribunal should look at the conduct of the employee not with reference to the triviality of the last incident but over the whole period. Just as the employer may be found liable in a constructive dismissal case as a result of conduct over a period of time, so the more normal and more sensible way of assessing contribution by the employee should be to pay very little attention to the finality of the situation but to look at it much more broadly over the whole period.

Moyes v   **[1986] IRLR 482 EAT**
Hylton Castle Working
  Men's Social Club & Institute Ltd
Even where a dismissal is unfair because of a breach of natural justice, the tribunal can consider whether the employee contributed to the dismissal and, if so, reduce compensation accordingly.

Allders International Ltd v   **[1981] IRLR 68 EAT**
Parkins
Questions of the employee's conduct alone are relevant to the question of whether the loss resulting from the dismissal should be reduced on grounds of contributory fault, unlike the question of fair or unfair dismissal where questions relating to the employer's conduct as well as the employee's are relevant.

Frith Accountants Ltd v   **[2014] IRLR 510 EAT**
Law
It will be unusual, though there is no test of exceptionality, for a constructive dismissal to be caused or contributed to by any conduct on behalf of an employee. This is because where there is a breach of the implied term of trust and confidence, by definition there will be no reasonable or proper cause for the employer's behaviour.

Parker Foundry Ltd v   **[1992] IRLR 11 CA**
Slack
In deciding whether or not to reduce compensation under [s.122(2)] and [s.123(6)], the employment tribunal is confined to taking into account the conduct of the complainant and not what happened to some other employee. Accordingly, that another employee involved in the incident leading to the complainant's dismissal had only been suspended was irrelevant.

Allen v   **[1982] IRLR 89 EAT**
Hammett Ltd
An employment tribunal is entitled to reduce compensation on grounds of contributory fault under [s.123(6)] of the Act by reason of the acts before dismissal not of the employee but of his solicitors. The general principle that a man is held responsible for the acts of his agents, so that the culpability of a party to proceedings takes into account the acts or omissions of that party's agent, applies also in the context of industrial relations legislation.

Crosville Wales Ltd v   **[1997] IRLR 691 HL**
Tracey (No.2)

In a case of selective re-engagement of employees dismissed while taking part in industrial action, participation in the industrial action itself cannot amount to "conduct" or "action" of the complainant justifying a reduction in compensation. That conclusion gives effect to the statutory requirement that any reduction in the compensation of an individual employee should be such as is "just and equitable". In deciding whether compensation should be reduced on grounds of contributory fault, the relevant question is whether the employee contributed to the dismissal, not to the failure to re-engage. In the case of collective action by a number of employees against their employer, it is impossible to allocate blame for the industrial action to any individual complainant, without reference to the conduct of the other employees concerned, including those who were re-engaged, and to that of the employer. However, individual blameworthy conduct additional to or separate from the mere act of participation in industrial action must in principle be capable of amounting to contributory fault.

Colwyn Borough Council v   **[1980] IRLR 420 EAT**
Dutton

The fact that pressure from other employees has to be left out of account in deciding whether a dismissal was unfair does not mean that the conduct of the employee which resulted in his fellow workers putting pressure on the employer to dismiss him could not be a contributory or causative factor in the chain such as to justify a reduction in compensation on grounds of the employee's contributory fault.

Edmund Nuttall Ltd v   **[2005] IRLR 751 EAT**
Butterfield

Committing pre-planned criminal offences and then concealing the true position from the employers was plainly culpable behaviour justifying a reduction in compensation.

Property Guards Ltd v   **[1982] IRLR 175 EAT**
Taylor and Kershaw

Failure by an employee to disclose a criminal conviction which is considered "spent" within the terms of the Rehabilitation of Offenders' Act cannot be grounds for reducing compensation for unfair dismissal. Since there is no obligation to disclose a spent conviction, failure to make such a disclosure cannot be treated as a fault by the employee.

Ladup Ltd v   **[1982] IRLR 7 EAT**
Barnes

Where a claimant is dismissed for an alleged criminal offence and is subsequently found guilty of that offence, the interests of justice require a review of the employment tribunal's decision not to reduce compensation on grounds of contributory fault. On review, the employment tribunal is entitled to go back and reduce his compensation by 100% on grounds of the employee's contribution to the dismissal.

Rao v   **[1994] IRLR 240 CA**
Civil Aviation Authority

Since the fact of there already having been a deduction under [s.123(1)] can affect what is just and reasonable under [s.123(6)], it may turn out that the deduction from the compensatory award on grounds of the employee's contributory conduct may not be the same as the deduction which it is just and equitable to make from the basic award on that ground.

G McFall & Co Ltd v   **[1981] IRLR 455 NICA**
Curran

The basic award and the compensatory award must be treated the same as far as a reduction on grounds of the employee's contributory fault is concerned. The use of the words "just and equitable" in the relevant provisions do not give the employment tribunal an uncontrolled discretion to apply in a different way to the basic award and the compensatory award a criterion which, once the facts are found and an opinion based thereon, is clearly meant to be the same in each case. The two awards must be treated consistently.

TBA Industrial Products Ltd v   **[1984] IRLR 48 EAT**
Locke

The amount included in respect of loss of pension rights can be reduced on grounds of contributory fault even though the same conduct has been taken into account in applying a withdrawal factor since, although the employee's conduct has been taken into account twice, the purposes for which it has been taken into account are separate.

Deductions

Babcock FATA Ltd v   **[1987] IRLR 173 CA**
Addison

In the absence of an agreement, express or implied, to the contrary effect, an employer is to be given credit for all payments he has made to the employee on account of claims for wages and other benefits. Therefore, sums paid or payable by the employer in lieu of notice should be taken into account in the assessment of unfair dismissal compensation. An employee is not entitled to both payment in lieu of notice and a compensatory award for loss of wages during the notice period.

Optimum Group Services plc v   **[2013] IRLR 339 EAT**
Muir

Where a claimant/pursuer seeks compensation from more than one respondent/defender, sums already received from one of them (including pursuant to a settlement agreement) must be deducted when assessing what, if anything, is the remaining loss which he is seeking to lay at the door of the others.

Digital Equipment Co Ltd v   **[1998] IRLR 134 CA**
Clements (No.2)

A redundancy payment in excess of statutory redundancy pay should be deducted from a compensatory award after any percentage reduction to reflect the chance of a claimant remaining in employment if the dismissal had not been procedurally unfair has been made. Section 123 draws a clear distinction between, on the one hand, 'the loss sustained by the complainant in consequence of the dismissal' which is to make up the amount of the compensatory award and, on the other hand, the compensatory award itself. Section 123(7) requires that an excess redundancy payment is not to be taken into account in ascertaining the loss but is to go to 'reduce the amount of the compensatory award'. Accordingly, excess redundancy payments which have actually been made by the employer are treated differently from the way the Court of Appeal treated the loss of earnings claim in *Ministry of Defence v Wheeler*. The employer who pays compensation for redundancy on a more generous scale than the statutory scale is entitled to full credit for the additional payment against the amount of the loss which makes up the compensatory award.

Heggie v   **[1999] IRLR 802 CS**
Uniroyal Englebert Tyres Ltd
The employers conceded that a payment made by an employer in lieu of notice must be deducted before applying a percentage reduction under s.123(6) of the Employment Rights Act to reflect the employee's contributory conduct.

Leonard v   **[1998] IRLR 693 CS**
Strathclyde Buses Ltd
An excess redundancy payment should be offset against a compensatory award before the statutory maximum laid down in s.124(5) is applied. As a straightforward matter of statutory construction, the statutory maximum falls to be applied to the compensatory award calculated in accordance with s.123, which must include the deduction of any excess redundancy payment under s.123(7). There is nothing in the decision of the Court of Appeal in *Digital Equipment Co Ltd v Clements,* that an employer should get full credit for any excess payment, which points to any different view.

Darr and another v   **[1993] IRLR 257 EAT**
LRC Products Ltd
Where the amount of the employee's loss following dismissal on grounds of redundancy is reduced by a severance payment from the employer, the correct method of calculating the compensatory award is first to assess the employee's loss of earnings over an appropriate period, then to deduct the part of the severance payment which has not already been set against the basic award, and finally to apply the statutory limit to the net sum.

McCarthy v   **[1985] IRLR 94 EAT**
British Insulated Callenders Cables
[Section 124(5)] makes clear that the amount of an ex gratia payment received by an employee in connection with his dismissal must be taken into account before the statutory maximum for compensatory awards is applied.

Walter Braund (London) Ltd v   **[1991] IRLR 100 EAT**
Murray
On a proper construction of [s.124(5)], the statutory upper limit applies to the final compensatory award, after making any reduction under [s.123(6)] by reference to the employee's actions.

Puglia v   **[1996] IRLR 70 EAT**
C James & Sons
Where there is no provision in the contract of employment entitling an employee to receive full wages in addition to sickness benefit, the compensatory award should be reduced by the amount any sickness benefit received by the employee during the period covered by the award.

Hilton International Hotels (UK)   **[1994] IRLR 267 EAT**
  Ltd v
Faraji
Invalidity benefit received by an employee following dismissal does not fall to be deducted from unfair dismissal compensation.

Puglia v   **[1996] IRLR 70 EAT**
C James & Sons
The weight of authority indicates that invalidity benefit should be deducted from a compensatory award. *Hilton International Hotels (UK) Ltd v Faraji* was decided without the EAT's attention being drawn to all the relevant authorities and would not be followed.

Rubenstein and Roskin t/a   **[1996] IRLR 557 EAT**
  McGuffies Dispensing Chemists v
McGloughlin
An unfair dismissal compensatory award does not have to reflect the "all or nothing" approach to the question of deductibility of benefits applicable to common law damages. In the case of benefits, such as invalidity benefit, to which a claimant has contributed but are not in the category of pure "insurance" monies, fully funded by the employee, the just and equitable solution is to deduct one-half of the amount of benefit received by the employee from the compensatory award.

Morgans v   **[2005] IRLR 234 EAT**
Alpha Plus Security Ltd
A compensatory award should be reduced by the full amount of incapacity benefit received by the employee during the period covered by the award. There is no jurisdiction, whether by reference to the previous practice in personal injury claims or by reference to authority, to disregard receipts or to claim and recover a sum in excess of actual loss. To treat something which is not a loss as being a loss by disregarding receipts, is to reward an unfairly dismissed employee by awarding a bonus. The inconsistency between the decisions of the EAT in *Puglia v C James & Sons Ltd* and in *Rubenstein v McGoughlin* (and a fortiori in *Hilton Hotels International (UK) Ltd v Faraji*) would be resolved in favour of *Puglia*.

Savage v   **[1998] IRLR 182 EAT**
Saxena

Housing benefit and income support should be excluded from the computation of an unfair dismissal compensatory award.

Knapton v   **[2006] IRLR 756 EAT**
ECC Card Clothing Ltd

Pension payments which an employee has chosen to receive early following dismissal should not be offset against an award of compensation.

MBS Ltd v   **[1983] IRLR 189 EAT**
Calo

In the ordinary case, it is neither necessary nor desirable for an employment tribunal to concern itself with the detailed tax implications of a dismissal, some of which may be to the employee's advantage, others to his detriment. In cases involving higher earners, however, it may be appropriate for a tribunal to go into the tax repercussions of the dismissal in producing justice and equity.

Bentwood Bros (Manchester) Ltd v   **[2003] IRLR 364 CA**
Shepherd

As a matter of principle, employment tribunals should take account of the fact that an employee receiving compensation has the benefit of receiving immediately what he or she would otherwise have had to wait to receive in instalments over the period of loss. This should be done on the basis of an appropriate year-on-year percentage deduction, not by a single deduction. However, it was arguable that the conventional discount of 5% applied by employment tribunals to take account of accelerated payment is on the high side and out of line with rates in other areas of the law, in particular the 2.5% now applied by statute in personal injury cases.

Deductions for contributory fault – where dismissal is for trade union membership/activities

155. *(1) Where an employment tribunal makes an award of compensation for unfair dismissal in a case where the dismissal is unfair by virtue of s.152 or 153, the tribunal shall disregard, in considering whether it would be just and equitable to reduce, or further reduce, the amount of any part of the award, any such conduct or action of the complainant as is specified below.*

(2) Conduct or action of the complainant shall be disregarded in so far as it constitutes a breach or proposed breach of a requirement –

    (a) to be or become a member of any trade union or of a particular trade union, or of one of a number of particular trade unions,

    (b) to cease to be, or refrain from becoming, a member of any trade union or of a particular trade union or of one of a number of particular trade unions,

    (c) not to take part in the activities of any trade union or of a particular trade union or of one of a number of particular trade unions, or

    (d) not to make use of the services made available by any trade union or by a particular trade union or by one of a number of particular trade unions.

For the purposes of this subsection a requirement means a requirement imposed on the complainant by or under an arrangement or contract of employment or other agreement.

(2A) Conduct or action of the complainant shall be disregarded in so far as it constitutes acceptance of or failure to accept an offer made in contravention of s.145A or 145B.

(3) Conduct or action of the complainant shall be disregarded in so far as it constitutes a refusal, or proposed refusal, to comply with a requirement of a kind mentioned in s.152(3)(a) (payments in lieu of membership) or an objection, or proposed objection (however expressed), to the operation of a provision of a kind mentioned in s.152(3)(b) (deductions in lieu of membership).

156. *(1) Where a dismissal is unfair by virtue of s.152(1) or 153, the amount of the basic award of compensation, before any reduction is made under s.122 of the Employment Rights Act 1996, shall be not less than £5,676*.*

(2) But where the dismissal is unfair by virtue of s.153, subsection (2) of that section (reduction for contributory fault) applies in relation to so much of the basic award as is payable because of subsection (1) above.

TRADE UNION AND LABOUR RELATIONS (CONSOLIDATION) ACT 1992 (as amended)

TGWU v   **[1992] IRLR 170 EAT**
Howard

The provision in [s.155(2)(a)] that an employee's breach of a requirement "to be or become a member of any trade union or of a particular union" should be disregarded in considering whether the employee's own conduct contributed to the dismissal, does not preclude the tribunal from having regard to the manner in which the employee exercised the right to non-membership.

Interim relief – employee representatives etc

128. *(1) An employee who presents a complaint to an employment tribunal that he has been unfairly dismissed and –*

    (a) that the reason (or if more than one the principal reason) for the dismissal is one of those specified in –
    (i) section 100(1)(a) and (b), 101A(1)(d), 102(1), 103 or 103A, or
    (ii) paragraph 161(2) of Schedule A1 to the Trade Union and Labour Relations (Consolidation) Act 1992, or

    (b) that the reason (or, if more than one, the principal reason) for which the employee was selected for

---

* It is anticipated that this sum will be increased by statutory instrument where the appropriate date falls on or after 6 April 2015.

dismissal was the one specified in the opening words of section 104F(1) and the condition in paragraph (a) or (b) of that subsection was met,

may apply to the tribunal for interim relief.

(2) The tribunal shall not entertain an application for interim relief unless it is presented to the tribunal before the end of the period of seven days immediately following the effective date of termination (whether before, on or after that date).

(3) The tribunal shall determine the application for interim relief as soon as practicable after receiving the application.

(4) The tribunal shall give to the employer not later than seven days before the date of the hearing a copy of the application together with notice of the date, time and place of the hearing.

(5) The tribunal shall not exercise any power it has of postponing the hearing of an application for interim relief except where it is satisfied that special circumstances exist which justify it in doing so.

129. (1) This section applies where, on hearing an employee's application for interim relief, it appears to the tribunal that it is likely that on determining the complaint to which the application relates the tribunal will find –

    (a) that the reason (or if more than one the principal reason) for the dismissal is one of those specified in –

        (i) section 100(1)(a) and (b), 101A(1)(d), 102(1), 103 or 103A, or

        (ii) paragraph 161(2) of Schedule A1 to the Trade Union and Labour Relations (Consolidation) Act 1992, or

    (b) that the reason (or, if more than one, the principal reason) for which the employee was selected for dismissal was the one specified in the opening words of section 104F(1) and the condition in paragraph (a) or (b) of that subsection was met.

(2) The tribunal shall announce its findings and explain to both parties (if present) –

    (a) what powers the tribunal may exercise on the application, and

    (b) in what circumstances it will exercise them.

(3) The tribunal shall ask the employer (if present) whether he is willing, pending the determination or settlement of the complaint –

    (a) to reinstate the employee (that is, to treat him in all respects as if he had not been dismissed), or

    (b) if not, to re-engage him in another job on terms and conditions not less favourable than those which would have been applicable to him if he had not been dismissed.

(4) For the purposes of subsection (3)(b) "terms and conditions not less favourable than those which would have been applicable to him if he had not been dismissed" means, as regards seniority, pension rights and other similar rights, that the period prior to the dismissal should be regarded as continuous with his employment following the dismissal.

(5) If the employer states that he is willing to reinstate the employee, the tribunal shall make an order to that effect.

(6) If the employer –

    (a) states that he is willing to re-engage the employee in another job, and

    (b) specifies the terms and conditions on which he is willing to do so,

the tribunal shall ask the employee whether he is willing to accept the job on those terms and conditions.

(7) If the employee is willing to accept the job on those terms and conditions, the tribunal shall make an order to that effect.

(8) If the employee is not willing to accept the job on those terms and conditions –

    (a) where the tribunal is of the opinion that the refusal is reasonable, the tribunal shall make an order for the continuation of his contract of employment, and

    (b) otherwise, the tribunal shall make no order.

(9) If on the hearing of an application for interim relief the employer –

    (a) fails to attend before the tribunal, or

    (b) states that he is unwilling either to reinstate or re-engage the employee as mentioned in subsection (3),

the tribunal shall make an order for the continuation of the employee's contract of employment.

130. (1) An order under section 129 for the continuation of a contract of employment is an order that the contract of employment continue in force –

    (a) for the purposes of pay or any other benefit derived from the employment, seniority, pension rights and other similar matters, and

    (b) for the purposes of determining for any purpose the period for which the employee has been continuously employed,

from the date of its termination (whether before or after the making of the order) until the determination or settlement of the complaint.

(2) Where the tribunal makes such an order it shall specify in the order the amount which is to be paid by the employer to the employee by way of pay in respect of each normal pay period, or part of any such period, falling between the date of dismissal and the determination or settlement of the complaint.

(3) Subject to the following provisions, the amount so specified shall be that which the employee could reasonably have been expected to earn during that period, or part, and shall be paid –

    (a) in the case of a payment for any such period falling wholly or partly after the making of the order, on the normal pay day for that period, and

    (b) in the case of a payment for any past period, within such time as may be specified in the order.

(4) If an amount is payable in respect only of part of a normal pay period, the amount shall be calculated by reference to the whole period and reduced proportionally.

(5) Any payment made to an employee by an employer under his contract of employment, or by way of damages for breach of that contract, in respect of a normal pay period, or part of any such period, goes towards discharging the employer's liability in respect of that period under subsection (2); and, conversely, any payment under that subsection in respect of a period goes towards discharging any liability of the employer under, or in respect of breach of, the contract of employment in respect of that period.

(6) If an employee, on or after being dismissed by his employer, receives a lump sum which, or part of which, is in lieu of wages but is not referable to any normal pay period, the tribunal shall take the payment into account in determining the amount of pay to be payable in pursuance of any such order.

(7) For the purposes of this section, the amount which an employee could reasonably have been expected to earn, his normal pay period and the normal pay day for each such period shall be determined as if he had not been dismissed.

131. (1) At any time between –

    (a) the making of an order under section 129, and

    (b) the determination or settlement of the complaint,

the employer or the employee may apply to an employment tribunal for the revocation or variation of the order on the ground of a relevant change of circumstances since the making of the order.

(2) Sections 128 and 129 apply in relation to such an application as in relation to an original application for interim relief except that, in the case of an application by the employer, section 128(4) has effect with the substitution of a reference to the employee for the reference to the employer.

132. *(1) If, on the application of an employee, an employment tribunal is satisfied that the employer has not complied with the terms of an order for the reinstatement or re-engagement of the employee under section 129(5) or (7), the tribunal shall –*

(a) *make an order for the continuation of the employee's contract of employment, and*

(b) *order the employer to pay compensation to the employee.*

(2) Compensation under subsection (1)(b) shall be of such amount as the tribunal considers just and equitable in all the circumstances having regard –

(a) *to the infringement of the employee's right to be reinstated or re-engaged in pursuance of the order, and*

(b) *to any loss suffered by the employee in consequence of the non-compliance.*

(3) Section 130 applies to an order under subsection (1)(a) as in relation to an order under section 129.

(4) If on the application of an employee an employment tribunal is satisfied that the employer has not complied with the terms of an order for the continuation of a contract of employment subsection (5) or (6) applies.

(5) Where the non-compliance consists of a failure to pay an amount by way of pay specified in the order –

(a) *the tribunal shall determine the amount owed by the employer on the date of the determination, and*

(b) *if on that date the tribunal also determines the employee's complaint that he has been unfairly dismissed, it shall specify that amount separately from any other sum awarded to the employee.*

(6) In any other case, the tribunal shall order the employer to pay the employee such compensation as the tribunal considers just and equitable in all the circumstances having regard to any loss suffered by the employee in consequence of the non-compliance.

EMPLOYMENT RIGHTS ACT 1996 (as amended)

Ministry of Justice v Sarfraz   **[2011] IRLR 562 EAT**

In ERA 1996 s.129(1), "likely" does not mean simply "more likely than not" – that is, at least 51% – but connotes a significantly higher degree of likelihood. It connotes something nearer to certainty than mere probability.

Interim relief – trade union membership/activities

---

161. *(1) An employee who presents a complaint of unfair dismissal alleging that the dismissal is unfair by virtue of s.152 may apply to the tribunal for interim relief.*

(2) The tribunal shall not entertain an application for interim relief unless it is presented to the tribunal before the end of the period of seven days immediately following the effective date of termination (whether before, on or after that date).

(3) In a case where the employee relies on s.152(1)(a), (b) or (ba), or on s.152(1)(bb) otherwise than in relation to an offer made in contravention of s.145A(1)(d), the tribunal shall not entertain an application for interim relief unless before the end of that period there is also so presented a certificate in writing signed by an authorised official of the independent trade union of which the employee was or proposed to become a member stating –

(a) *that on the date of the dismissal the employee was or proposed to become a member of the union; and*

(b) *that there appear to be reasonable grounds for supposing that the reason for his dismissal (or, if more than one, the principal reason) was one alleged in the complaint . . .*

162. *(1) An employment tribunal shall determine an application for interim relief as soon as practicable after receiving the application and, where appropriate, the requisite certificate . . .*

163. *(1) If on hearing an application for interim relief it appears to the tribunal that it is likely that on determining the complaint to which the application relates it will find that, by virtue of s.152, the complainant has been unfairly dismissed, the following provisions apply.*

(2) The tribunal shall announce its findings and explain to both parties (if present) what powers the tribunal may exercise on the application and in what circumstances it will exercise them, and shall ask the employer (if present) whether he is willing, pending the determination or settlement of the complaint –

(a) *to reinstate the employee, that is to say, to treat him in all respects as if he had not been dismissed; or*

(b) *if not, to re-engage him in another job on terms and conditions not less favourable than those which would have been applicable to him if he had not been dismissed.*

(3) For this purpose "terms and conditions not less favourable than those which would have been applicable to him if he had not been dismissed" means as regards seniority, pension rights and other similar rights that the period prior to the dismissal shall be regarded as continuous with his employment following the dismissal.

(4) If the employer states that he is willing to reinstate the employee, the tribunal shall make an order to that effect.

(5) If the employer states that he is willing to re-engage the employee in another job, and specifies the terms and conditions on which he is willing to do so, the tribunal shall ask the employee whether he is willing to accept the job on those terms and conditions; and –

(a) *if the employee is willing to accept the job on those terms and conditions, the tribunal shall make an order to that effect; and*

(b) *if he is not, then, if the tribunal is of the opinion that the refusal is reasonable, the tribunal shall make an order for the continuation of his contract of employment, and otherwise the tribunal shall make no order.*

(6) If on the hearing of an application for interim relief the employer fails to attend before the tribunal, or states that he is unwilling either to reinstate the employee or re-engage him as mentioned in subsection (2), the tribunal shall make an order for the continuation of the employee's contract of employment.

164. *(1) An order under s.163 for the continuation of a contract of employment is an order that the contract of employment continue in force –*

(a) for the purposes of pay or any other benefit derived from the employment, seniority, pension rights and other similar matters; and

(b) for the purpose of determining for any purpose the period for which the employee has been continuously employed;

from the date of its termination (whether before or after the making of the order) until the determination or settlement of the complaint . . .

165. *(1) At any time between the making of an order under s.163 and the determination or settlement of the complaint, the employer or the employee may apply to an employment tribunal for the revocation or variation of the order on the ground of a relevant change of circumstances since the making of the order.*

TRADE UNION AND LABOUR RELATIONS (CONSOLIDATION) ACT 1992 (as amended)

Taplin v   **[1978] IRLR 450 EAT**
C Shippam Ltd

In order to determine for the purposes of an application for interim relief under [s.161] of the Act whether it is likely that an employee will be found to have been dismissed on grounds of trade union membership or activities, the correct approach is for the employment tribunal to ask itself whether the employee has established that he has a "pretty good" chance of succeeding in the final application to the tribunal. In order to obtain an order under [s.163], the employee must achieve a higher degree of certainty in the mind of the tribunal than that of showing that he had just a "reasonable" prospect of success.

London City Airport Ltd v   **[2013] IRLR 610 EAT**
Chacko

"Likely" requires more than a balance of probabilities as regards ultimate success. *Taplin v C Shippam Ltd* should still be followed, so that it must be established "that the employee can demonstrate a pretty good chance of success". This is despite the House of Lords ruling in the very different context of disability discrimination legislation that "likely" means "could well happen".

British Coal Corporation v   **[1988] IRLR 7 EAT**
McGinty

The provision in [s.165(1)] relating to an application to the tribunal for revocation or variation of an order for interim relief does not require that such an application be heard by the tribunal which originally made the order.

Bombardier Aerospace/Short   **[2008] IRLR 51 NICA**
    Brothers plc v
McConnell

This decision was taken under the provisions in Northern Ireland that mirror s.161. Although s.161 does not refer to s.153, and therefore no application for interim relief can be made where an employee is selected for a genuine redundancy as a result of trade union membership or activities, this decision holds that interim relief can be claimed where it is alleged that the redundancy itself is a fabricated pretext for a trade union reason for dismissal.

McConnell v   **[2009] IRLR 201 NICA**
Bombardier Aerospace/Short Brothers plc (No.2)

If it is likely that the principal reason for a dismissal was redundancy, rather than trade union activities, then a claim for interim relief cannot succeed, even if unfair selection for redundancy was likely to be established. Observed: "principal" means "primary" so that there is only ever one primary reason, all other reasons are subordinate.